York St John
Library and Information Services
Normal Loan

Please see self service receipt for return date.

		1 1 JUN 2023

Fines are payable for late return

London Narratives

CONTINUUM LITERARY STUDIES SERIES

Also available in the series:

Character and Satire in Postwar Fiction by Ian Gregson
Fictions of Globalization by James Annesley
Joyce and Company by David Pierce
Masculinity in Fiction and Film by Brian Baker
Novels of the Contemporary Extreme edited by Alain-Philippe Durand and Naomi Mandel
Romanticism, Literature and Philosophy by Simon Swift
Women's Fiction 1945–2005 by Deborah Philips

Forthcoming titles:

Active Reading by Ben Knights and Chris Thurgar-Dawson
English Fiction in the 1930s by Chris Hopkins

London Narratives

Post-war Fiction and the City

Lawrence Phillips

continuum
LONDON • NEW YORK

Continuum
The Tower Building, 11 York Road, London SE1 7NX
80 Maiden Lane, Suite 704, New York, NY 10038

British Library Cataloguing-in-Publication Data
A catalogue record for this book is available from the British Library.

ISBN: 0–8264–8452–2 (hardback)

Library of Congress Cataloging-in-Publication Data
A catalog record for this book is available from
the Library of Congress.

Typeset by YHT Ltd, London
Printed and bound in Great Britain by Biddles Ltd,
King's Lynn, Norfolk

Contents

Introduction: Rewriting London   1

1   **Blitz Retrospective**   10
2   **The Centre Cannot Hold**   35
3   **Love in a Cold Climate**   56
4   **Stress Fractures**   80
5   **The New Londoners**   106
6   **London Revenant**   132
7   **Coda**   158

Bibliography   161
Index   171

For Laila and Justin, with love

Introduction
Rewriting London

... the tendency of humanity is to crowd into the large cities, and within their bounds to live semi-migratory lives. Of the history and of the thought of the great number of men with whom we come into contact we have no knowledge at all ... of their lives and passions we know nothing. So that unless the imaginative writer helps us in this matter we are in great danger of losing alike human knowledge and human sympathy.

Ford Madox Ford, *The Critical Attitude*

In his seminal study of urban design, *The Image of the City* (1960), Kevin Lynch observes that 'the city is a construction in space, but one of vast scale, a thing perceived only in the course of long spans of time' (Lynch 1). London is an ancient city by any measure and yet much of its fabric, geographical footprint and population level are little over a century in age. Certainly, cities replenish themselves and are remodelled in response to a range of stimuli that are economic, social, cultural and even natural in origin, but looking back over the long history of the city, modern London has been shaped by two relatively recent phenomena. The first is the quite remarkable growth in London's population in the latter years of the nineteenth and early years of the twentieth centuries. At the beginning of the nineteenth century the city had fewer than one million inhabitants. By the 1880s the population had risen to 5 million, and by the outbreak of the First World War in 1914, 7.5 million. In 1800 the city had not expanded much beyond the environs of the medieval walled City and the seat of political power, Westminster. Greater London today, measured by the Metropolitan Police District, covers over 720 square miles. Nearly all of what modern Londoners know as their city didn't exist as a metropolitan space before the nineteenth century, and a sizeable proportion of it is no older than the last century. Before the nineteenth century it is possible to assume that most people living in London had a familiarity with the city as a whole – it was a single town. By the twentieth century, most inhabitants would be unlikely to claim intimacy with the city much beyond their home district and place of work. The second major upheaval in the city's modern history is the destruction of the Blitz. The financial district of the city lost half its office space. Nearly 120,000 houses were destroyed or beyond repair; 288,000 more houses were seriously damaged and a further two million, slightly (J. White 39). While much of London remained intact, destruction on this scale created a prevailing sense of beleaguerment during the war, and a sense that the entire city was being rebuilt in the post-war reconstruction; it took decades to fill the gaping holes left by the bombs.

The pattern of this recent history, remarkable growth, devastating destruction and a slower process of reconstruction has created a distinctive fabric and image for the city in the post-war imagination of its inhabitants and artists. Pre-eminent among both groups are London's post-war novelists. London has long attracted considerable literary attention not least by virtue of being the centre of the publishing industry, and its wealth, power, sheer size and diversity in proportion to the rest of the country. Yet the newness of much of the city exists in tension with a prevailing sense of the city's age that has embedded a contradiction at the heart of the image of the city, as Gavin Weightman and Steve Humphreys observe: 'Its physical fabric is not even very old, though much is made in tourist brochures of its "historic past"' (Weightman and Humphreys 9). This newness becomes clear when one considers that the pre-war growth of the city and its post-war reconstruction has created an urban space notable for its scattered nature and suburban sprawl – the city in 2000 had a similar population to the city in 1914 but was geographically twice its size (Inwood 9). The uniqueness of this issue over the space and historicity of the post-war and contemporary city has – often subconsciously – fascinated post-war novelists in a variety of forms, but has received little sustained critical attention. There is a growing body of work on several aspects of post-war fiction and the city – most recently on 'postcolonial' London – and a growing corpus of essays and studies on particular authors and the city, but none that has attempted an overview of London fiction since the war even though such a survey or surveys would include many major figures and numerous minor talents in British fiction.

This book is attuned to the post-war history, culture and development of the city through an overview of a selection of the most significant fictional engagements with London, while being neither a history nor a literary survey. The number of texts examined here is of necessity selective and emblematic rather than offering the pretence that it is exhaustive and definitive. This is vital to ensure that readings achieve a sufficient level of detail to support the argument of this book rather than offering some form of taxonomic listing best left to readers' guides. Equally, there are many substantial histories of London by both historians and, intriguingly, literary artists to preclude the burning need for one more. This book is, however, a first step in the establishment of a consolidated cultural analysis of post-war representations of the city. A first step because it is limited to fiction and makes no pretence to exhaust the material available for analysis – an invitation, I hope, for other studies. In this vein the book offers a series of interventions across six chapters with what I have identified as significant literary, cultural and developmental trends in London in pursuit of three major underlying representational modes in relation to the city – image, history and narrative.

The image of the city quite consistently revolves upon the size of the city, its integration and its effect on the individual consciousness. There is a long history of constructing an image of London as monstrous, threatening and functioning like some enormous body, but it is as well to emphasize again the exponential growth of London in the late nineteenth and twentieth centuries which adds some credence to the figure. This is in many ways a very modern trope that has considerable representational significance. The image is expressively flexible. For example, during the war and thanks to the black-out and bomb damage, night-time London was the stuff of nightmares – a threatening, hellish, monstrous landscape. Likewise, London was conceived as an enormous body bravely soaking up the damage meted out by the bombs and a signifier of national pride, spirit of resistance and perhaps pity. Even the monster image can be on the side of the Londoner as in Churchill's famous wartime observation that the city could swallow an entire invading army. Above all, such literary and psychological images are responsive both to collective reinforcement and to individual variation; expressive possibilities to which London writers are particularly attuned.

History, memory and the integration of the past into the present city is also a potent motif. A common city image is that of the historical palimpsest as over time, the physical remains of former cities accrete in urban space, and from thence to the accretions of associated memories tied to place and space. Yet much of modern London has no such ancient history (unless one counts the former villages buried beneath London's sprawl). For London, history is a potentially troubling concept as the new struggles under the weight of the old city that encompasses such a small sum of its physical totality. The ancient and the modern live in uncomfortable proximity in the imaginary of London. As London in the post-war period has become even less the industrial metropolis of the nineteenth century and more the consumerist tourist city of the contemporary moment, the tension is even more acute. The past is celebrated but has increasingly become something that can disturb, disrupt and dominate the contemporary inhabitant even as social and cultural progress inexorably shifts towards the 'new' fabric of the city. It has taken a fundamental reformulation of the Londoner to provoke a reconsideration of the past – the social and economic liberation of the urban working classes and the successive waves of mass migration to the city from former British colonies. Yet the monumental, tourist and national history of the city continues to be reiterated. It is as well to remember that Freud described the uncanny as linked to the 'compulsion to repeat', so the past of London has the ability to disturb as well as monumentalize the modern city.

The question of narrative and the city will have a less familiar ring to those engaged with urban representation. The impetus for its inclusion here is the connection between cognitive mapping, spatial stories and spatial form both literal and representational. In particular it is the convergence between time and space in the city – which encompasses both the image of the city and its past – and issues of time and space in narrative that reveal significant underlying processes taking place in the psychological apprehension of the city, as H. G. Wells's Time Traveller ruminates: 'There is no difference between Time and any of the three dimensions of Space except that our consciousness moves along it' (Wells 2005a 4). The city is the artificial environment par excellence and as such it is constructed around humanity's perception of time and space. Yet perceptions change while the physical structure that expresses them remains until reformulated and reconstructed – a process that is never total as Martin Heidegger argues in *Being and Time* (*Sein und Zeit*) (1962): ' "the past" has a remarkable double meaning; the past belongs irretrievably to an earlier time; it belonged to the events of that time; and in spite of that, it can still be present-at-hand now' (Heidegger 378). To produce meaning from the 'space' between the past and the 'present-at-hand' there is narrative. In literary narratives of the city one finds both recognition of past modes of city experience and a component of that reformulation. Such spatial redundancy and reformulation can be rapid and disjunct, but it is a process that is vital to expressions of the lived experience of the city that are fully ontological and mythic. If that seems like a contradiction too far, Ernst Cassirer observes that 'language does not merely contain signs or designations for a being; rather, language is a form of being itself' (Cassirer 82). I would extend this to argue that this is even truer of narrative. Spatial metaphors are replete among several schools of critical thought, but in relation to the physical artefacts of the city and the narratives that create and formulate the experience of place and space are more than just analytical or existential metaphors. They actively create being *in* space. Of course this book is concerned with representations of space and place (London) through literary narratives, not nar-ratives of experience, of the city. Yet there is an unavoidable relationship between the two. In many respects literary narratives – and other representation forms founded on narrative – codify experiential narratives formed from lived experience. The codification of course also alters that relationship, but the connection remains all the same. In relation to the city there is an ongoing negotiation between images, histories and memories, literary narrative, and lived experience that flows both ways. Lynch observes that 'our perception of the city is not sustained, but rather partial, fragmentary, mixed with other concerns. Nearly every sense is in operation, and the image is the composite of them all' (Lynch 2). Yet what negotiates between perception of the city and our images of it? The composite image by which we make sense of our experience in the city and the various feelings, memories, histories, experiences, preoccupations, etc. is translated and codified through the *process* of narrative – a narrative of consciousness.

This brings me to the underlying theoretical coordinates of this study. These are various and range from literary metaphors, architecture, to cultural geography. I am most clearly indebted to Michel de Certeau's work on both 'walking in the city', spatial syntaxes, and spatial stories from *The Practice of Everyday Life* which gave me the means to articulate the key role of narrative in analysing representations of the lived experience of the city. As de Certeau argues:

> In modern Athens, the vehicles of mass transportation are called *metaphorai*. To go to work or come home, one takes a 'metaphor' – a bus or a train. Stories could also take this noble name: every day they traverse and organize places; they select and link them together; they make sentences and itineraries out of them. They are spatial trajectories. (de Certeau 115)

'Stories' and thence 'spatial trajectories' cannot be articulated without the narrative through which they are transmitted. Henri Lefebvre's work on space and materiality provided the necessary corrective to ensure that the passage between material and discursive spaces was never forgotten and from hence comes my emphasis on process. Like de Certeau, Lefebvre emphasizes the influence of everyday life: 'everyday life also figures in representational spaces – or perhaps it would be more accurate to say that it forms such spaces' (Lefebvre 116). De Certeau's metaphors of movement – walking, transportation, itineraries – develop and trace the 'journey' between everyday life and representational space. Yet the physical city is not just a matter of routes, which places undue emphasis on streets and roads at the expense of buildings and dwellings. Such an emphasis on movement becomes excessively synchronic and would have little to do with the lived experience of the city. Places that store or solidify the energy of past inhabitants of the city exist in creative tension with the kinetic energy of the present. The nature of buildings as both contemporary dwelling and a crystallization of the past is a significant contributor to the imaginative flux of the city, and as Gaston Bachelard observes: 'Space that has been seized upon by the imagination cannot remain indifferent space subject to the measures and estimates of the surveyor. It has been lived in, not in its positivity, but with all the partiality of the imagination' (Bachelard xxxvi). Buildings have a powerful psychological dimension that is underrepresented in studies of space and place.

Even though cities are vast conglomerations of dwellings, analytical emphasis tends to rest on the alienating scale of the modern city. Anthony Vidler argues in *The Architectural Uncanny* (1992) that, 'the uncanny ... was also born out of the rise of the great cities, their disturbingly heterogeneous crowds and newly scaled buildings demanding a point of reference that, while not refuting a certain instability, nevertheless served to dominate it aesthetically' (Vidler 4). The thrust of this argument suggests that inasmuch as the modern city produces increased alienation via an aesthetic domination that is out of scale to the individual, the more localized, human scale of the residential dwelling becomes increasingly 'unhomely'. As Karl Marx noted in the *Economic and Philosophical Notebooks* of 1844, the rent system that dominates in the centre of modern cities undermines what should be the certainty of the 'homely': ' "Here I am at home" – but where instead he finds himself in *someone else's* house, in the house of a *Stranger* who always watches him and throws him out if he does not pay his rent' (Marx 314). It is significant that many of the protagonists in the novels examined in this book live in temporary rather than permanent accommodation, while the experience of those who enjoy a permanent 'home' in the city creates a different attitude towards and image of the city.

The past is also a feature of both estrangement and the uncanny, able to both dispossess and alienate. The city preserves in its fabric the practices of previous generations that can be as dehumanizing as the loss of human scale in modern high-rise architecture. Moreover, as already noted, London's history is in fact only the history of a tiny proportion of the modern city. The past is like a lurking spectre that is disconcertingly a familiar and appropriate facet of the image of the city, but also has the power to introduce the inappropriate and inexplicable, as Walter Benjamin argues, 'for without exception the cultural treasures he surveys have an origin which he cannot contemplate without horror' (Benjamin 2000 120). The horror is accentuated when no origin is evident at all and devolves into myth and mystery. Hayden White argues that the 'tropic is the shadow from which all realistic discourse tries to flee' (H. White 2), and yet within the modern tradition of representing London – and perhaps all major cities – there is a constant pull towards both the tropic (image, memory) and the discursive (narrative, history) in creative tension with the physical presence and lived experience of the city. Despite Peter Ackroyd's question – 'Is London, then, just a state of mind? The more nebulous its boundaries, and the protean its identity, has it now become an attitude or a set of predilections?' (Ackroyd 2001 750) – it is not so easy to shake off the materiality of the city even if the relationship is discursively and aesthetically complex as the readings that follow will demonstrate.

The following chapters are best read as six interventions into the post-war image, history and narrative of the city, through significant London texts around six significant social and cultural themes: post-war reflections on the Blitz, dystopian visions of the city, the reformulation of personal relationships, the reformulation of class identities, immigration to the city and the historical representation of the city. Despite the separate chapters and texts, the texts and themes are closely interrelated. What occurs are a series of reformulations of the tropic and discursive that has much to do with changes and developments in the social and material fabric of the city over this period. Ways of writing the city are reformulated rather than rejected between the texts and there are thematic, tropic, and discursive, continuities with earlier writing on London which I have identified when significant. In Chapter 1 I explore the immediate post-war representation of the Blitz through novels by Graham Greene, Elizabeth Bowen and Patrick Hamilton. Each of these three novels take life during wartime as their subject and are shaped by the immediate hardships of tightening rationing and the blasted remnants of the city. Contrary to subsequent popular myth, the Blitz these novels reveal is neither comradely nor egalitarian. The vestiges of pre-war fascism focused in London had not gone away, and lives as well as buildings remained shattered. Above all, there is a prevailing sense of malaise in British society that would not be renewed from above by the re-imposition of the pre-war social dispensation, but by a certain degree of faith that has its locus in the city.

By contrast, Chapter 2 reveals the flip-side of post-war representations of London that is dystopian in tone and would persist throughout the period. This chapter takes us from the late 1940s to the mid-1970s, although each version of the city in extremis has a different social and cultural base. In *Nineteen Eighty-Four* (1949) George Orwell's immediate post-war fears centre on totalitarian government and a shattered social, material and political infrastructure. Anthony Burgess's *A Clockwork Orange* (1962) would register a similar unease of authoritarian government, but also contemporary fears of the new assertiveness of a distinct youth culture. J. G. Ballard's *High-Rise* (1975) registers considerable disgust at the social consequences of communities disconnected from the city in new high-rise developments suggesting that they have enervating and debilitating consequences. In each of these three novels there is a distinct predilection for the close sociability and proximity of the city and its ability to signify community, that contrasts with the modernist anxiety of anonymity and anomie of the previous generation. The city is in each novel a potential source of redemption against some of the exaggerations of post-war political and social trends. Chapter 3 draws us directly back into the contemporary lived city through David Lodge's first novel *The Picturegoers* (1960), Lynne Reid Banks's *The L-Shaped Room* (1960) and Rodney Garland's novel of Gay London *The Heart in Exile* (1953). Still informed by the consequences of the war and social upheaval, teenage identities and community, this chapter explores how relationships in the new urban milieu are sustained in an era of shifting sexual mores but also porous class boundaries. I argue that retrospective periodization labels such as 'swinging' London and 'the permissive society' have little writ in literary engagements with the city during the period.

Chapter 4 develops further the representation of class realignments in the city, particularly as this is manifested in attitudes towards the material fabric of London through gentrification or the aspirations of class mobility, in readings of Stella Gibbons's *A Pink Front Door* (1959), B. S. Johnson's *Albert Angelo* (1964) and Doris Lessing's *The Four-Gated City* (1969). Again, issues of community come to the fore as a major motif in post-war literary representations of London, but also revealing a tension between the permanently settled and the transient, traditional notions of national and class identity, and the rebuilding of London and British society. Lessing's novel will swing us back to a dystopian vision of the future, but here with a more explicit notion of redemption based around the ties that bind communities and families together. Chapter 5 explores the social, material and cultural consequences of the remaking of London, not on grounds of class – although this remains a factor – but ethnicity. It is no exaggeration to observe that post-war immigration to London from former British colonies and beyond has been a – if not the – most significant social change in London's population in the post-war period. Through Sam Selvon's *The Lonely Londoners* (1956), Colin MacInnes's *City of Spades* (1957), V. S. Naipaul's *The Mimic Men* (1967), and Buchi Emecheta's *Second-Class Citizen* (1974), I explore how coming to terms with and remoulding the social spaces of London presents a major challenge in the search for new urban identities. Rather than any sort of homogenous experience, the draw of the imperial capital has produced a diverse range of experiences and identities. While racist attitudes are a major factor in these novels, of more importance is the utility of the city as a 'contact zone' for exiles, migrants and the socially ambitious. Identification with and within the city, partial, limiting, but sometimes successful, is the basis for a unique identity that demonstrates considerable continuity with social and literary strategies for representing the city explored in earlier chapters.

Chapter 6 draws together the major thematic strands of the post-war city – image, history and narrative – in consideration of a literary trend that emerges in the late 1970s that reflects upon London as trope, discourse and material space. Resonating back through the preoccupations of the previous chapters, this is a form of meta-writing that operates through a high degree of self-conscious engagement with the conception of the city, its formulation, identity and ability to both embrace and provoke moments of the utmost uncanny. Moving into the political and social upheaval of the Thatcher era, the loss of a unitary government for the capital engenders a crisis of urban identity, a sense with which Maureen Duffy's *Capital* (1975), Peter Ackroyd's *Hawksmoor* (1985) and Michael Moorcock's *Mother London* (1988) are replete. London becomes a revenant whereby history returns as the repressed, the disjunctive and the uncanny – a sense only countered by Moorcock's novel that returns the reader to earlier notions of urban and historical community, but through memory and friendship rather than an abstract notion of the city. As Jonathan Raban concluded his groundbreaking 1974 study *Soft City*: 'We need – more urgently than architectural utopias, ingenious traffic systems, or ecological programmes – to comprehend the nature of citizenship, to make a serious imaginative assessment of that special relationship between self and the city; it unique plasticity, its privacy and freedom' (Raban 250). London's writers have responded.

1

Blitz Retrospective

Violence comes to us more easily because it was so long expected not only by the political sense but by the moral sense. The world we live in could not have ended any other way ... One feels at home in London ... or in any of the bombed cities ... because life there is what it ought to be. If a cracked cup is put in boiling water it breaks, and an old dog-toothed civilization is breaking now.

Graham Greene, *Collected Essays*

London between 1945 and 1951 was a city coming to terms with a radically changed metropolitan landscape. The legacy of the war was everywhere to be seen. The destruction of vast tracts of the city, the docks and other districts in the Blitz of 1941 was further compounded by the random devastation of the V1 and V2 'vengeance' weapons of 1945, revealing urban vistas not seen for centuries. Building materials would remain in short supply for years, as would almost everything else, lending the city a worn, shattered façade compounded by an air of stale decay: 'London looked broken, drab, patched, tired out and essentially Victorian still' (J. White 44). A regime of sharp rationing would continue its grip on everyday life and would not begin to ease until 1950. In fact in the short term rationing increased in severity, amplifying what was already a thriving black market. As if to add to the misery, 1947 would see one of the worst winters on record, hitting London particularly harshly and exacerbated by coal shortages. The population of London had changed too. The war years had seen evacuations, huge civilian casualties, swarms of allied troops lending the city an exaggerated cosmopolitanism, and a semi-permanent population sleeping underground at night: 'During the first quarter of 1945 the number of shelterers remained fairly constant at 12,500 in the underground and about 5,000 in the new deep tube shelters' (Waller 138). It would not be until 1951 that greater London as a whole would approach its pre-war population of over 8 million, but inner London at 3.4 million was 15 per cent below its 1939 population, indicating a definite demographic shift. By contrast, the outer suburbs had rapidly expanded in the same period. Such population shifts would significantly affect the post-war reconstruction of London and, inevitably, its culture.

The war years had seemingly broken down what Georg Simmel has described as the 'reserve' of the city-dweller, the defensive mechanism by which the individual negotiates the 'touch-and-go elements of metropolitan life' (Simmel 412). Certainly, sentiments of the kind expressed by one woman who was still living in Elephant and Castle underground station at the end of April 1945, even though not homeless, can be found throughout the war period: 'I stay here because I like it', she said, 'I like the company and the noise of the trains. I shall be sorry to go home' (Waller 138). This sort of public sentiment and camaraderie, encouraged by wartime government propaganda and amplified by post-war nostalgia, represents a powerful conceptualization of wartime London that has been challenged by Angus Calder in *The Myth of the Blitz* (1991). Regardless of the actuality of this camaraderie during the war years, the social perception of the period in the history and culture of London has been one of mutual support, steadfastness and grim determination powerfully contributing to the war effort. The contemporary observation of Macdonald Hastings that 'Throughout the long war, from beginning to end, London has been the wedge that's kept the door of freedom open' expresses a common sentiment that still has considerable power (Waller 1). By contrast, the acute austerity of the immediate post-war period has received no such mythologization. Despite the political euphoria that swept a Labour government to power in 1945, the multitude of problems between 1945 and 1951 soon led to disillusionment as grim as the cracked and crumbling façade of the city.

A similar disillusionment can be discerned in the cultural expectations of the early post-war years. The auspices for an artistic revival were good after the hiatus of the war years. Even government support was forthcoming, with the Arts Council receiving a royal charter in 1945. Mollie Panter-Downes noted in the spring of that year that there was an audience in London starved of new work:

> During the war years, more and more Londoners have taken to reading poetry, listening to music, and going to art exhibitions, although there is less and less of all three to be had in this shabby, weary capital. Most of the poets are too personally involved in the war to have attained that state of impersonal tranquillity which generates good poetry. (Waller 92)

The paucity of artistic gratification for London's population reinforces the general sense of disappointment and malaise in the early post-war years, registered in contemporary and modern surveys of post-war fiction. The period is constructed in cultural terms as a hiatus; a lying fallow in expectation of a new literary renaissance after the cataclysm of world war. As John Lehmann wrote in 1950, the tomorrow of this intellectual rebirth was still awaited: 'Is it merely that an altered situation, a changed mixture of feeling is waiting, as so often before, for a new catalyst, a new formula, a new innovation of genius to lead the dance of our tomorrow?' (Sissons and French 212). Thence the despair of the leading literary periodical of the war, *Horizon* in 1947: 'It is disheartening to think that twenty years ago saw the first novels of Hemingway, Faulkner, Elizabeth Bowen, Rosamund Lehmann, Evelyn Waugh, Henry Green, Graham Greene, to name but a few, for no new crop of novelists has arisen commensurate with them' (Sissons and French 212). By contrast, the war years saw a notable surge in interest in literature among servicemen and women, with hours to pass between repetitive duties and with limited outlets for entertainment. However, Bernard Bergonzi notes that while 'Editors and critics in the late Forties tended to see the contemporary literary scene as exceptionally barren, and it is usually presented as a dull and empty period', those 'writers who were already established – especially novelists – produced outstanding work, and the years between 1945 and 1951 were much more interesting and productive than is often thought' (Bergonzi 84). Moreover, many of the best examples of that work were of and about London.

Inevitably the literary situation, especially in relation to significant representations of London, is more complex than these critical overviews would suggest. Certainly, initial responses to the war years and immediately after were set by writers who had established themselves in the 1930s or earlier, and who continued to write through the war to considerable critical acclaim. This chapter will consider work by three of the most important of those authors, whose work plotted the changing physical and social map of London – Patrick Hamilton, Elizabeth Bowen and Graham Greene. One could undoubtedly continue this train of literary association since the London Blitz has continued to hold the imagination of writers, particularly in popular fiction. Yet the authors selected here represent a specific analysis of the destruction, realignment and rewriting of London's physical, social and cultural matrix, different in form and intent to later nostalgia-laden, romanticized, historical fictions. Yet there is a link between the sparse gloom, anger and paranoia of representations of wartime London in the 1940s and 1950s, and the romanticized city of later popular fictions. Such nostalgia masks the real depravations of the period, evoking more positive memories of the past that creates not only a 'myth of the Blitz' as Calder suggests, but an ongoing mythologization of London. As Sallie Westwood and John Williams observe, 'such feelings are lived in the present as sentiments, as pleasures and yet are also bound to loss and discomfort with a familiar world removed and now remodelled within the imagination' (Westwood and Williams 12). The novels featured in this chapter do not rely on the temporal distancing of nostalgia and 'remodelled imagination'. Their loss, and the loss of their generation, is tackled by an unflinching engagement with the complex social reformulation facing the country, and seen with greatest intensity in London, the setting and symbolic subject of their novels.

The additional factor of London introduces another narrative structure into these texts that has resisted the influence of 're-remembering' the Blitz. The city brings to the fore another narrated history and psychological palette. As Simmel observes: 'The metropolis reveals itself as one of those great historical formations in which the opposing streams which enclose life unfold, as well as join one another with equal right. However, in this process the currents of life, whether their individual phenomena touch us sympathetically or antithetically, entirely transcend the sphere for which the judge's attitude is appropriate' (Simmel 419). The psychological experience of the metropolis is antithetical to the type of totalizing 'myth' that Calder identifies. Cities are comprehended by historically sensitive metaphors experienced alongside and mutually influencing the material city. As Homi Bhabha reminds us: 'Remembering is never a quiet act of introspection or retrospection. It is a painful re-remembering, a putting together of the dismembered past to make sense of trauma of the present' (Westwood and Williams 12). Bhabha's anatomic register of 'dismemberment' and 'trauma' evokes a persistent metaphor for London as a body with a heart, veins and vital organs, that breathes and broods. Indeed, soon after the fall of France, Churchill spoke of the ability of London to swallow up an entire army by herself. Peter Ackroyd is sensitive to the ubiquity of such metaphors in *London: The Biography*:

> London is a labyrinth, half of stone and half of flesh. It cannot be conceived in its entirety but can be experienced only in a wilderness of alleys and passages, courts and thoroughfares, in which even the most experienced citizen may lose his way; it is curious too, that this labyrinth is in a continual state of change and expansion. (Ackroyd 2001 2)

A labyrinth is akin to a narrative. Michel de Certeau argues that the act of walking the city is comparable to the relationship between the act of speaking and the language spoken (de Certeau 97). The novels examined in this chapter are awkward, disturbing, edgy, angry, contradictory and elegiac, much as the bombed city might be described. By inscribing that experience they evoke a particular language or narrative of the city and create what Walter Benjamin has called a 'materialistic historiography' (Wolfreys 9). This is not mimetic, but a structure of feeling that resists the sentimentalization of the past and of the city.

In 1945 before the end of the war, Elizabeth Bowen had observed of London: 'It is no doubt an old and interesting city but to me it has come unstuck' (Glendenning 165). On one level, this registers Bowen's sense of yearning for her native Ireland and an aversion to an ascendant post-war Labour government after the fervour of the war years defined by Churchill, whom she greatly admired. Yet there is more here. A city that has come unstuck is certainly symbolic of a civilization perceived to be in decline, or at least dramatic readjustment to a very different world dominated by two emerging superpowers, the USA and the USSR. An equally dramatic social revolution was also in progress, as Anthony Howard observed:

> For 1945 was not merely a political watershed: it had at least the potentiality for being a social one too. The war had not only buried the dinner jacket – it had reduced famous public schools to pale, evacuated shadows, it had destroyed the caste system in the Civil Service, it had eroded practically every traditional social barrier in Britain. (Sissons and French 30)

The Heat of the Day was partly written during the final year of the war. The first five chapters were completed by 1944 but then put aside when Bowen turned to her short stories. An explanation for this hiatus can be found in an essay written in 1942: 'One cannot reflect, or reflect on, what is not wholly in view'. As Renee Hoogland observes: 'fragmentation on the level of empirical reality effects a measure of disintegration that transgresses the limits of subjective comprehension. The war produced a degree of meaninglessness that fell outside anyone's imaginative scope' (Hoogland 109). Bowen returned to the novel in 1945, but it was not published until 1948 (1949 USA). Given that the 'empirical reality' of the novel is in fact London in wartime rather than simply 'the war', Hoogland's reading of Bowen's difficulties invites further consideration, especially when related to Bowen's 1942 comments about critical distance. This novel is a hybrid text, written both during and after the war, embedded both in the social and cultural experiences of the war years and in the volatile and difficult early post-war period during which London had come 'unstuck' in Bowen's imagination. Knowledge of the division of the narrative into two such distinct compositional blocks also invites evaluation of the strong impression created of London throughout the novel as well as changing social and cultural perceptions. While 1944, 1945 and 1947 are chronologically close, they represent tectonic upheavals in historical terms.

The plot structure of the novel certainly owes something to two important wartime books that also share a strong London focus: Patrick Hamilton's *Hangover Square* (1941) and Graham Greene's *Ministry of Fear* (1943). Hamilton's novel charts the final year in the career of the schizophrenic George Bone, obsessed by desire for the feckless manipulative Netta and her nasty friend and sometime lover, the car dealing proto-spiv Peter. Despite the ever-present homicidal tendencies exacerbated by his illness, the sympathy of the reader is all with George, from whose perspective the narrative largely unfolds. This sympathy is further underlined when it becomes clear that Netta

and Peter are keen pre-war appeasers and closet fascists who celebrated Chamberlain's accommodation with Hitler (unlike the
strongly opposed George). In a burst of violence releasing the
incremental tension of the novel, George finally kills Peter and Netta,
on the day in 1939 that Germany invades Poland. The dazed, confused and mentally unstable George heralds the oncoming war by
finally turning his fury and repulsion on the novel's two fascists – later
killing himself. The symbolism is hard to miss. The appropriately
named 'George' evokes England's national saint, and his experience
suggests something of the national 'repression' consequent to
appeasement, but action and war seem to herald self-destruction;
appropriate enough, perhaps, from the perspective of the Blitz when
the novel was written.

The Ministry of Fear is set at the height of the Blitz and features
another triangle of two men and one woman. The hero and narrative
focalizer is another seriously damaged man. Where George Bone
displays schizophrenia, Arthur Rowe killed his terminally ill wife a few
years before the outbreak of the war. Given a nominal sentence by a
sympathetic court that is mirrored by the press, who dub his act a
'mercy killing', he lives a life of voluntary social exclusion, deliberately
cut off from family and friends. But the war, and his accidental
entanglement with an Austrian brother and sister, the Hilfes, marks
the beginning of his reintegration into society. The novel turns upon
an attempt by the spy ring he has stumbled upon to blow him up with
a parcel bomb. Suffering severe amnesia, Rowe refashions himself
after the questionable 'Boy's Own' adventure values of his youth,
which enable him ultimately to vanquish the plot against him. Having
effectively forgotten his past long enough to alert the authorities and
ultimately tackle the fascist spy brother, and to fall in love with the
more sympathetic sister, the traditional adventure ending of the
better man 'getting the girl' provides narrative closure but along the
way raises more concerns than it lays to rest. While central London is
being bombed, the spy ring Rowe encounters is located at the heart of
the suburban middle classes, suggesting something rotten at the heart
of British culture – echoed in the epigraph from Greene that heads
this chapter – and Bowen's estimation that the city, and thereby
Britain, has become 'unstuck'. Similarly, the revival of adventure
sentiments and moral judgements cast in black and white simplicity
sits uneasily in a complex and compromised London milieu.

Like Hamilton's Bone, Rowe thwarts the evil and seductive fascists,
but at the expense of revealing something rotten at the core of British
society. The logic of Bone's suicide is here replaced with a fabricated
identity that only serves to repress the past. Moreover, Rowe's
attachment to Anna Hilfe clearly anticipates the liberation of Europe
from the grip of the fascists. Yet the characterization of occupied and
fascist Europe as a woman is problematic. Anna is rescued and

'occupied' by a man who has killed his wife. There is a shared symbolism here with Hamilton's novel. In both cases, the suppression of the past seems to be founded on the death of a woman. If this is intended to point to the purging of a compromised pre-war history and a renewal of British vitality, it can also be said to be a reassertion and validation, based on masculine values of violence. In this context, it is difficult not to read the pre-war appeasement of Hitler by Chamberlain as 'feminine' compromise and weakness set against Churchill's promise of masculine action and violence. Yet both George Bone and Arthur Rowe act in unbalanced psychological states. Rowe has yet to recover properly from amnesia and Bone has given in to his schizophrenia.

The Heat of the Day is also structured around a love triangle between two men and a woman that is explicitly related to the ideological and social struggles attendant on the war. Yet while sharing the noiresque atmosphere of *Hangover Square* as well as elements of the city's wartime hedonism, there is a significant change in gender perspective since it is the two men who present disturbing insights into the underbelly of wartime London. The solid Stella ostensibly fits the bill as a conventional femme fatale as the guilty party in a divorce long before the war. Her lover Robert is revealed to be selling secrets to the enemy, and hunted by the odious counter-spy Harrison who proposes not to implicate Robert to the authorities if Stella sleeps with him. Despite what we know of Stella in an age much less sympathetic to divorce than our own and scarcely tolerant of sex outside marriage despite the war, she is an extremely sympathetic character. The strategy is similar to that used by Hamilton and Greene. Instead of schizophrenia and 'mercy' killing, Stella is tarnished by the double standards of social and sexual betrayal. The reader's sympathies are later rewarded when we learn that she was in fact the innocent party in her divorce – betrayed rather than betraying. That Stella has allowed herself to be seen as an adulteress provides a crucial insight into her character and the themes of the book. Stella elaborates on her past to Harrison, the counter-spy:

> What I am talking about is the loss of face ... How do you suppose that felt? All the world to know. To be the one who was left – the boring pathetic casualty, the 'injured' one ... It was a funny day when the other, the opposite story came round to me – the story of how I had walked out on Victor. Who was I to say no to it: why should I? Who, at the age I was, would not rather sound a monster than look a fool? (*Heat* 224; second ellipsis original)

This decision shapes her into the strong, self-sufficient woman that we see in the novel, well prepared for the social realities of the war. As Hermione Lee observes of Bowen's wartime writing: 'All the war-time stories are concerned with a diminishment of feeling and with an international – not merely a personal – loss of innocence' (Lee 162–3). As with George Bone and Arthur Rowe, Stella's history and character has a broader symbolic import within the novel. She both remains loyal to her country by abhorring Robert's espionage, while remaining true to her social attachments by not simply rejecting him when the truth is known. Her former loss of innocence and the need to resist negative social approbation gives her the strength to avert complicity with both Robert's actions and the sordid option offered by Harrison. Each man, both spies, is seen to be equally flawed. As representatives of the two sides in the war their very natures question the ideological underpinnings of the conflict, initiating a debate that looks forward to the conclusion of the war and Britain's future.

Underlying these psychological, social and political tensions is London, the 'unstuck' city. Bowen was later to observe of her wartime writing that: 'I see war ... more as a territory than as a page in history' (Bloom 1987 81). This imaginative and textual spatialization of the war is formally 'placed' in London. Place is an important aspect of Bowen's writing, as Lee argues: 'What has always ominously characterized her treatment of place is the loss of self. When places cease to function properly, their inhabitants lose selfhood, and are doubly "disinherited"' (Lee 158). Wartime London in *The Heat of the Day* is certainly such an ominous place, as can be seen from the descriptive passage that precedes Harrison's first revelations about Robert's activities:

> This fairly old house in Waymouth Street, of which her flat took up the top floor, was otherwise in professional – doctors' and dentists' – occupation and was accordingly empty at most week-ends: below her now were nothing but empty rooms; the caretakers living in the basement almost always went out on Sunday evenings. Silence mounted the stairs, to enter her flat through the door ajar; silence came through the windows from the deserted street. In fact, the scene at this day and hour could not have been more perfectly set for violence – but that was not on the cards. She had recognized in him, from the first, the quietness of a person perpetually held back from some extreme: it had not, however, been until this morning, on the telephone, that the quietness became an extreme itself. (*Heat* 23)

The uncanny weekend emptiness of the city's commercial premises is accentuated by the wartime atmosphere. The uncanniness permeates both inside and outside the building; the empty, deserted building is threatening but it is the violence that seeps in from the city streets paradoxically as silence that heralds the devastating consequences of Harrison's revelations about Robert. For Stella at this moment, there is none of the wartime camaraderie or the thronging streets of the metropolis to relieve her isolation. The entire passage creates a gothic atmosphere that accentuates Stella's potential vulnerability. The passage also draws upon a specifically urban trope of the alienated individual, although the scene lacks the direct impression of the impersonal city crowd. Instead, Stella is, paradoxically, crowded by silence. The suppression of the London evening by blackout regulations comes to be personified in Harrison, the threatening gothic male, a lone wanderer of the city streets but also a covert soldier in a secret war. He is the ultimate urban stranger whom Stella continually struggles to place and categorize.

The effect of this city of silence in *The Heat of the Day* is to accentuate the individual against the homogenized suffering of the war and the seething crowds of the metropolis. Certainly the blackout is a manifestation of the war, as is the Blitz of the early days of Stella's and Robert's relationship. All of the principal characters are employed in the war – Robert is a wounded soldier and works in the Ministry of Defence, which is where he gains access to sensitive information; Stella with her language gifts works for the Ministry of Information; Harrison presumably works in an official agency as a counter-spy. Of the more minor characters, Roderick, Stella's son, is in the army, Stella's young counterpart Louie works in a factory on war-related work, and her friend Connie works for the Civil Defence. And yet the atmosphere of the novel is intensely isolating. London had originally signified for Stella an 'opportunity to make or break, to free herself' (*Heat* 25). Even after her first meeting with Harrison at the funeral of her cousin Francis, Stella still feels release from his oppressive gaze as her train approaches London: 'As the suburbs thickened on either hand she felt less constricted, and bolder' (*Heat* 86).

Yet the city has become a place of oppressive silence and violence, no longer the site of freedom or boldness by the time of her second meeting with Harrison at her flat. It is a curious detail that Stella leaves the door ajar for both the atmosphere of violence and Harrison to enter her personal space. When we learn that the flat is only partly her space being rented furnished: 'It's not mine ... Nothing in this flat is' (*Heat* 28), it is another instance of Stella being misread by appearances as she had been in her divorce. Yet Stella still almost invites Harrison into her home, suggesting some consciousness of the import of what he represents and what she will learn. This becomes evident from another London image that has the wartime city counting down time like a monstrous antique clock, even though her curtained and blacked-out room lacked an 'apprehension of time':

> It was imperfect silence, mere resistance to sound – as though the inner tension of London were being struck and struck on without breaking. Heard or unheard, the city at war ticked over – if from this quarter, from these immediate streets, the suction of cars in private movement was gone, there was all the time a jarring at the periphery, an unintermittent pumping of vital traffic through arterial streets into arterial roads. Nor was that quite all: once or twice across the foreground of hearing a taxi careered as though under fire. (*Heat* 56)

This is, of course, a manifestation of the organic trope associated with London, and hints at Ackroyd's identification of cities with labyrinths. Here it reinforces the interaction of these few characters as in some way localized, or disconnected from the metropolis as a whole. Here there is both anonymity and the threat of the unknown in 'arterial streets' and 'arterial roads'. It is significant that an established city trope is being used to accentuate the uncanny atmosphere of the narrative. As Burton Pike argues: 'The inhabitant or visitor basically experiences the city as a labyrinth, although one with which he may be familiar. He cannot see the whole of a labyrinth at once, except from above, when it becomes a map. Therefore his impressions of it at ground level at any given moment will be fragmentary and limited: rooms, buildings, streets' (Pike 9). Indeed, across this no man's land of silent violence, Stella imagines that a taxi 'careered as though under fire'. The city has become a living landscape of projected anxiety, threat, a battleground and augur of imminent change upon which Stella steadies herself to fight, but on a field that is increasingly obscured the further one looks beyond herself and her close associates. Moreover, the image suggests that her relationship with Robert is running out of time and looking towards the obscurity of future events. Published in 1948, this obscurity is set against an eminently known wartime temporal and physical landscape to which the novel is tied. Stella's affair with Robert starts during the 1941 Blitz, and the conclusion of the novel brings us to the first V1 raids of 1944. The issue is just how far the affair is keyed into the rhythm of what is rapidly becoming the myth of wartime London.

The time and space of this narrative is one of the most inventive aspects of the novel. With this setting established, it is not until chapter 5 – the last of the chapters written during the war – that the unravelling of Stella and Robert's relationship from inception in 1941 until the night if the second meeting with Harrison is revealed in an extended anterior narrative:

> The first few times they had met she had not noticed the limp – or, if, vaguely, she had, she had put it down to the general rocking of London and one's own mind ...
> They had met one another, at first not very often, throughout that heady autumn of the first London air raids. Never had any season been more felt; one bought the poetic sense of it with the sense of death. Out of the mists of morning charred by the smoke from the ruins each day rose to a height of unmisty glitter ... All through London, the ropings-off of dangerous tracts of street made islands of exalted if stricken silence, and people crowded against the ropes to admire the sunny emptiness on the other side. The diversion of traffic out of blocked main thoroughfares into byways, the unstopping phantasmagoric streaming of lorries, busses, vans, drays, taxis past modest windows and quiet doorways set up an overpowering sense of London's

organic power – somewhere here was a source from which heavy motion boiled, surged and, not to be damned [*sic*] up, forced for itself new channels. (*Heat* 90–1)

The equation between Robert's limp, the bombing of London and Stella's state of mind is a further symbolic indication of how closely the city is tied to both character psychology and narrative structure in the novel. Robert is maimed by enemy action but survives, the severity of his limp fluctuating with the intensity of the bombing. Likewise, the 'body' of the city is injured, but 'London's organic power' reasserts itself and the 'arterial' flow of the city's lifeblood – traffic – finds other routes to flow: 'boiled, surged and, not to be damned up, forced for itself new channels'. The link between the injured Robert and the ravaged city does, however, raise important questions. One of the consequences of Robert's experience and wounding at Dunkirk is an intense disillusionment that leads directly to his subsequent espionage. Rather than buy into the myth of triumph associated with the gallant retrieval of men by civilian boats, Robert recalls that the military action leading up to that point was an ignominious defeat: 'Dunkirk was waiting there in us – what a race! A class without a middle, a race without a country. Unwhole. Never earthed in – and there are thousands of thousands of us, and we're still breeding – breeding what?' (*Heat* 272–3). The implication is that London and, by extension, Britain is similarly damaged, is at risk of imploding. In Robert's view British culture is materially and psychologically in a terminal state and, like Bowen's reading of London, 'unstuck'.

Robert's justification for his treason looks ahead to post-war disillusionment, and it is significant that the explanation he offers Stella emerges in the portion of the book written after the war. Yet it is Stella's engagement with the city that creates the counter experience of Robert and his 'injured' London. A further reading of the above passage points to how life flows on in London despite the extravagant injury of the bombing. Much as Stella weathers the vicissitudes of her own life, 'life' in London goes on regardless. Stella's experience of London and her romance closely references the seasons and more locally, the cycle of the day. From sunrise to sunset throughout 'that heady autumn ... Never had any season been more felt' (*Heat* 90). The nightly destruction is followed by a daily sense of hope: 'the daytime as pure and curious holiday from fear.' Hope arises from the dust and ashes of despair, while people are forcing for themselves 'new channels' like the relentless traffic, which is itself a signifier for the unchastened energy of the city. Stella emerged from her divorce injured but took the opportunity to remake herself, to rechannel herself; her move to London and relationship with Robert heralds one change, and the advent of Harrison another. Beyond Robert's nihilism and self-loathing, Stella is a counterpoint for life, change, reinvention and a full-blooded grasp of the future rather than the past; a past that stultifies Robert, emblemized by his family and their uncomfortable suburban house. And yet the freedom Stella discerns in the city is a debatable commodity, an illusionary liberation, as Jonathan Raban observes: 'The city our great modern form, is soft, amenable to a dazzling and libidinous variety of lives, dreams, inter-pretations. But the very plastic qualities which make the city the great liberator of human identity also cause it to be especially vulnerable to psychosis and totalitarian nightmare' (Raban 15).

Nightmare and psychosis could easily be read onto Robert and Harrison, yet London is also a city of the dead – the difference between night and day. The day brings life and a reprieve from fear, the night the death and danger of the Blitz. Significantly, Harrison visits during the night, and Robert will eventually leap to his death into night-time darkness from Stella's rooftop. Thence if the days produced moments of 'stricken silence' and 'dazzlingly silent lakes' (91), static moments of spatialized anticipation, the silence of the night is of threatened violence. The silence of the night is life anticipating death and is associated with Harrison and, latterly, Robert:

> The night behind and the night to come met across every noon in an arch of strain. To work or think was to ache. In offices, factories, min-istries, shops, kitchens the hot yellow sands of each afternoon ran out slowly; fatigue was the one reality. You dared not envisage sleep. Apa-thetic, the injured and dying in hospitals watched light change on walls which might fall tonight. Those rendered homeless sat where they had been sent; or, worse, with the obstinacy of animals retracted their steps to look for what was no longer there. Most of all the dead, from mor-tuaries, from under cataracts of rubble, made their anonymous pre-sence – not as today's dead but as yesterday's living – felt through London. Uncounted, they continued to move in shoals through the city day, pervading everything to be seen or heard or felt with their torn-off senses, drawing on this tomorrow they had expected – for death cannot be so sudden as all that. Absent from the routine which had been life, they stamped upon that routine their absence ... (*Heat* 91–2)

There is a clear echo of T. S. Eliot's *The Waste Land* in this passage, which is itself a reference to Dante's *Inferno* (iv. 25–7): 'I had not thought death had undone so many.' The dead have undone – 'unstuck' – the living. Or more precisely, it is Robert and Harrison who are unstuck and undone by turns, through the motif of night-mare and paranoia. Moreover, the familiar city trope, the anonymity of the urban crowd is, as with Eliot's poem, equated with death. Thence in both texts, the state of the people in the post-war city – albeit the First World War in Eliot's poem – merely serves to accentuate the dilemma or decline of the living city. The vocabulary of this passage blurs the distinction between the routine patterns of

everyday life and the extraordinary events of the war, superimposing a
numb despair – 'strain', 'ache', 'fatigue', 'apathetic', 'obstinacy',
'cataracts', 'torn', 'death'. Life in the city grinds on in accordance
with a logical regularity, like the machinery of a clock or some great
living organism, which are metaphors carefully chosen by Bowen.
Stella meets Robert during the death and destruction of the Blitz,
and then meets Harrison for the first time at the funeral of her ex-
husband's cousin. Both characters are tied into the 'unreal' wartime city
and death – 'absent from the routine which had been life' – undone.

The absence of routine is of course war; its persistence the hope of
life and survival. Both Robert and Harrison persist in their battle over
information and allegiances among the visible dead of battlefield
London. They never inhabit the daytime where death is repressed as
an absence, a 'stricken' or 'dazzling' silence. Instead over the 'catar-
act' of the destruction, they are engaged in a life and death struggle
over the rubble that conceals the silent dead below. That they also
compete over Stella as part of the same struggle points to the lumi-
nescence suggested by her name. She remains part of the continued
'routine' of the city's life. She has a family and persists with family
rituals – Francis's funeral, her son's inheritance, the family visits with
her son. These are activities that simply do not exist for Harrison, and
are dysfunctional for Robert. Robert's final refusal to participate in
the family conference over whether to accept the offer made on the
family home underlines this detachment and inability to reconnect.
When Stella later reflects on their relationship she finally senses the
extent of his isolation: 'All the time, all the same, the current had
been against his face. The war-warmed impulse of people to be *a*
people had been derisory; he had hated the bloodstream of the
crowds, the curious animal psychic oneness, the human lava-flow'
(*Heat* 275). Notice how Robert has been excluded from the symbolic
organism of London. This is significant since the inability to belong
to the life of the city is representative of his inability to reconcile the
contradictions of a culture that he has condemned as 'never earthed
in' (*Heat* 272). As Burton Pike observes:

> The idea of the city seems to trigger conflicting impulses, positive and
> negative, conscious and unconscious. At a very deep level, the city
> seems to express our culture's restless dream about its inner conflicts
> and its inability to resolve them. On a more conscious level, this
> ambivalence expresses itself in mixed feelings of pride, guilt, love, fear,
> and hate toward the city. The fascination people have always felt at the
> destruction of a city may be partly an expression of satisfaction at the
> destruction of an emblem of irresolvable conflict. (Pike 8)

The Heat of the Day plays out this ambivalence through Stella, Robert,
Harrison and the agonies of London's destruction. The conclusion of
the novel takes the reader away from London. Roderick contemplates

his new estate in Eire; Louie leaves London with her new child, returning to her home town; Harrison has been stationed abroad; and Stella is about to be married again and will herself, one assumes, leave London. This epilogue to the novel sees London again being pounded by bombs, this time the V1 and V2 rockets of the 'mini Blitz'. London is once more facing destruction, but the characters and thence their stories are leaving its textual environs. A traditional novel concludes by looking forward to the fate of the characters, but here the abandonment of the city suggests also the abandonment of an 'emblem of irresolvable conflict' – London and British culture 'has come unstuck' (Glendenning 165).

Bowen's representation of the time and space of London within the narrative structure of *The Heat of the Day* provides a useful baseline for comparison with the remaining texts in this chapter. Kevin Lynch has suggested that for the inhabitant or visitor the cacophony of impressions of the city at street level is akin to a labyrinth and, as we have seen, it is a recurrent image in textual representations of cities. At street level, the city is fragmentary and limited to the individual's perception. 'He cannot see the whole of a labyrinth at once, except from above, when it becomes a map' (Lynch 1–2). Literary representation, unlike individual perception, has the ability to narrate the local but also generalize across the city providing an extended canvas to explore the feelings of both the individual character and the city as a whole, even if, in empirical terms, the latter is impossible. Bowen's strategy is to work from the local, usually from Stella's perception as the main focalizer for London, to impressions of London based on her emotional response to the scene in which she is involved, for example the silence of the street and the underlying violence of Stella's first encounter with Harrison. Stella's sense of threat and the oppressiveness of the moment are projected onto the street, and in a wider angle the city. These impressions do not totalize London as they remain Stella's impression based on local stimuli – distant traffic noise or the uncanny silence of the blackout. There are passages where London is totalized, but the significant occasions where this occurs are when Stella narrates and contemplates the two years of her relationship with Robert. The London of these major anterior narratives projects Bowen's own hesitation over writing contemporary events – 'One cannot reflect, or reflect on, what is not wholly in view' (Hoogland 109) – into Stella's narrative. Bowen is aided in this process by existing traditions of writing the city or, rather, the city as image: 'It is as if, by displacing the city backward in time ... they wished to ensure its metaphorization, to place it as firmly as possible in the realm of the imaginary while at the same time presenting it as a ''reality'' ' (Pike 13).

Other post-war writers would take a different approach to representing the space and time of wartime London and produce very different narratives as a consequence. Graham Greene's *The End of the Affair* (1951) and Patrick Hamilton's *The Slaves of Solitude* (1947) share several similarities with the plot structure of *The Heat of the Day*. Both novels feature a love triangle which provides the main narrative conflict, a feature they share not only with *The Heat of the Day* but also the two earlier war novels by Hamilton and Greene, *Hangover Square* and *The Ministry of Fear*. *The Slaves of Solitude* is set in late 1943, outside London in a fictionalized commuter town, Thames Lockdon (based on Henley-on-Thames), to which the protagonist, Londoner Miss Roach, has retreated during the Blitz. The main action is set around the vicissitudes of her experience in the boarding house where she stays, the Rosamund Tea Rooms. Here she has two foils, the appalling Mr Thwaites who revels in tormenting her, and Vicki Kugelmann, a German who had been living in Britain before the war and chose to remain. To round off the similarities to Greene's and Hamilton's earlier novels, Mr Thwaites was a pre-war fascist sympathizer and Vicki clearly does not have the critical attitude towards her country that her choice of residence might lead one to expect – Miss Roach even refers to her half seriously as 'a lonely "German spy" she had taken under her protection' (*Slaves* 49). The love triangle in this novel is formed between Miss Roach, Vicki and an American lieutenant stationed nearby, Dayton Pike. Once she moves into the Tea Rooms, Vicki consciously sets herself in competition with Miss Roach, vying for the attentions of the lieutenant and siding with Mr Thwaites in his persecution. The action peaks with the sudden death of Thwaites and Vicki being given notice to quit, precipitating Miss Roach's own return to her preferred environment and home, London.

The End of the Affair is, by comparison, an unusual narrative. Set in the south London suburbs immediately following the end of the war, it represents the unravelling of an affair between a writer, Maurice Bendrix, and the wife of a senior civil servant, Sarah Miles. Her husband, Henry Miles, works initially in the Ministry of Pensions but is then redeployed to the Ministry of Home Security as a consequence of the war. The affair encompasses the entire period of the war. Bendrix first meets Sarah in 1939 while conducting research for a novel which features a senior civil servant. They soon begin an affair and it is quickly apparent that, although not oppressive, Sarah's marriage to Henry has long been a sexless one. While London is seldom directly used as a palimpsest for the characters' emotions, as was evident in *The Heat of the Day*, the three-way relationship between Bendrix, Sarah and Henry is played out to the rhythm of wartime London. The most striking feature of the novel is the dramatic shift in narrative point of view when Bendrix obtains Sarah's diary from the private detective he has hired – recalling the private detectives in *The Ministry of Fear* and the spies in *The Heat of the Day*. At this point it is clear that Bendrix's attempts at understanding why Sarah broke off her relationship with him have been woefully inadequate, leading to a radical thematic shift. We learn that following a V1 bomb attack on the house in which she and Bendrix have been having an assignation, she swore an oath that if God spared her lover she would break off their 'sinful' relationship. When Bendrix does survive, the novel charts Sarah's attempt to come to terms with this oath which leads her into an internal struggle over faith and belief. As Paul O'Prey observes, the Blitz 'is the setting for the mysterious actions of a God who, to use the terminology of the novel, "seduces" His sinners to believe in Him, so that, in the midst of total violence, "sanctity and fidelity and the courage of human beings" are rediscovered' (O'Prey 89).

It is the representation of London in these two novels that is revealing of the thematic and structural similarities and differences between them and *The Heat of the Day*. While *The Slaves of Solitude* does not appear to be a London novel at all, being set outside London, the city remains the determining factor that gives Thames Lockdon its meaning. Yet there is a contradiction at the heart of this representation of London. It is a preferable locale to the stifling Tea Rooms and the small-town atmosphere of Thames Lockdon, but also a vast monster on the village's doorstep, consuming and drawing the inhabitants inwards and ejecting them when no longer needed:

> London, the crouching monster, like every other monster has to breathe, and breathe it does in its own obscure, malignant way. Its vital oxygen is composed of suburban working men and women of all kinds, who every morning are sucked up through an infinitely complicated respiratory apparatus of trains and termini into the mighty congested lungs, held there for a number of hours, and then, in the evening, exhaled violently through the same channels.
>
> The men and women imagine they are going into London and coming out again more or less of their own free will, but the crouching monster sees all and knows better.
>
> The area affected by this filthy inhalation actually extends beyond what we ordinarily think of as the suburbs – to towns, villages, and districts as far as, or further than, twenty-five miles from the capital. Amongst these was Thames Lockdon, which lay on the river some miles beyond Maidenhead on the Maidenhead line.
>
> The conditions were those of intense war, intense winter, and intensest black-out in the month of December. (*Slaves* 3)

This daemonic London is a variation on the city-as-body images evident in *The Heat of the Day*. In Bowen's novel it was traffic and roads as arteries within the body of the city; here it is the exhalation of the city beyond its physical confines which has, it appears, a malignant effect on the surrounding Home Counties. The two images have a history of association, as the geographer and statesman Halford Mackinder observed in 1902: 'The life of the great metropolis ... exhibits the daily throb of a huge pulsating heart. Every evening half a million men are sent in quick streams, like corpuscles of blood through the arteries, along the railways and the trunk roads outwards to the sub-urbs' (Porter 397). The transformation of this trope into the city as monster represents a familiar enough antagonism to the propensity of the city to expand and consume its hinterland, and the drudgery of commuter life in a similar vein to Eliot's workers crossing London Bridge: 'I had not thought death had undone so many'.

While there may be a common echo of Eliot's *The Waste Land* in both novels, there is a marked difference of intent, tone and theme to the trope in Hamilton's novel. In *The Heat of the Day*, the pulsating arteries of London's roads and inhabitants are signs of endurance if not resistance in the face of nightly bombing. London is wounded, but will endure. It is a hope that faces down the despair of the Blitz. Hamilton opens his novel with a negative image of London to which the war is incidental – in fact the war only impinges on the image in the last few lines of the passage. And yet, beyond this opening metaphor, London is represented positively throughout the rest of the novel from Miss Roach's point of view. It is a source of pride to her – 'She felt a sudden, delightful, modest, gin and french pride in her experience as a 1940s Londoner' (*Slaves* 28) – the location of useful and rewarding occupation – 'But there was not enough to occupy her in any sense fully or satisfactorily, and she often wished that she was going up to London and back again each day by train' (*Slaves* 148) – and socially and personally far more amenable place than the small world of Thames Lockdon and the Rosamund Tea Rooms – 'when at last she alighted at Thames Lockdon station (from London), instead of feeling composed, consoled, and refreshed, she was invariably filled with anxiety, apprehensiveness, and dejection' (*Slaves* 77). The city and Thames Lockdon are counterweights in the novel. London has the association of freedom and the release from stifling social constraints that Stella enjoyed when she came to London at the beginning of the war, only to discover that some constraints offer protection from risk, danger and betrayal. It is through the relaxed sensibilities of wartime London society that she comes to meet Robert and Harrison. For Miss Roach, the oppressiveness, bullying, sneering and immobility of the society at the Tea Rooms draws her back towards London. Indeed, the society of the Tea Rooms dominated by Mr Thwaites, and later Vicki, raises similar questions about the decline and decay of British society to the equally suburban home of Robert's family, with another very middle-England name 'Holme Deane' to compare with Thames Lockdon. As Harrison remarks when Stella tells him of her visit to the family, she 'Went to look at at the first place where the rot could start' (*Heat* 131). Robert would later cite his upbringing as a major source of his disillusionment and subsequent spying: 'A class without a middle, a race without a country. Unwhole. Never earthed in' (*Heat* 272). The English spy ring uncovered by Rowe in *The Ministry of Fear* is of course also located in the suburbs, and it is the same 'rot' that Miss Roach encounters at the Rosamund Tea Rooms.

None of these novels are a simple attack on the middle classes as a whole, but rather a distinction is drawn between characters who are rooted and secure with their identity and those who are not. The latter, in both *The Heat of the Day* and *The Slaves of Solitude*, are dangerous and often associated with fascism. For Stella the distinction is one of knowing where you are from, even while admitting she 'had come loose from her moorings' (*Heat* 114): 'Having been born to some idea of position, she seldom asked herself what her own was now – still less, what position was in itself' (*Heat* 115). In the latter novel, Mr Thwaites, Vicki Kugelmann, and also Lieutenant Pike are more radically cut asunder from their moorings. The lieutenant and Vicki are resident in a foreign country and are easily explicable in those terms, but it is Mr Thwaites who comes closest to the despair evidenced by Robert, although he lacks the sophistication of self-awareness, being a more instinctual creature. Significantly, he is adrift in middle-England and its boarding houses: 'He had money of his own and he had lived, resounded through boarding-houses and private hotels all his life' (*Slaves* 12). Moreover, he had squandered a connection with London and retreated into the world of transient suburban lodgings: 'He had at one time had a family connection with a firm of solicitors in London; but here he had never worked seriously, save at the task of torturing clerks and typists' (*Slaves* 12). And he of course retains his fascist sympathies: 'Mr Thwaites had, since 1939 slowly learned to swallow the disgrace of Hitler, whom he had been from the beginning, and still secretly remained, a hot disciple' (*Slaves* 14). By contrast, Miss Roach resembles Stella in her sense of identity and association with London both as workplace and as preferred home. This is most clearly signified by her understated resistance to Mr Thwaites and latterly Vicki.

Yet despite this intriguing reversal of the usual literary and thematic distinction between the country and the city, images of London continue to be negative in the first half of the novel, providing variations on the opening image of London as monster, creating a tension in the novel that replicates the conflict between the characters:

> At such moments the countryside, stealthily informing her of its immense size, would seem, of course, in grandeur, wildness and stillness, completely to dominate and submerge all things appertaining to men and towns, and to reduce, in particular, to microscopic, thread-like smallness the railway-tracks by which these communicated with each other – the noise of the trains thereon distantly falling on her straining ear like something less than minute rumblings in the enormous belly of the enormous supine organism enveloping her and everything. By this

adjustment of her sense of dimensions, Miss Roach's spirit, bathed in moonlight, would be composed, consoled and refreshed.

The train on the other hand, which Miss Roach normally took down from London to Thames Lockdon, had opposite ideas. So far from being aware of its doll-like magnitude in the night, of being diminished practically to the point of extinction by the surrounding void of fields, woods, and hills, it came crashing on, like a huge staggering bully, from station to station, lashing out right and left at the night, on which the tables were turned, which was itself relegated to nothingness, and whose very stars had less importance in the eyes of the train than one of the sparks from the funnel of its engine. (*Slaves* 76–7)

The first paragraph of this passage reminds the reader that Thames Lockdon is a small country town. The railway lines are a symbol of provincialism, connecting the town with the main lines of urban communication which have been reduced to small 'threads' suggesting a rather slim or fragile connection with the metropolis. Yet this is less a sign of preference for the small world of Thames Lockdon, than an obliteration of 'all things appertaining to men and towns' which provides Miss Roach with composure and relief. Yet the 'minute rumblings of a mighty belly of the enormous supine organism enveloping her and everything' recalls the great 'crouching monster' (*Slaves* 3) from the novel's opening paragraph. The trains are the rumble of the 'belly' but also Miss Roach's lifeline to London. It is less than clear whether 'the enormous supine organism' represents the calm countryside or the calm of the metropolis 'enveloping her and everything'. Given the relationship between the insularity of Thames Lockdon and the hope of London, the latter would seem the most likely reading and would correspond with her feelings towards the town. The crashing progress of the train obliterates the peace of the night and in turn Thames Lockdon for it is, of course, the London train.

Where this passage becomes less positive is the equation between the thundering progress of the train and 'a huge staggering bully', which at once suggests Mr Thwaites rather than Miss Roach's positive association with London. Indeed, it is clear that Miss Roach thinks of him as such early in the novel (*Slaves* 12). Yet it is important to note that it is the train 'down from London' towards Thames Lockdon and her torment at the Rosamund Tea Rooms. Whereas the first paragraph seems to emphasize the positive effects of the countryside over the looming city, it is the journey *from* the city, and more explicitly *to* Thames Lockdon, that is the source of horror. Given the context of these two passages it is likely that a distinction is intended between the countryside, the city, and the small-town Englishness of Thames Lockdon which increasingly becomes an overt issue in the novel thanks to the presence of Vicki Kugelmann. The passage is the reverse of Stella's experience on returning to London from the country, when she enjoys a gradual alleviating of pressure as she moves further into the heart of the city. Moreover, there is something of the cosmopolitan metropolitan's puzzlement over the suburban akin to this observation from John Buchan's *The Thirty-Nine Steps* (1915): 'But what fellows like me don't understand is the great comfortable, satisfied, middle-class world, the folk that live in villas and suburbs' (Buchan 226). The closet fascist sympathizer Thwaites is the doyen of this world, and as the trains emerge from London and approach Thames Lockdon they adopt his persona – the 'huge staggering bully' (*Slaves* 76).

Self-assertion over and escape from this suburban world is the ultimate goal of the novel. For Miss Roach, this is a problem. When pressured it is clear she would rather return to London but 'she was still too scared of the bombs. They had left London alone a long while now, but you never knew when they would return' (*Slaves* 122). But return she does after facing down – or rather pushing down – Mr Thwaites who then, coincidentally, takes ill and promptly dies, revealing the underlying weakness of his robust appearance. With the fascist tormentor vanquished, and a small inheritance in hand, Miss Roach has the confidence to return to London. Her return is, how-ever, prefigured by that of Archie Prest. Prest is another London exile yearning for his life in the city. Unlike Miss Roach, he has not fled the bombing but is a retired music-hall performer and comedian. Cru-cially, and significantly, he does not fit in at all with the Rosamund Tea Room idea of middle-class respectability: 'Though speaking, when he did, with a "common" accent, and dressing in a "common" way ... Though too quiet in his manners, and too seemly in his comings and goings, to give offence, he was yet regarded as being somehow beyond the pale' (*Slaves* 69). Prest is at the beginning of the novel merely part of the background to the guest house, being used to give an occasional outside view of the struggle between Miss Roach, Thwaites and Vicki, but he is symbolically important in understanding the relationship explored in the novel between the suburb, Thames Lockdon, and the metropolis, London. For Prest, retirement and exile from London is acutely debilitating:

> Mr Prest was, however, conscious of never having fully succeeded in life, of now belonging to the past, of being in more or less enforced retirement, and of being utterly unknown as a personality outside a circle of acquaintances in London which diminished year by year. He was, therefore, a miserable man – his sense of failure and futility showing in his demeanour. He had, in fact, something of the character and manner, as well as the external semblance, of a certain sort of ex-pugilist – an air of having been battered silly by life, of submissiveness to events, of gentleness, of willingness to please, of dog-like gloom and absent-mindedness as he floated through the day. (*Slaves* 70)

His only release is an occasional reconnection with that life in Lon-don when he revisits the pubs and restaurants frequented by his old colleagues in the city where he assumed 'an air of freshness and rejuvenation' (*Slaves* 71). Like Miss Roach, his link to London distinguishes him – professionally and personally – from the other inhabitants of the Tea Rooms, but also marks him out as alien. He and Miss Roach are the only members of the guest house to have actively defined professional careers. Of the two 'villains' of the novel, Thwaites has been idle much of his life bar his feeble flirtation with the legal profession, and Vicki is tied locally as the secretary to a vet. Both resent the perceived importance of Miss Roach's employment in London and her connection to 'high' culture as a publisher's assistant: 'she had sensed in Vicki, the vet's secretary, a certain distaste in regard to her connection and activities with a publishing firm in London', of which Mr Thwaites also expresses his 'vast resentment' (*Slaves* 98).

The class affiliations are significant and again underline the tripartite structure identified in relation to London, the countryside and the suburb. Miss Roach is middle class but, like Stella, has a sense of where she is from. Her father was a dentist and therefore a member of the established professions. Her family has at least some money, evidenced by the legacy that comes to her from her aunt enabling the material escape back to London. Perhaps most importantly, and emphasizing her cultural qualifications, she is a university graduate having 'matriculated', and has been a schoolmistress at a prep school. By comparison, Mr Thwaites seems only to read cheap thrillers and Vicki has no cultural aspirations at all, constantly shocking the retired Miss Roach by her crudeness. Mr Prest, while working class, is also tied to London's culture, albeit the popular culture of the music hall. A clear distinction is evident between the cultural desert of the suburbs dominated here by Thwaites and Vicki, and the social and cultural vibrancy of London. This reminds us that the monstrous apparition of London at the beginning of the novel represents a view of London tied to the lower middle class of suburbia fearing for their faux countryside idyll and showing their aversion to the cultural diversity and richness of the city.

Writing of the country/city binary in the inter-war years, Judy Giles and Tim Middleton observe that 'The cosy domesticity of suburbia was frequently attacked for its isolationism and cultural paucity … which hides deep villainy …' (Giles and Middleton 195). Greene's *The End of the Affair* is another suburban novel which certainly builds on these themes against the backdrop of wartime London and after. Whereas the city in both *The Heat of the Day* and *The Slaves of Solitude* is represented as a living entity, the London of *The End of the Affair* lacks this key element. The city is the container of the narrative; all of the action takes place either around the common of an anonymous south London suburb or in central London. This would suggest a structural affinity with Bowen's novel, but the reciprocal relationship between characters' emotions and the city landscape is not replicated. Ostensibly, London in Greene's novel is not a presence; it fails to become a symbolic landscape and thence underlines the isolation of the main characters whose struggles, jealousies and inadequacies expand to overwhelm the narrative space of the novel. Peter Mudford observes that: 'Few modern novels are so skilful or so relentless within a narrow compass in showing that frontier which exists between emotional exhaustion and suicidal despair' (Mudford 26). The form that the London setting takes in this novel adds to the 'narrow compass' that Mudford identifies. Yet by setting the novel in London and, more specifically, in wartime London and the first year of peace, he ties the novel to a very specific literary tradition in relation to the representation of the city.

The opening coordinates of the novel are specific in actualizing the class preoccupations of the suburb, while also bringing to the fore the frame of the war even though we are told the action begins in January 1946. In very quick succession we learn that the first-person narrator, Bendrix, lives on 'the wrong – the south – side of the Common' (*End* 7), and that his home shows evidence of bomb damage: 'I closed the stained-glass door behind me and made my way carefully down the steps that had been blasted in 1944 and never been repaired. I had reason to remember the occasion and how the stained glass, tough and ugly and Victorian, stood up to the shock as our grandfathers themselves would have done' (*End* 8). The implication of the final sentence is that there was something in the Victorian character that would have stood up to the shock of the Blitz which is lacking among their descendants. Through Bendrix we experience the same train of thought encountered in *The Heat of the Day* – of the nation in decline. While a common conservative trope – the past was always better than the present – in this instance the attitude is tied closely to the physical fabric of the city. The Victorian city, both actually and as moral underpinning, is very specifically not 'unstuck', to return to Bowen's phrase, but that London 1946 has become so. This recalls Jerry White's observation: 'London looked broken, drab, patched, tired out and essentially Victorian still' (J. White 44). London has not become the modern city that it should and rests on a Victorian glory that is becoming 'patched [and] tired out'. The sense of exhaustion itself echoes Mudford's reading of the novel as an exploration of 'emotional exhaustion and suicidal despair'. The place, post-war London is, therefore, an important if understated factor in understanding the novel. The connection would not be lost on a contemporary reader; not least because, as noted earlier, London saw little progress in a programme of repairs during 1946 and suffered an acute housing crisis, while food rationing actually became harsher than during the war. As the novelist Susan Cooper wrote: 'after the war and victory, where was the transformation scene?' (Sissons and French 35).

Yet transformation is one of the themes of this novel, as is healing and understanding as well as something in short supply following the war, hope and faith. Like many of Greene's novels that touch on religious themes, it is a reading rooted in secular concerns. In 'At home', an essay on the Blitz written in 1940, Greene observed: 'There are things one never gets used to because they don't connect: sanctity and fidelity and the courage of human beings abandoned to free will: virtues like these belong with old college buildings and cathedrals, relics of a world with faith' (O'Prey 89). Bendrix's Victorian home is a relic of the past, but it is also the site of the key moment in the narrative. This is alluded to early in the novel when Bendrix refers to some bomb damage to the building and reflects: 'I had reason to remember'. This was the site of the final assignation between Bendrix and Sarah Miles that ends their relationship. It is heralded by the advent of the V1 rockets across London, an event which is symbolically tied to their relationship:

> The glass from the old windows crumbled under our feet. Only the old Victorian stained glass above the door had stood firm. The glass turned white where it powdered like the ice children have broken in wet fields or along the side of roads. She told me again, 'Don't be scared.' I knew she wasn't referring to those strange new weapons that still, after five hours, droned steadily up from the south like bees .... . It passed low across the Common and we took it for a plane on fire and its odd deep bumble for the sound of an engine out of control. A second came and then a third. We changed our mind then about our defences. 'They are shooting them like pigeons,' I said, 'they must be crazy to go on.' But go on they did, hour after hour, even after the dawn had begun to break, until we realized that this was something new. (*End* 69–70)

Note how Bendrix's narrative again emphasizes the stained glass above the Victorian door. The obvious association is with the stained glass of a church or cathedral, echoing Greene's observation from 1940. When Sarah says 'Don't be scared', Bendrix reads this as a platitude anticipating the end of their relationship, which further links this new weapon with the imminent change in their lives. While Sarah's diary will reveal that Bendrix has at least partially misled himself, the final line 'that this was something new' is indeed prescient. When the house is hit by a rocket it is this Victorian door that will save Bendrix's life: 'But when memory did return it was not in that way. I realized first that I was lying on my back and that what balanced over me, shutting out the light, was the front door' (*End* 71). It is also under this door that Sarah sees Bendrix's inert arm and assumes he is dead, only to see him then emerge alive, like Lazarus. It is at this point that Sarah takes her oath: 'Let him be alive, and I *will* believe' (*End* 95).

Despite early impressions, the plot is closely aligned with the contemporary London landscape in which it is set. Not so much in terms of mimetic representation, but as a psychological space. For the modern reader, wartime London, including 1946, is a historical landscape old enough to be smothered by the mythologizing of government propaganda, academic and popular history, and popular media. The relatively low-key representation of London locations seems to diminish the significance of the city. Yet on publication in 1951 the physical remnants of the ravages of war on the city were everywhere to be seen. The last few years of war and the first few years of peace were contemporary events. As Steven Connor argues, 'the novel [is] not just ... passively marked with the imprint of history, but also as one of the ways in which history is made and remade' (Connor 1). Recalling its original context, Greene's strange story of the fine line between love, hate and faith is not just about the localized relationship between Bendrix, Sarah and Henry Miles but a wider social commentary inextricably tied to its London setting. Sarah's 'faith' is a way forward rather than a simple matter of newly awakened religious sensibility.

This faith is embedded in the narrative through striking metaphors of the Resurrection, Bendrix's escape from the house rubble and the post-mortem 'miracles'. First of these is the disfigured rationalist to whom Sarah had turned in an attempt to overcome her oath whose skin condition disappears; and secondly the son of the private investigator hired by Bendrix to track down the identity of Sarah's new lover whose appendicitis miraculously heals. Each ailment is suggestive: Smythe's skin deep disfigurement and the young Parkis's internal swollen organ – a disfigured surface and an internal festering, a man and a child – suggests London's and Britain's post-war dilemma. Physically battered but still living by a pre-war social order, this novel seems to cry out for renewal, a rebuilding of London's battered ruins and social change symbolized by the cured child. The religious imagery in the novel therefore points towards the need for a renewal of faith in the nation which is symbolized by London. To recall the epigraph from Greene that heads this chapter, 'the world we lived in could not have ended in any other way' and 'an old dog-toothed civilization is breaking now'; the war is the cleansing agent anticipating the rebirth of British society and presumably more broadly, Western civilization. Intriguingly, Greene's observation closely approaches the desire for change expressed in Robert's self-justification in *The Heat of the Day*, 'Of course: they have started something ... You may not like it, but it's the beginning of a day. A day on our scale' (*Heat* 274). The key difference is that Robert seeks change from outside rather than within, which is the option held out by Stella.

While it would be too much to suggest that all three novels share the same political, ideological, or even aesthetic outlooks, they all point towards change. *The Heat of the Day* is the most conservative, and thence least positive, in outlook. Change here is seen but the novel sidesteps its implications by seeing the future in tradition and convention – Stella's son is to become a land-owning patriarch and Stella is to marry into respectability, and both will leave London. *The Slaves of Solitude* sees the future as the breaking down of barriers between the 'good' middle and working classes, high and popular culture, exemplified in Miss Roach and Mr Prest who both return to London where this future is situated but scarcely mapped out. And finally, *The End of the Affair* where change remains in London but requires a renewal of faith and it is significant that it is the older, very traditional generation, Bendrix and Miles, who seem most challenged and scarcely reconciled to this future. All Bendrix can plea for at the end of the novel is to be left alone, literally passed by: 'O God, You've done enough. You've robbed me of enough. I'm too tired and old to learn to love, leave me alone for ever' (*End* 192). Yet those directly touched by Sarah's 'miracles', Smythe and the young Parkis, are transformed and gesture towards the future. Connor observes that 'in the post-war period, Britain came progressively to lose its confident belief that it was the subject of its own history' (Connor 3). All three of these novels of the immediate post-war moment see this, and to varying degrees see further towards the effects of both post-war decline and inevitable transformation. The place, space and narrative of this prescience is London. It seems appropriate to conclude this chapter with a paraphrase of Winston Churchill: 'We shape our cities, then they shape us' (Reader 9).

2

The Centre Cannot Hold

Their reaction to the London of the immediate post war period was of the blackest description. It was like encountering one's oldest friend selling matches in the gutter, with a face altered by disease.
                                                                Wyndham Lewis, *Rotting Hill* (1951)

While London was to prove the cauldron in which the future of modern Britain would unfold, early post-war anxieties about the city and the social, political and cultural future of the country initiated a series of near-future dystopian visions of the city. Never an extensive tradition – and here I am only going to identify three novels ranging from the late 1940s to the 1970s, George Orwell's *Nineteen Eighty-Four* (1949), Anthony Burgess's *A Clockwork Orange* (1962) and J. G. Ballard's *High-Rise* (1975) – it has nonetheless marked a continuing sense of loss of national prestige and acute anxiety. Strikingly, given the known liberal credentials of these authors, such anxieties are manifested in these novels as a conservative fear of change, whether represented by a socialist government, a burgeoning youth culture, or technological development.

Some sense of the political miasma of what should have been a triumphant left following the general election victory of 1945, can be detected in Kingsley Amis's attack on Orwell in his 1957 pamphlet 'Socialism and the Intellectuals': the 'present political apathy of the intelligentsia' was largely the fault of Orwell who had become 'a right-wing propagandist by negation, or at any rate a supremely powerful – though unconscious – advocate of political quietism' (Feldman and Gartenberg 262–3). And yet following the darkest days of the later 1940s, London and Britain began to turn around – rationing was finally to disappear, London gradually began to rebuild, and a national festival culminated the years of Labour government. Moreover, a consensus was formed among the planners and architects, if not the inhabitants of the city: 'London needed modernising' (J. White 47). So how was pessimism snatched from the jaws of growth and an easing of harsh post-war conditions? And why did this dystopian vision of the city of the near future persist? The issue can be seen clearer in the writing of an arch conservative, Wyndham Lewis. His *Rotting Hill* (1951) is a patchily effective 'blast' against post-war depravations and loss of national status:

> The majority of the nation was highly stimulated: and if the landed society was taxed out of existence, the middle class in rapid dissolution, on the whole England became brighter rather than a darker place. To symbolize this extraordinary paradox the capital city burst into festivities all along the south bank of the Thames; there was whoopee at Battersea, there was a thunder of orchestras in a new national concert-hall, a thousand peep shows, culminating in a Dome of Discovery lower down the river. This was staged in the ward sanctified by Shakespeare. In the Parliament the lamb lay down with the lion; the Tory bleated softly and snoozed beside the rampant socialist lion: all England seemed to have decided to forget that it had lost everything, and to live philosophically from day to day upon the Dole provided by the United States. (Lewis viii)

Lewis's distrust of 'stimulation' to mask the underlying 'rot' conjures an image that is not dissimilar to Bowen's 'unstuck' metropolis, Robert's 'unwhole' suburban upbringing, the retreat of Bendrix in *The End of the Affair*, or the monsters of middle-England found in Hamilton's Rosamund Tea Rooms. Yet as I argued in the preceding chapter, these visions of decay, betrayal and loss are invariably located in the suburbs, leaving London as a whole a more positive force. By contrast Lewis locates the 'rot' squarely in the city, although he does identify the decay in class terms. Surprisingly given Lewis's politics, it is not the poor or working classes who are the source of decay for 'the Nazis were such great gentlemen they mostly bombed the poor' (Lewis 91), but the abdication of power and responsibility by the middle and upper classes. While most of London's districts received some bomb damage, it is only in poorer districts that major bombing destroyed the fabric of the city. The rest of London, middle and upper class, is beset by a symbolic dry rot that the present rulers – the Labour government – is in no hurry to 'reconstitute' (Lewis 91). The implication is of course that this London, Lewis's city, is not a voting base for a socialist government, pointing to what is really bothering Lewis: the loss of political ascendancy by the establishment – the Tory lamb that has lain down beside the socialist lion. Moreover, the first signs of major regeneration in London, the Festival of Britain and the redevelopment of the South Bank as a cultural centre, take place in formerly working-class and industrial areas: 'twenty-seven acres of war-blasted Victorian warehousing and backstreet industry' behind County Hall (J. White 46). Lewis also points to several other conservative preoccupations through the changing political and social landscape of the city. The national decline attendant not only to economic dependence on the United States, but the loss of empire: 'Like Vienna, this city has no meaning henceforward. It is too vast a head for so puny a body – since most of the gargantuan colonial padding that made Britain (Great Britain!) look so enormous has been shed' (Lewis 92). In tandem with the loss of empire there comes an influx of much-needed workers to rebuild London and the country from those very same former colonies: 'Up on Rotting Hill, beamed on by Negroes, shadowed by Afrikanders, displaced by queues of displaced persons, ignored by Brahmins, run over by hasty "fiddlers" of various extraction, we are foreign' (Lewis 92), is matched by the emergence of a financially successful working-class entrepreneur – 'We are famous for our *spivs*' (Lewis 92). This essentially conservative discourse takes many forms in post-war writing, but it provides the essential fear, the underlying 'rot', necessary for the metropolitan dystopia.

George Orwell's *Nineteen Eighty-Four* is without question the immediate post-war instigator of this genre in the UK, and while critical attention has focused on the novel's political warning against Stalinist totalitarian government and the implications of 'doublethink' and 'Newspeak', much less attention has been paid to how the narrative is inextricably grounded in London. At best, one might find an acknowledgement that the fabric and living conditions of London in *Nineteen Eighty-Four* are a direct response to London during and immediately after the war. George Woodcock, for example, draws upon his own personal memory of Orwell during the war to observe:

> But in *Nineteen Eighty-Four*, with true polemic genius, Orwell made a virtue of his weakness of invention by setting the dread world of the future in an even more decayed version of the wartime London in which he and I walked in the last decade of his life. There are the rundown, unrepaired 1930s blocks of flats, the tumbling shored-up buildings, the vacant lots red with fireweed, the rockets unpredictably crashing down, and even, served in the canteen of the Ministry of Truth, a stew with 'amongst its general sloppiness, cubes of a spongy pinkish stuff that might have been a preparation of meat,' which astonishingly resembled a wartime dish that Orwell and I and some of our friends would eat when we went for lunch to the Bodega in Fleet Street. (Woodcock 24)

Woodcock's reminiscences are interesting insofar as they alert us to several aspects of the novel that demand critical attention. Firstly, and unusually in a futurist novel, there is a particular evocation of nostalgia for post-war London that was already emerging in the late 1940s. This emerges early in Woodcock's recollection by virtue of his own experience of wartime London and friendship with Orwell, and is used by him to underline the realist credentials of the novel. Yet while this is an aspect of the novel to which I will return, to leave it at that is to do a disservice to the complexity of Orwell's narrative. Even in the late 1940s, the 'myth' of London's and England's resistance to

Germany – a 'people's war' – was well established, not least thanks to the propaganda of the war years themselves to which Orwell contributed at the BBC. In this respect, locating the Ministry of Truth of the novel in the same building as the temporary home of the Ministry of Information during the war where Orwell (and, indeed, Bowen) had worked, underlines the association – notwithstanding the further irony that the building is better known as Senate House, the usual home of the governing body of the University of London and its central library. Naming the principal character 'Winston' further evokes the wartime atmosphere. Indeed, as Giles and Middleton observe: 'the versions of Englishness occasioned by the Second World War have remained potent tools ... of the "English Character" *in extremis*' (Giles and Middleton 9). Shorn of such propaganda and nationalist sentiment, the mismatch between an image of a heroic city and a heroic country provides a disturbing contrast to the crushing tawdriness and fear in the London of the novel, which is stark and deliberately drawn.

Secondly, while nostalgia is a notably politicized deployment of the past, the issue of history has a wider resonance within the novel. It is the obliteration of any sort of reliable historical record by the Party that is a key plank in the ideological apparatus by which it retains power. While the idea of an objective history is a concept open to debate – histories are interpretations of factual material not 'the truth' – it is the stifling of historical debate, of contestation over the meaning of the past, which makes this form of thought-control so disturbing. Despite Winston's memory of discovering an unexpunged document that disproved the Party's version of the past, such evidence is, on the whole, unimportant in a system where 'All history was a palimpsest, scraped clean and reinscribed exactly as often as was necessary' (*Nineteen Eighty-Four* 39). Moreover, the collective memory of the Proles seems equally ineffectual, although this is more to do with a failure of communication: 'Within twenty years at the most, he reflected, the huge and simple question, "Was life better before the Revolution than it is now?" would have ceased once and for all to be answerable. But in effect it was unanswerable even now, since the few scattered survivors from the ancient world were incapable of comparing one age with another' (*Nineteen Eighty-Four* 83). Time, rather ironically, would seem to be on the Party's side.

Yet the one aspect of Winston's world that challenges the stifling of historical debate, the erasure of the written record of the past, and the inability to communicate across class and generational boundaries, is the material fabric of the city. As Pike observes: 'The overall impression of the physical city to one who observes it ... is of buildings and streets deposited in sedimentary fashion over a long period, and implying a future' (Pike 16). Peter Ackroyd goes further by noting that 'Contemporary theorists have suggested that linear time is itself a figment of the human imagination, but London has already anticipated their conclusions. There are many different forms of time in the city, and it would be foolish of me to change its character for the sake of creating a conventional narrative' (Ackroyd 2001 2). An elaboration of Pike's metaphor demonstrates Ackroyd's point: while the laying down of sedimentary layers fits in well with our notions of a comprehensible chronology that forms the essence of historical interpretation, the erosion and physical interference of subsequent ages produces the situation Ackroyd describes. The chronological inconsistency between the buildings which embody the development and planning of previous eras permeates the contemporary material experience of the city.

The nursery rhyme 'Oranges and Lemons' is a major motif of the novel that attests to Orwell's complex engagement with materiality and the past in the novel. The significance of the rhyme is that it points to material locales in the fabric of London that physically demonstrate a pre-Revolutionary usage and history. This is crucial since the Party, in line with its policy of rewriting the historical record and the complementary control of memory to suit its purposes, has also attempted to appropriate material history, and more specifically, the material history evident in London's fabric, to their version of the past:

> Winston wondered vaguely to what century the church belonged. It was always difficult to determine the age of a London building. Anything large and impressive, if it was reasonably new in appearance, was automatically claimed as having been built since the Revolution, while anything that was obviously of an earlier date was ascribed to some dim period called the Middle Ages. The centuries of capitalism were held to have produced nothing of any value. One could not learn history from architecture any more than one could learn it from books. Statues, inscriptions, memorial stones, the names of streets – anything that might throw light upon the past had been systematically altered. (*Nineteen Eighty-Four* 88)

Yet the circulation of what amounts to a trivial historical artefact, a children's rhyme, and the unavoidable sediment of London's development, ultimately point to the weaknesses of the system despite its appearance of overarching power. It is memory rather than history that presents this challenge, and gains power by its association with the material city. Even while only remembered in fragments and by different people, none of whom seem to know the whole, the power of the rhyme points to the difficulty of controlling and restricting this nexus of memory, language and physical place. While the Party may seek to control language through Newspeak and appropriate physical space by giving it a new history, that control only extends very imperfectly to the Proles where, presumably, memory and tradition still exist. In many respects this is Winston's tragedy. Trained by the Party to think only in conventional historical terms which he rewrites daily at work, when he questions the Prole in the pub he fails to recognize the value and power of memory: 'A sense of helplessness took hold of Winston. The old man's memory was nothing but a rubbish-heap of details' (*Nineteen Eighty-Four* 82). The old man's reminiscences, based in a physical experience of the city, do in fact provide Winston with an answer; clearly the 'capitalists' did not dominate the city in the way the Party histories would have it, providing a chink in their ideological armour but he fails to see it. He is right to identify hope in this respect with the Proles, but he is constitutionally unable to decode the form that that hope might take.

In many respects, Orwell has through the old man identified an aspect of the spatiality of memory that Michel de Certeau elaborates in the following terms: 'Stories traverse and organize places; they select and link places together making sentences and itineraries out of them' (de Certeau 115). In this respect, the experiential fabric of London is a vast network of individual itineraries and stories that create, circulate and preserve the very past that the Party's attempts to rename, appropriate, or rewrite clearly fail to repress entirely. The fact that Party members can sally out into London (even if at the risk of being picked up by a patrol) points to the ongoing risk that individual consciousness of the past might emerge beyond Party control. Indeed, the very scarcity of day-to-day consumables forces the outer-party member to undertake such expeditions: 'Party members were supposed not to go into ordinary shops ... but the rule was not strictly kept, because there were various things, such as shoelaces and razor blades, which it was impossible to get hold of in any other way' (*Nineteen Eighty-Four* 11). The failure by the Party to supply personal necessities draws Winston and presumably others before and, one must presume, after him into the streets of London and among the Proles.

The state regulation, or rather alienation, of sexual desire – 'Sexual intercourse was to be looked on as a slightly disgusting minor operation, like having an enema' (*Nineteen Eighty-Four* 60–1) – is another example of Party prohibition having the opposite effect to what was intended. The painful tale Winston commits to his diary of an encounter with a prostitute is both resonant of location as well as the spatialized plot of Winston's memory, which has become a story associated with place, in de Certeau's terms:

> *It was three years ago. It was a dark evening, in a narrow side-street near one of the big railway stations. She was standing near a doorway in the wall, under a street lamp that hardly gave any light. She had a young face, painted very thick. It was really that paint that appealed to me, the whiteness of it, like a mask, and the bright red lips. Party women never paint their faces. There was nobody else in the street, and no telescreens.* (*Nineteen Eighty-Four* 59; italics original)

While the act itself is recalled as a form of rebellion against the strictures of the Party (despite the self-revulsion revealed later in the chapter), by narrating his own story within a material locale in the city, Winston recalls his own actions into memory which he then translates into a personal history in the diary. Significantly, Orwell is also projecting an aspect of the contemporary city into the future city. Most readers with even a passing familiarity with London (if not other cities) would be aware of the attraction of the major railway termini for prostitution that grew in the nineteenth century alongside the expansion of rail travel. As Jerry White observes: 'The area west of Eastbourne Terrace, by Paddington Station, became known for its "sleazy hotels" where prostitutes lived and took their clients – Graham Greene was a punter there in the 1930s and 1940s' (J. White 22). Like the recognizable London of war damage and austerity, this creates a recognizable London in which the reader's present is translated into the future city. The persistence of this practice around the railway termini of Winston's London reinforces the persistence of the past in the material places and spaces of the city in a similar way to the 'Oranges and Lemons' motif. Moreover, the city's implacability to the Party's attempted control of the past creates stories and narratives that can in turn form the very individuality that it seeks to abolish; as Pierre Janet observed: 'Narration created humanity' (de Certeau 115).

Orwell's acute sensitivity to this aspect of the city as lived space and the practices, memories and narratives that accrete around those places can usefully be codified in de Certeau's terms as a 'practiced place' (de Certeau 117) – 'Stories thus carry out a labour that constantly transforms places into spaces or spaces into places' (118); a place that is created not from the bare physical skeleton of the street, building, or monument, but by usage, by practice. In contradiction to the Party's palimpsest of an endlessly redefinable discursive history, this is the past and memory codified around material spaces. The codification of usage is a form of independent reading (experiential), contrasted with the written (proscriptive) and, thence, malleable history promoted and largely created by the Party (the Party's *langue* to the city's *parole*, perhaps). Practice, by its very dependence on the engagement of the individual, is a challenge to the monolithic official, corporate, recorded history of the Party. This analogy of the city as text recalls Roland Barthes's *scriptable* (readerly) text 'that calls for active involvement on the part of the reader in the production of the text' (Jefferson and Robey 111). In the novel, this works on two levels. On the one hand, Winston increasingly becomes a *reader* of the city through the relationship between his thoughts, memories, and the narrative in his diary and the material spaces of the city in which he lives and moves. Parts One and Two of the novel chart an increasing awareness of his essential humanity before the brutal repression of

Part Three. On a more literary level, the narrative by translating the contemporary London of the late 1940s also encourages the reader to experience resistance to the Party discourse that continually threatens to overwhelm Winston's tentative exploration of his own story. The exploration of his memories and the formulation of a personal narrative of the past can be measured by his traverse across and experience of a recognizable image of the everyday city. For example, alongside the record of his marriage and the visit to the prostitute, Winston begins to recall memories of his mother and sister again, anchored to a recognizable (if generic) aspect of the city – the underground railway: 'His mother, in her slow, dreamy way, was following a long way behind them. She was carrying his baby sister – or perhaps it was a bundle of blankets that she was carrying: he was not certain whether his sister had been born then. Finally they emerged into a noisy, crowded place which he had realized to be a Tube station' (*Nineteen Eighty-Four* 33). Once more, this passage engages the reader by drawing upon memories of the war and the use of the deep central Tube stations as air-raid shelters, but it also takes this general sympathetic reminiscence and generic London space to solidify a personal memory. As Winston moves through his life, and particularly when he is formulating a forbidden personal itinerary through London, he is increasingly characterized and humanized with a past and feelings that are morally comprehensible to the reader unlike the grim ideology of the Party. This contrasts with the callousness he shares with other Party members at the beginning of the novel, noted in his first entry in the diary:

> *then there was a wonderful shot of a child's arm going right up into the air a helicopter with a camera in its nose must have followed it up and there was a lot of applause from the party seats but a woman down in the prole part of the house suddenly started kicking up a fuss and shouting they didn't oughter of showed it not in front of the kids they didn't it ain't right not in front of the kids it aint until the police turned her out i dont suppose anything happened to her nobody cares what the proles say typical prole reaction they never –* (*Nineteen Eighty-Four* 13; italics original)

This passage shows just how far Winston changes. His automatic reaction here is to share the mirth at the massacred child and to repeat Party opinion about the Proles, '*typical prole reaction*'. Indeed, the reader's distance from Winston is emphasized since the shock expressed by the woman reflects a more acceptable moral response.

London in *Nineteen Eighty-Four* is a spatialized narrative by which we perceive far more structurally than, say, a typical romance (Rabkin 79). This is of course an aspect of the broader literary tradition of utopian/dystopian fictions by which the plot is often spatialized to provide a checklist of comparisons to the contemporary society it is challenging. Yet Orwell goes beyond these expected generic

conventions which tend not to involve extensive narrative characterization, to explore the material basis of both the humanity of society
and the individual to which the city is crucial. The city is a vast
mechanism of social control in a Foucauldian sense, as a consequence
of the various panoptic technologies of observation and regulation
from the telescreens to other Party members and their children. It
has equally been physically transformed in some measure to
demonstrate that power, for example the enormous disconcerting
posters and statues of Big Brother pasted on every other wall and atop
existing monuments (Big Brother has replaced Nelson in Trafalgar
Square). A more potent symbol is manifested in the four towers of the
ministries:

> Winston kept his back turned to the telescreen. It was safer, though, as
> he well knew, even a back can be revealing. A kilometre away the
> Ministry of Truth, his place of work, towered vast and white above the
> grimy landscape. This, he thought with a sort of vague distaste – this
> was London, chief city of Airstrip One, itself the third most populous of
> the provinces of Oceania. He tried to squeeze out some childhood
> memory that should tell him whether London had always been quite
> like this. Were there always these vistas of rotting nineteenth-century
> houses, their sides shored up with baulks of timber, their windows
> patched with cardboard and their roofs with corrugated iron, their
> crazy garden walls sagging in all directions? And the bombed sites
> where the plaster dust swirled in the air and the willow-herb straggled
> over the heaps of rubble; and the places where the bombs had cleared
> a larger patch and there had sprung up sordid colonies of wooden
> dwellings like chicken-houses? But it was no use, he could not
> remember: nothing remained of his childhood except a series of
> bright-lit tableaux occurring against no background and mostly
> unintelligible.
> ... The Ministry of Truth contained, it was said, three thousand
> rooms above ground level, and corresponding ramifications below.
> Scattered about London there were just three other buildings of similar
> appearance and size. So completely did they dwarf the surrounding
> architecture that from the roof of Victory Mansions you could see all
> four of them simultaneously. They were the homes of the four Minis-
> tries between which the entire apparatus of government was divided.
> (*Nineteen Eighty-Four* 8–9)

Several aspects of Orwell's narrative technique in this passage have
already been discussed, although it is significant to see this ensemble
in action so early in the novel. This is a recognizable post-war London
vista, even down to the fireweed ('willow-herb' or *Epilobium angusti-
folium*) that grew profusely among the burnt-out remains of bombed
buildings. Even the temporary shacks that sprang up later in the war
in response to the housing crisis are included in the description.
Towering over this prospect is the 'enormous pyramidal structure of
glistening white concrete' of the Ministry of Truth, and the similar

buildings of the three other Ministries (*Nineteen Eighty-Four* 9). As already noted, this is modelled on Senate House in Bloomsbury, appropriated as the Ministry of Information during the war. And yet this is and is not the same building. In appearance, the description fits well with the white concrete and tiers as well as the authoritarian severity suggested by its early 1930s neo-classicism. However, the scale of the fictional building in the novel dwarfs the real building. Moreover, where did the three other Ministry buildings come from? They are of course symbolic additions to the central London skyline of the novel and are the only post-war buildings to be identified in the novel. The tallest buildings in this essentially Victorian city, they are of course manifestations of power and domination. Phallic and panoptic, they both induce fear and awe as well as suggesting a 'panorama city' that is 'a "theoretical" (that is, visual) simulacrum' suggesting a '"geometrical" or "geographical" space of visual, panoptic, or theoretical constructions' (de Certeau 93). The height and visual domination of these buildings expresses a desire to define, control and 'idealize' the city and the social interaction of its inhabitants, which from their height are effectively invisible. These buildings express the Party's desire to map out and control.

This view of the ministry buildings is shared by the reader with Winston at near ground level. From ground level this unassailable vision of complete power is rather diminished despite the presence of the technological adjunct of scopic domination, the telescreen. As Winston demonstrates, one can, with care, simply turn one's back on such observation giving a lie to the total visibility and thence total power claimed by the gleaming white towers of government, countered perhaps by the areas of privacy sectioned out by forms of residential architecture that predates the Revolution of which the telescreen is designed to minimize. What this suggests is that an inner life can never be entirely eradicated. Further, while the Party attempts to dominate the city and its inhabitants, the structure of the city is a development of earlier ages when power was far more contingent, requiring voluntary complicity founded on a desire for privacy. Moreover, the Party shows no sign of renewing the fabric of London in its image. The Party claims that capitalism produced no buildings of distinction is instead an accurate statement of the period of Party-rule rather than the past. The society created and maintained by the Party exists in a physical environment that is alien if not inimical to its strictures. When Winston looks out at London it is not the towering ministry buildings that determine his thoughts, but the evidence of an earlier society represented by 'rotting nineteenth-century houses' and his own Victory Mansions 'built in the 1930s or thereabouts' and 'falling apart', as well as the evidence of the inability of the Party to provide even basic housing for some of its citizens, evident from the wooden shacks that have grown up in the larger bomb-sites. This leads

Winston to dwell upon the past. With this clear evidence of decay –
these buildings must have been new and maintained at one time – the
obvious question that emerges is 'has it always been like this?' Winston's inability to recover the past as memory at this point is really
neither here nor there; the evidence of the material city has initiated
the desire to know and understand.

The Party tacitly acknowledges the limitations of its control of the
material realm, and by implication the circulation of stories and
memories, by the implementation of both Doublethink and Newspeak. Doublethink can only be thought of as an imperfect system of
thought-control that is considerably weakened by the conjunction of
materially anchored memory. The very need for the existence of the
concept is an acknowledgement of failure, demonstrated by Winston's attempts to recall his mother and sister and thereby the
repressed guilt over the circumstances of their disappearance (this
confrontation with repressed guilt is another aspect of Winston's
psychological humanization), and the power of the 'Oranges and
Lemons' rhyme to raise questions about the city's and the individual's
past. Newspeak also seems to have very uncertain foundations. Saussure's distinction between *langue* and *parole* provides a useful
demonstration of the issue. The Party's avowed aim 'to narrow the
range of thought' (*Nineteen Eighty-Four* 49) relies upon the assumption
that the system of language they create will be identically reproduced
in the minds of potential speakers. Yet the gap between system (*langue*) and use (*parole*) is wide and dynamic, which Saussure acknowledges by side-stepping the issue, merely noting that *parole* was a very
difficult subject for scientific analysis and concentrating on a synchronic analysis of the abstracted system instead. Winston's linguist
acquaintance Syme, who is working on the latest version of Newspeak,
is an example of the limitations of the thought-control explicit in
Newspeak. Despite his orthodoxy and work engaged in the 'destruction of words' he is plainly excited by the language itself even if in a
destructive sense, 'it's a beautiful thing' (*Nineteen Eighty-Four* 48), he
notes, and Winston plainly sees his doom expressed in this enthusiasm. Regardless of his deep belief in Insoc and Big Brother, Symes
has been led into dangerous revolt through language. The city holds
the promise of a similar form of resistance, as de Certeau observes:

> The ordinary practitioners of the city live 'down below,' below the
> thresholds at which visibility begins. They walk – an elementary form of
> this experience of the city; they are walkers, *Wandersmanner*, whose
> bodies follow the thicks and thins of an urban 'text' they write without
> being able to read it. These practitioners make use of spaces that
> cannot be seen; their knowledge of them is as blind as that of lovers in
> each other's arms. The paths that correspond in this intertwining,
> unrecognized poems in which each body is an element signed by many
> others, elude legibility. It is as though the practices organizing a

> bustling city were characterized by their blindness. The networks of
> these moving, intersecting writings compose a manifold story that has
> neither author nor spectator, shaped out of fragments of trajectories
> and alterations of spaces: in relation to representations, it remains daily
> and indefinitely other. (de Certeau 93)

The route of Winston's rebellion is through the repressed memories
and questions for which the city is the catalyst, leading to ever-
frequent sallies onto the streets and spaces of London. He is captured
only when that movement ceases and he becomes a static target for
the Thought Police. At the point when he and Julia settle into a
permanent place of liaison above Charrington's shop, the connection
between his physical trajectory through the city and his memories
ceases. Equally, his own thoughts and the practical independence of
his memory are subsumed by the reassertion of historical discourse
through the conventional explanation and chronology of Goldstein's
book – the Party controls and dominates this form while memory is
the real threat. Winston ceases to counter the absolutism of the Party
with tantalizing, incomprehensible and amorphous 'series of fragments of trajectories and alterations of spaces' but has re-entered the
visible, controllable realm of the Party.

Yet *Nineteen Eighty-Four* is far from the pessimistic novel that its
reputation suggests. Only if one assumes that Winston and Julia are
unique and alone in their experience of the city and their resistance
could this be so. But if the Party has gone to the trouble of maintaining the bait of Charrington's shop among the Proles and Goldstein's book as a rumour and actuality among Party members, and
while the failure to provide minimal standards of material necessities
to its members, then the promise of the novel is that the lure of the
city will remain, and experiences like Winston's and Julia's will continue. So long as there are people who continue their trajectories in
the city as the elaborate apparatus of bait and capture suggests, these
'practitioners' of the 'urban text' will provide an alternative reality to
that frantically imposed by the Party.

Viewed in a broader context, the deft representation of history
rooted in discourse as a form of oppression, versus memory anchored
in the material as an expression of freedom (even if of severely limited scope) has, ironically, created considerable problems for critics
dissatisfied with the imperfect alignment of the novel with 'the historical and political circumstances to which it alludes' (Sinfield 101).
In a very real sense, it is the danger of the constructedness of history
that forms the foundation of Orwell's warning and it is interesting to
note the consternation among those who wish, in turn, to simply limit
the relevance of the novel to a facet of post-war history. The narrative
itself resists this. Alan Sinfield has sought to explain this characteristic
of the novel with reference to Barthes's elaboration of myth:

> It abolishes the complexity of human acts, it gives them the simplicity of essences, it does away with all dialectics, with any going back beyond what is immediately visible, it organizes a world which is without contradictions because it is without depth, a world open and wallowing in the evident, it establishes a blissful clarity: things appear to mean something by themselves. (Barthes 143)

This certainly helps to explain what the Party is striving for; no less than mythic status, but the counter established by the novel is to advance the specificity of individual experience and memory founded on the material space and place of the city. In its particulars, in walking the street, contemplating its sedimented history, or evoking memories, the city goes, as Raban observes, 'soft': 'it awaits the imprint of an identity. For better or worse, it invites you to remake it, to consolidate it into a shape you can live in' (Raban 9). *Nineteen Eighty-Four* explores the significance of the micro-politics of the individual in conflict with the broad, totalizing sweep of the macro-politics of history and the 'system'. The individual shapes the lived spaces of the city, while the latter seeks to impose meaning and order discursively; a mapped space in which inhabitants are invisible.

In narrative terms, the structures and 'spaces' of myth provides the necessary link between *Nineteen Eighty-Four*, Burgess's *A Clockwork Orange*, and Ballard's *High-Rise*. The two later novels lack the emphasis placed by Orwell on the past and memory which affects the space, or image, of the city produced by their narratives. This creates a city space that is more abstract and mythic. Indeed, Burgess was praised by one US reviewer of having written 'that rare thing in English letters – a philosophical novel' (Morrison xvii), and Ballard has long been recognized for 'his interest in types, rather than characters, as well as his penchant for allegories or visions, rather than stories or "plots"' (Delville 4). By comparison to *Nineteen Eighty-Four*, the two later novels are less obviously historically situated. They certainly do not present the contemporary reader with a London vista that is as specific as the wreckage and privations of the post-war city. This divergence requires careful examination. Paul Werth argues that in sociolinguistic terms 'conceptual space is modelled upon physical space' and this process is carefully represented in the central antagonism between Winston and the Party in *Nineteen Eighty-Four* (Werth 7). Winston's conceptual space is increasingly shaped by the physical fabric of the city which the Party has failed to remake in its image, and thence fails to control the mental space it creates. This physical city was familiar, at least in being contemporary if not intimately known, to the original readers of the novel. Yet we need to bear in mind Lefebvre's warning that such 'mental space then becomes the locus of a "theoretical practice" which is separated from social practice and which sets itself up as the axis, pivot or central reference point of knowledge' (Lefebvre 6). Lefebvre is, of course, attacking a tendency in critical discourse, but that tendency has a broader resonance to developments in post-war society to which *A Clockwork Orange* and *High-Rise* are attuned. By choosing, by and large, to ignore the past, the city space created in these novels becomes abstract and non specific.

In *A Clockwork Orange*, the city has been almost entirely reduced to schematic vagueness with blandly named streets, anonymous 'flat-blocks' and locations named by function. Thence we never learn more of the central area of the city other than its designation – significantly following North American spelling – 'center'. Other areas are similarly identified: the Industrial Canal, the Municipal Power Plant and Staja ('state jail'). The relationship between the city and its hinterland is reduced to the simplest conceptual relationship, the town and country. In *High-Rise*, the narrative unfolds within the 'container' of a giant high-rise apartment block and the city is reduced to a vista that is looked out on and, crucially, down upon; a network of streets, the river and the commercial centre a smoky presence on the horizon. In each case, life in the city has been reduced to a theoretical abstraction. The former representing the disassociation of a violent youth culture unengaged with the life, and arguably the 'lived' experience of the city to the point where it becomes merely an undefined space in which random acts of violence can occur. The tower block in *High-Rise* represents the artificiality of the planned and contained environment, built on utopian socio-logical and architectural ideas at the expense of the 'organic' sediment of the liveable, 'soft' city.

That both representational environments lead to or encourage individual, rather than state, acts of extreme violence is an important point of distinction from *Nineteen Eighty-Four*. The built environment in both *A Clockwork Orange* and *High-Rise* creates alienation. In each case a planned environment releases rather than controls antisocial behaviour, suggesting that it is physical constraint that is the focus of these two novels rather than the psychological control sought by the Party in *Nineteen Eighty-Four*. The city in Orwell's novel is a richly suggestive realm of individual practice where the psychologically imprisoned might rediscover their humanity, whereas the city in Burgess's and Ballard's novels is of bland, dehistoricized constraint which liberates not as a civilizing force, but through the release of the most basic, atavistic instincts. Clearly the latter form of 'liberation', the equivalent of the free play of the Freudian *id*, is hardly socially desirable and, as a result, the vision of the near future offered by both Burgess and Ballard is far bleaker than that posited by Orwell.

While there are important differences between the narrative spaces created by Burgess and Ballard, this basic similarity cannot be underemphasized, as the following two examples demonstrate. First, this passage from *A Clockwork Orange* immediately follows an inter-rupted gang fight as police sirens wail in the distance:

Then we slooshied the sirens and knew the millicents were coming with pooshkas pushing out of the police-auto-windows at the ready. That little weepy devotchka had told them, no doubt, there being a box for calling the rozzes not too far behind the Muni Power Plant. 'Get you soon, fear not,' I called, 'stinking billygoat. I'll have your yarbles off lovely.' Then off they ran, slow and panting, except for Number One Leo out snoring on the ground, away north towards the river, and we went the other way. Just round the next turning was an alley, dark and empty and open at both ends, and we rested there, panting fast then slower, then breathing like normal. It was like resting between the feet of two terrific and very enormous mountains, these being the flat-blocks, and in the windows of all the flats you could viddy like blue dancing light. This would be the telly. Tonight was what they called a worldcast, meaning that the same programme was being vidded by everybody in the world that wanted to, that being mostly the middle-aged middle-class lewdies. (*Orange* 15)

The immediate consequences of the interrupted violence still resonate through this passage. The woman ('devotchka') that Billyboy's gang were about to practise 'ultraviolence' upon comes back into the narrative frame and has called the police. Alex, the protagonist, threatens Billyboy with the crude machismo of ripping off his testicles ('yarbles') – 'I'll have your yarbles off lovely' – while another of Billyboy's gang lies seriously injured on the ground. Yet our attention is drawn away from the breathless, post-combat adrenalin of this moment and resolves into an awareness of the physical city. The concealment offered by the no-man's-land alley between two vast tower blocks facilitates the sense of impunity felt by the combatants, but is 'like resting between the feet of two terrific and very enormous mountains'. The language suggests the feelings provoked by a sublime landscape, the tower blocks are transmuted into mountains, in a striking transferral of the 'terrors' of a natural landscape into the urban. This is no casual switch of register. Alex and his gang are not the subjects of this landscape, cowed by Burke's 'mode of terror or pain'. Rather they and their extravagant violence belong to it. The real subjects of its 'terror' are the 'middle-aged middle-class lewdies' residing within. The tower block is the rampart of their security from the lawlessness of the night, but also part of the urban landscape, a 'mode of terror or pain'. The sense of vast community evoked by the technology of the 'worldcast' – an interesting anticipation of expressions like 'global village' – only serves to highlight the disproportionate power of the violence of the night streets that has been transformed into the terrors of an untamed natural landscape, but disturbingly within the civilized, controlled artificial environment of the city. Above all, the residential city of tower blocks is marked by its banality of which violence is the obvious adjunct. It is a significant aspect of the novel that Alex and the nasdat gangs never operate in the 'Center'. This area of the city is the least delineated in the narrative and presumably expresses a vital identity, a symbolism that deters the gangs who prefer to operate in a semiotic vacuum to assert their own identity and narrative. It is, no doubt, better policed in acknowledgement of its specular and symbolic power. As Stephen Barber observes: 'The street gangs conglomerate on the periphery of the city, as though its centre were alien, its identity possessing a vital component which the street gang cannot assimilate'. Moreover, they remain 'in the housing blocks, consuming the blankness which the suburbs feed out incessantly, comfortingly, dependably – since violence needs its structure and nourishing support system' (Barber 27).

By contrast to the ministry buildings of *Nineteen Eighty-Four*, these residential tower blocks do not represent a symbolism of specular power, but an essential powerlessness. Yet they do seem to offer a degree of safety. When Alex's gang comes to commit a substantial robbery, it is to the conventional houses of a wealthy area which they turn. Indeed, while what we do see of the tower blocks is vandalized – 'there was no need to press the electronic knopka to see if it was working or not, because it had been tolchocked real horrorshow this night' (*Orange* 25) – there is no suggestion of attacks on individual apartments. While the blocks represent a withdrawal from the city as a whole due to the danger of the night streets, they also represent an exclusion from the heart of the city as well as identification with its symbolic narratives. It is an attraction to the cultural landscape of London which begins to awaken Winston's memories and individuality in *Nineteen Eighty-Four*, most obviously through the rhyme tied to those most ubiquitous of London landmarks, its churches. Such a possibility is closed off in the city of *A Clockwork Orange*. Indeed the initial consequences of the post-war housing boom which lasted into the 1970s produced many of London's lamentable tower blocks. The following description of the Holly Street Estate, Dalston (Hackney) demonstrates a clear similarity to the use to which Alex and his gang put the topography of the tower block estate: 'The corridor is a thieves' highway ... At the corners where blocks join are dark passages, blind alleys, gloomy staircases. It is easy to get lost in these labyrinths and easy for robbers to lurk or to lose their pursuers' (Harrison 230). This bland, anonymous, landscape of concrete towers generates a crisis of identity to which the gangs are the response. Their violence, drug-taking and ever more bizarre fashions are desperate attempts to achieve meaning. Indeed, as Barber argues: 'the street gangs embody that moment of traversal between chaos and the void, snatching at any appropriating identity or imagery that will constitute a presence in the streets' (Barber 27).

The tower block of Ballard's *High-Rise* represents a different proposition. Rather than the resettlement and containment of the urban poor in high-density council estates, Ballard's tower block expresses a desire for exclusivity among its middle- and upper-class inhabitants. In this respect, the relationship between these massive towers (there are five in total on the estate, at various stages of completion and occupation) and the rest of London does share in the specular 'will to power' that was harnessed by the Party in *Nineteen Eighty-Four.*

> The high-rises seemed almost to challenge the sun itself – Anthony Royal and the architects who had designed the complex could not have foreseen the drama of confrontation each morning between these concrete slabs and the rising sun. It was only fitting that the sun first appeared between the legs of the apartment blocks, raising itself over the horizon as if nervous of waking this line of giants. During the morning, from his office on the top floor of the medical school, Laing would watch their shadows swing across the parking-lots and empty plazas of the project, sluice-gates opening to admit the day. For all his reservations, Laing was the first to concede that these huge buildings had won their attempt to colonize the sky. (*High-Rise* 19)

The domination of the city's skyline is palpable – challenging even the sun – and yet there is a crucial difference between the consequences of the power exerted here and in *Nineteen Eighty-Four.* The towers built and maintained by the Party are visual reminders of its power and project an overwhelming sense of repression and thought-control by which the Party governs. For example, the specular and symbolic menace offered by the windowless façade of the Ministry of Love concerned with 'law and order ... was the really frightening one' (*Nineteen Eighty-Four* 9). Orwell's towers exude power but are also mechanisms for the exercise of that power. They are not residential buildings. Nor does Ballard's high-rise resemble the tower blocks of *A Clockwork Orange,* which totally lack their assertion and confidence, even if at another level they represent the State's power to contain the poorer segment of the population in uniform high-density estates, the street gangs reflect how that control is ultimately ineffective. Ballard's high-rise, by contrast, promises the specular power of wealth and exclusivity which attracts the professional middle classes. It is no accident that many of the inhabitants are members of the techno-cratic professional elite, with a smattering of minor celebrities who could be understood as professional manipulators of media tech-nologies in any event. Yet the abrogation of such power here has no object. Beyond the social separation and exclusivity evident from the deliberate separation from the rest of London – 'For all the proximity of the City two miles away to the west along the river, the office buildings of central London belonged to a different world' (*High-Rise* 8) – the towers are meaningless. There is an overdetermination of power that has no other outlet than through and against the inhabitants themselves, which is where the similarity to Burgess's vision lies.

This is most clearly seen in Richard Wilder, a maker of gritty TV documentaries resident on the second floor of the building and, as such, 'more exposed to the pressures generated within the building' (*High-Rise* 42). These pressures soon resolve themselves into a vision of the weight of the building bearing down with greater force the lower you are on its 40 floors. In a structural sense this is of course correct, since it is the lower building and the foundations which dissipate the energy forced downward by the weight of the building. However, for Wilder the weight becomes psychological and phobic: 'He was constantly aware of the immense weight of the concrete stacked above him, and the sense that his body was the focus of the lines of force running through the building' (*High-Rise* 48). Wilder resolves to rise physically and socially through the building, which points to Ballard's central allegory. The building itself is a representation of society divided along class terms. There are those at the top who reside in the upper five floors of the building, a large middle class between the 10th and 35th floors and a lower class residing in the lower nine floors. The 10th and 35th floors are given over to amenities marking physical, social and increasingly psychological barriers mapped onto the building's levels. These divisions rest on little more than the level of residence since the block's residents are remarkably homogenous in terms of social class and education: 'What angered Wilder most of all about life in the apartment building was the way in which an apparently homogenous collection of high-income professional people had split into three distinct and hostile camps. The old social sub-divisions, based on power, capital and self-interest, had reasserted themselves here as anywhere else' (*High-Rise* 52–3).

Aside from the psychological prestige that height seems to impart, the reasons for this sub-division require examination. The first point to make is that this is a constructed environment that is ideologically driven. Now, cities are also constructed environments but their spaces and places are subject to the flux of usage and history. While cities are the home to extreme economic and social disparities, the city, the space itself, is relatively fluid over time as is evident in London, where historically well-to-do areas can become relatively deprived and vice versa, with all the possibilities in between. Indeed, the Docklands area in which Ballard's fictional development is sited was the subject to just such a 'regeneration' that began only a few years after *High-Rise* was published. As Pike observes: the city seems to express our culture's restless dream about its inner conflicts and our inability to resolve them' (Pike 8). In a very real sense the city grows and fluctuates to express the culture that it physically concentrates. The 'city in the sky' of *High-Rise* is an attempt to bypass such a connection between the people, their culture and the built environment to resolve social and structural conflict. The project is essentially authoritarian and is Ballard's comment on the consequences of planned, socially artificial communities that were popular with planners in the post-war years. Ballard makes clear that it is the building and its philosophy that fails not the people, since the failure in this middle-class 'city' is identical to those seen in the working-class ghettoes of the high-rise council estate: 'In principle, the mutiny of these well-to-do professional people against the building they had collectively purchased was no different from the dozens of well-documented revolts by working-class tenants against municipal tower-blocks that had taken place at frequent intervals during the post-war years' (*High-Rise* 69).

The ideological foundation behind such engineered communities is most directly exemplified by the Swiss-French architect, Le Corbusier. His observation that 'A house is a machine for living in' underpins the functionalism of Ballard's high-rise and points, perhaps surprisingly, to the extreme individualism that it produces: 'The high-rise was a huge machine designed to serve, not the collective body of tenants, but the individual resident in isolation' (*High-Rise* 10). Of course, Ballard has extrapolated Le Corbusier's functionalist philosophy of the single living unit and placed them in a huge conglomeration of such units such that this 'city in the sky' is, in fact, inimical to the basic idea of city living. While cities have and continue to produce enormous tensions, individualism and alienation areas are created that serve the collective population such as shopping areas and markets, parks and civic celebrations. Le Corbusier's vision of easing urban congestion with high-rise accommodation – which held many post-war planners and architects spellbound – in fact undermines the city's social foundation, although his ideas were appropriated by planners who lacked his singular vision. The city becomes a structure rather than a social space, a mass of surfaces that encourage distance rather than the intimacy demanded by lived space. They create awe but not home:

> The square silhouettes of the terraced roofs stand clear against the sky, bordered with the verdure of the hanging gardens. The uniformity of the units that compose the picture throws into relief the firm lines on which the far-flung masses are constructed. Their outlines softened by distance, the sky-scrapers raise immense geometrical facades of glass, and in them is reflected the blue glory of the sky. An overwhelming sensation. Immense but radiant prisms. (Le Corbusier 324)

Alongside this aesthetics of distance, the construction of lived spaces has become the 'theoretical practice' against which Lefebvre warned, given concrete form and thence actually manufacturing the barbarity that the polis was originally conceived to keep at bay. This engineered environment destroys the social cohesion that the city, even if unacknowledged and far from the surface consciousness of its inhabitants, must maintain at a minimal level to function as a liveable environment. Its absence leads to a loss of civility, self-destructive atavistic drives, rebellion and open warfare between the three 'classes' of the building: 'Even the tone of voice of his neighbours as they described these outbreaks of hostility was calm and matter-of-fact, like that of civilians in a war-torn city dealing with yet another air-raid' (*High-Rise* 60). This image of the city at war is present in all three novels, but it is not the fear of an external threat. While the city of *Nineteen Eighty-Four* does appear to be responding to an external aggressor – Eurasia or Eastasia depending on the shifting sands of mysterious realignments – it is Winston's lover, Julia, who identifies the real aggressor, the state against its own citizens: 'she startled him by saying casually that in her opinion the war was not happening. The rocket bombs which fell daily on London were probably fired by the Government of Oceania itself, "just to keep people frightened"' (*Nineteen Eighty-Four* 135). Similarly, the violent alienation of the 'nasdat' (youth) of *A Clockwork Orange* is a response to the blandness and uniformity of the city, and the blandness of mainstream culture (such as mindless television) overseen by the authorities. The government even co-opts former gang members into the police indicating that the violent antagonism is mutual and endemic to the city at all levels leaving violence as the only common language: 'This one has been up to his old tricks, as we can well remember though you, of course, can't. He has been attacking the aged and defenseless, and they have properly been retaliating. But we must have our say in the State's name' (*Orange* 110).

In *High-Rise* of course, the inhabitants of the tower block are isolated from the city, each other and ultimately their humanity, and turn on the building and themselves. Excessive order, whether achieved through the psychological control of the Party in *Nineteen Eighty-Four*, the bland civility of the built environment and psychotropic control in *A Clockwork Orange*, or the inhumanly structured machine-living of Ballard's *High-Rise*, has undermined the relationship between order and disorder in the city. As Steve Pile and Nigel Thrift observe: 'It is not just that we find order in one place and disorder in another, but that there is an internal relationship, a tension maybe, between the two' (Pile and Thrift 2). The authoritarianism depicted in each novel upsets this balance which is central to the city as lived space and in each case leads to open rebellion. The remaking of the psychological and material landscape of the city in the post-war years provided the raw material for these dystopian projections. Yet London bears witness to the inability of such forced social control to attain a permanent hold on the life of the city. To recall de Certeau's phrase, the 'spatial stories' of the city tell a different tale to the literary trajectory of Orwell's, Burgess's and Ballard's novels although all, ultimately, are exaggerated narratives of the resistance that use and experience of the city has produced in the second half of the twentieth century, despite the experiments of government and city planners. As Jerry White observes:

Everywhere, it seemed, these local paradoxes were replicating themselves in different corners of London like botanical hybrids forced in
a greenhouse, however unlikely the aspect or unpromising the soil.
(J. White 74)

In response to authoritarianism, the city has become increasingly
heterodox. The decay or 'rot' that so appalled Wyndham Lewis was
actually the early stages of its salvation.

3

Love in a Cold Climate

Cinematic pleasure belongs to the range of erotic pleasures of the nomadic gaze first known to the traveller and the flâneur *and then embodied by way of panoramic spatio-visuality in the modes of inhabiting space of transitional architectures. Suggesting these historic aspects of the fascination of the apparatus, and highlighting its fantasmatic connection to travel and landscaping, one looks back not only to the early cinema but also 'back to the future'.*
Giuliana Bruno, *Streetwalking on a Ruined Map* (1992)

Arguably the most widely acknowledged social upheaval of the post-war period was the shift in sexual mores. The slogans 'swinging London' and the 'permissive society' are often linked to the improving economic situation of Britain from the later 1950s, particularly for the nation's and specifically London's working classes. Yet such historical watersheds are seldom as complete as they might at first appear. Social histories of London contrast the grey and grim early post-war years of shortages, tottering world empire and economic crisis with the burst of energy and liberation that first became discernable in the mid-1950s through a burgeoning youth culture based around American popular music. The opening of Shawn Levy's popular history of 'swinging London' reiterates this well-established before-and-after hypothesis:

> Grey.
> The air, the buildings, the clothing, the faces, the mood.
> Britain in the mid-1950s was everything it had been for decades, even centuries: world power; sire of glorious intellectual, aesthetic and political traditions, gritty vanquisher of the Nazis, civilising docent to whippersnapper America, bastion of decency, decorum and the done thing.
> But somehow it was less. (Levy 3)

Fast-forward a few years, and this image of a stuffy, traditional, powerful Britain and repressed society is transformed into a Britain shorn of such worldwide responsibilities (and respect), political and economic diminishment, and playing second fiddle to super-power America who soon signalled the basis of the new 'special relationship' through the Suez debacle, Britain's last roll of the imperial dice. And yet such decline brings liberation. Loss of responsibility leads to the valorization of irresponsibility, overturning the social and cultural reticence of centuries. Thence 'swinging London' (significantly the coinage of an American magazine). As Colin MacInnes was quick to point out, the shock troops of this new social dispensation were the newly dubbed teenagers:

> Contemporary England is peculiar for being the most organized country, in the social sense, for ensuring the moral and material welfare of everybody – pullulating with decent laws, with high-minded committees, with societies for preventing or encouraging this or that – and it has produced, in consequence, the *dullest* society in Western Europe: A society blighted by blankets of negative respectability, and of dogmatic domesticity. The teenagers don't seem to care for this, and have organized their underground of joy. (MacInnes 1961 58–9)

While compelling as a thesis, this seems a little too convenient, as do many instances of fundamental historical 'breaks'. In many senses this is the equivalent of London's and Britain's historical 'repressive hypothesis', to adapt Foucault's observation about sexual mores for the moment. The idea of a stolid, powerful, socially restrictive society about to be swept away crucially overlooks that repression and conformity in fact represents an acute anxiety, if not preoccupation, over what 'polite' society seeks to repress – an incitement to discourse. The celebration of power is to acknowledge the fear of its loss, and the high value placed on social conservatism reveals an awareness of rapid and fundamental social change. As we saw in the last chapter, a true social conservative like Wyndam Lewis was a finely tuned barometer for the radical shifts that were taking place in the very era Levy and MacInnes identify as the restatement of traditional Britain in the late 1940s and early 1950s. The recent history of the war years demonstrated a far more radical upheaval of social mores than anything the 1960s would produce (even if it was only a temporary laxity). Indeed, one can discern a similar pattern in earlier eras – London had been 'the gayest city in the world' in 1935 (J. White 327). The 'swinging' London I wish to discuss here is something other than these historical clichés.

City life itself represents a social erotic that is always a threat to traditional values, by contrast to the pastoral tradition which has signified its suspicion of the urban in the strongest terms. Regardless of the anonymity of the urban crowd and the indifference, if not outright animosity, of city-dwellers, cities bring people into ever closer physical, cultural and social proximity. Despite the 'reserve' of the city-dweller (Simmel 412), we are driven to touch one way or another. Writers of the metropolitan have long recognized this. Virginia Woolf's urban stream of consciousness in works like *Mrs Dalloway* or

'Kew Gardens' creates a psychological space which focuses on this facet of the urban experience, even when class and/or culture erect physical barriers such as in the street or park. One can stretch back further through all the great London authors of recent literary history, Gissing and Dickens being major figures in the nineteenth century. This urban communion entails a particular frisson:

> We spend so much of our time, after all, in crowds: our bodies are always colliding and rubbing, our hands brushing; our areas of privacy, in a society where land and space are constantly and dangerously rising in value, are being eroded. The modern city, of small apartments and densely occupied communications routes – trains, pavements, lifts, supermarket walkways – makes us live hugger-mugger, cheek to cheek. We need, apparently, to relearn how to touch each other amicably ...
> (Raban 12–13)

While London has its history of class-based separation as districts and streets rise and fall in fashion and value, as well as the great divides of east and west, centre and suburbs, life in the street has always reproduced this promiscuity of proximity. In modern London only among the very rich or the great suburban belts around the city can this separation be ostensibly maintained, and even here only in restricted spaces. For the former, wealth can buy physical separation if desired, but for the latter it is as much a psychological isolation than an actual one among streets of semi-detached houses peering at each other across the road, or their inhabitants peering over the garden fence through the privet. In the modern city, as Raban notes, the movement has been towards the smaller dwelling space and ever closer physical association with your neighbour, and even if ignored in wilful urban reserve or alienation it is difficult not to overhear other lives. The greatest challenge to the continued 'privatization' of city life is the street, and this is as true of the twentieth century as it has been of London through the centuries: 'The London streets provided entertainment, commerce, communication, information, politics, sex. All human intercourse was here' (J. White 309).

The guiding feature of the novels to be considered in this chapter is how intimacy is played through and worked out on London's streets. From the 'stepping out' between home and cinema, social taboos broken by single mothers, to the mixed economy of fear and display of Gay London in the 1950s and 1960s. These 'spatial stories' in de Certeau's terms – 'every day, they traverse and organize places; they select and link them together; they make sentences and itineraries out of them. They are spatial trajectories' (de Certeau 115) – represent an exploration of the shifting awareness of physical proximity in the city, of class identities, and the places and spaces of sexual encounter and regulation. They are not separate issues, but questions to which post-war writers of London have been particularly attuned. It is important to bear in mind, though, that while writing after the war might represent a new frankness in referring to sexual encounters, it would be wrong to associate such a discursive shift with a major social reformulation in quite the way suggested by Levy and MacInnes. After all, we are discussing stories here, not history. As Carolyn Steedman distinguishes: 'stories are not consciously ordered, whereas histories (like case stories) are interpretative devices, they suggest coherence' (Steedman 143). Class and sexuality in the city have long been staples of the urban novel (as is easily demonstrated by the novels examined in the previous chapters of this study), but not always explicitly. This chapter will consider how the physical and conceptual reformulation of London after the war prompted and offered new literary opportunities through new spatial itineraries for authors writing of the intimacies of city life. Rather than the over-simplified sexual and social revolution that has become lodged in the popular imagination, what these material and conceptual changes point to is a refocusing on the practices of intimacy in the city, which is a history of continuity rather than abrupt reformulation.

David Lodge's first novel, *The Picturegoers* (1960), is not, chronologically, the earliest engagement with post-war London youth culture and it is by no means representative of the clichés of the pop-culture teenager. Such texts are in fact relatively few and far between, perhaps being better memorialized in cinema and television. Indeed, one can hazard that post-war fiction has maintained a far more nuanced and interrogatory (if not bemused) stance to the boom in popular culture. This is largely a consequence of class. The novel is, and arguably remains, a predominately middle-class genre, while the youth-culture boom of the 1950s and 1960s was spearheaded by the working classes and thence a matter for the more 'democratic' media of film and television (and is, no doubt, a factor in the middle class's habitual suspicion of both, particularly the latter). As Steven Connor observes: 'For many novelists writing in the 1950s and 1960s, during the rise and heyday of public service broadcasting in Britain, television proposed itself not just as a glamorous alternative to literary culture but also as a competitor in speaking for and constructing a common culture' (Connor 29). The stars of this cultural reformulation were also working class, and more often than not Londoners to boot (David Bailey, Terrence Donovan, Terence Stamp, Michael Caine, the Dave Clarke Five, the Rolling Stones, the Kinks, Twiggy, the Pretty Things, Sandie Shaw, The Who, Helen Shapiro, the Small Faces, Adam Faith, etc.). As Jerry White observes:

> It was this demotic element of class mix that marked the 'Swinging Sixties' out from the Roaring Twenties in London and, indeed, from any previous decade. It is not unreasonable to consider the 1960s a genuine period of 'social revolution' for the way in which working-class

talent was plucked from obscurity and pitched into worldwide stardom and riches overnight – not a new phenomenon but new in its apparently inexhaustible cast list. Photographers, hairdressers, actors and actresses, models, above all rock musicians and singers loomed large among the new stars. (J. White 342)

Note the absence of working-class authors from that list. The 'high' cultural 'revolution' was one for another decade as some aspects of popular culture gained intellectual respectability, but it did give many writers from this period an outsider's view on the new London. This is not to overvalue the middle-class credentials of literature from this period, but to emphasize the marginalization of the novel from the new youth-led popular culture. As such, while full of prejudice and having the potential for misinterpretation, the literary representation of the 'trajectory' of London's spatial narrative of those years is less likely to be caught up in a wave of what, today, we would call hype and thence less likely to talk in terms of 'revolutions'. While the detachment of the social observer may be false, it is significant that the literary establishment in Britain, if only for a brief period, was out of step with its own cultural base.

David Lodge exemplifies this point. A new novelist in 1960 and, while relatively young and completing his National Service when writing the majority of this novel (it was begun when he was 21), he was neither young enough nor from the correct social class to be a part of the new popular culture, even though he was in a position to be an acute observer of London life as an undergraduate and then a postgraduate student in the city. Yet Lodge did grow up in the London he fictionalized; the Brickley of the novel a thinly disguised Brockley and New Cross, so he was in a position to be aware of pre-war patterns of life in London. Thence this inner-city residential area on the southern shore of the Thames – the wrong side, one might observe – represents a retreat for the student-protagonist, Mark Underwood from the faux hedonism of student London. Unlike Lodge, Underwood is from a prosperous outer-London commuter town 'in the no-man's-land between London and "the country"' called Blatcham (Picturegoers 39) – a cousin in the spirit of Hamilton's Thames Lockdon in *The Slaves of Solitude*, or Robert's suburban family home in Bowen's *The Heat of the Day*. Mark is alienated in this place and disgusted by his parents, observing that 'the men of the town exhausted themselves in the diurnal pilgrimage to the City and back' (*Picturegoers* 39). The draw to central London is familiar enough to be a cliché, being well established as long ago as the picaresque novels of the eighteenth century – a character like Mark Underwood is a modern echo of Henry Fielding's Tom Jones; the young man from the provinces finding himself, his place in life and his fortune through a journey narrative that culminates in the city. The modern version of the picaresque is, however, somewhat less resolvable. This 'city' narrative from outer commuter suburb, to centre inner suburb is carefully drawn in class terms – from the suburban middle classes of the City commuter belt, to the 'welfare bohemia' of student London (*Picturegoers* 41), to the newly prosperous urban working classes. The sense of spatial, social and cultural journey for Underwood is pronounced when he comes to lodge with the Mallorys, as is his contradictory attraction to and alienation from popular culture in the form – if not the figure – of film actress, Amber Lush:

> In the Mallorys he felt he had rediscovered the people. The phrase smacked somewhat of 'Thirties affectation, but there was no other way of stating the fact. And it was a fact. But the popular art he looked for to accompany this rediscovery was sadly lacking. What he was witnessing was a fair sample of popular entertainment, and it was quite artificial and valueless: a circus cynically provided for the bread-filled masses by big business. Surely there must be an alternative? Something solid, earthy.... But what could be more solid, more earthy than that? He reflected, as Amber, lifting a leg to examine a stocking, tensed her skirt over one of her famed buttocks. (*Picturegoers* 65; ellipsis original)

The undergraduate conceit of this passage is pronounced. To rediscover the people presumes earlier first-hand knowledge that Underwood does not have creating the facsimile of an older man's regrets. The trajectory of his development turns an affectation into reality. The sexual charge of the film scene he watches on the screen accentuates the sexual challenge of wooing of the Mallorys' eldest daughter, Clare, newly expelled from a convent under some, as yet, unnamed infractions, and quickly identifies the novel's unusual juxtaposition of 'spiritual' values that has some resonance with Greene's *The End of the Affair*. The strong Catholic content of the narrative – of which Clare's earlier vocation is but one example – is finely balanced against the equal power of that temple of mammon, the cinema. Both represent spaces in which physical urges are sublimated: the cinema shows graphic acts of violence and sexuality, providing a focus and outlet that is as effective a regulatory institution as the admonishments of the Church. Indeed, one might go further and observe that the extreme violence of the Crucifixion and other violent tableaux in the bible provides similar theatricalized sublimations. The connection between the psychological spaces created by the spectacle of the Church and the cinema had been noted before the war by Dorothy Richardson, for whom each theatre was a 'little bethel' serving 'a plain miraculous food, sometimes coarse, sometimes badly served, but still miraculous food served to feed our souls' (Richardson 168). The novel charts Underwood's cynicism towards both, his hesitation and confusion and then immersion into the Church with the reactivation of his faith and ambition to become a priest. Ironically,

Underwood's journey from worldliness to piety mirrors Clare's movement in the opposite direction. This psychological journey, and those of the other characters in the novel, is not just played out *in* the cinema and the church, but *out* in the streets between them and the Mallorys' home.

Such 'spatial syntaxes' (de Certeau 115) assume a particular character when elaborated into city streets that are 'accumulating a mass of vital imageries from the fluid matter of memory, nostalgia, evocation, and suturing that index of scars into the projection of the contemporary moment' (Barber 8). Underwood's hesitation and confusion extends beyond his class tourism and alienation from popular culture, into his grasp of broader society that is directly linked to his migration from the conservative certainties of the sub-urbs into the far more fluid zone of the city. He lacks an organizing principle and is unable to accept his inability to draw together the multifarious facets of the life he observes. He is ultimately unable or unwilling to take responsibility for himself when he seeks external government and regulation from the Church: 'The body was like the surly, recalcitrant electorate of a democratic state, with the mind a nervous, impatient, and ultimately helpless executive. The body required autocratic government' (*Picturegoers* 181). While this curious observation could be dismissed as an extended simile, it is none-theless a striking image. Its source stems from a negative attitude towards the mass cooperation of democratic government and a desire for autocracy that the 'order' of the Church promises. It is a pro-foundly egotistical self-realization that is at odds with the bustling intimacy represented by the Mallory family and the city for which they substitute. His predicament is familiar to us already. There is a start-ling correlation between Underwood's confusion and Robert's des-pair and desire for autocratic government in *The Heat of the Day*. It is Robert's intimacy with Stella that brings to the fore the contradictions of his desires and such a resolution, much as Clare does for Mark. Moreover, he is another refugee from a suburban commuter town and shares a comparable spiritual void to Underwood. Mark fails as an aspiring writer, is unable to realize his attraction to the grounded family unit of the Mallorys through Clare, and ultimately retreats into the metaphysical hiatus from life offered by religion. The city is both catalyst and symbol of his fundamental failure revealing the con-servative within the liberal, although he does not immediately realize this:

> I don't inspire faith in myself. And God can't help me, I'm afraid. My problems aren't religious. I'll try and explain. Look: out there is Lon-don; beyond is the world. I can't see it because of the fog. But even if the fog cleared, I wouldn't know what it all meant. Looking out over a city gives me a sort of sick feeling – a sense of the appalling multiplicity of life. I get a sort of dizziness – that helpless feeling you get when you

read that a star is ninety million light years from the earth. I think of
the sewerage pulsing through thousands of miles of pipes, of trains
crammed with humanity hurtling through the tube, of the people who
never stop walking past you on the pavements – such infinite variations
of appearance, none of them alike, each with his own obsession, his
own disappointment, his own set of values, his own magazine under his
arm catering for his own hobby – railway engines or beekeeping. One
feels that one wants to gather them all like a harvest; or stop one,
understand him, absorb his identity, and them pass on to the next one
– but there's no time, there are too many, and you're swamped. (*Picturegoers* 79)

This whole passage is resonant with an inability to negotiate the
intimacy of city life and again betrays a desire to dominate – 'absorb
his identity' – and the fear that such control is beyond his personal
ability among a multitude of difference (which also lies behind
Lewis's acerbic narrative in *Rotting Hill*). The post-war city is actually
an engine for producing new identities, new individualities – 'infinite
variations' – that the conservative mind cannot grasp. The fog is, of
course, both literal and figurative.

The vision of a popular metropolitan culture that both fractures
traditional identities and continually manufactures new ones is contrasted with the Church, which subsumes all into a single communion. This recalls the influential reading of popular culture by
Theodore Adorno and Max Horkheimer: 'The sociological theory
that the loss of the support of objectively established religion, the
dissolution of the last remnants of pre-capitalism, together with
technological and social differentiation or specialisation, have led to
cultural chaos is disproved every day; for culture now impresses the
same stamp on everything' (Adorno and Horkheimer 120). Underwood is unable to recognize this aspect of popular culture, although
he is able to argue that 'the menace of the cinema was not surely that
it was lewd and sensual, but that it encouraged people to turn their
backs on real life' (*Picturegoers* 107) – yet this is exactly what Mark
plans to do by pursuing a vocation in the Church. Both popular
culture and religion promise much the same ideological or spiritual
service in the novel. Each provides an outlet for frustrated desires and
a psychological and material (cinema, church) space in which to revel
in such desires and/or retreat from them. The opposition that the
novel establishes between the Church and the cinema is barely one at
all, continually inviting the reader to accept the similarity of both
'institutions'. The key difference, however, is that the cinema, or
popular culture more broadly, is reached through the streets and is
inherently communal in this sense, while the Church encloses and
contains – in essence a coerced, overtly disciplinary, community. It is
the city itself that is the defining element that encourages a positive
reading of the possibilities of popular culture. The space of this

communion, as Dorothy Richardson recognized in her identification of the religious aspects of the practice of going to the 'pictures', is exactly what Adorno and Horkheimer omit from their analysis, abstracting and criticizing its various forms rather than analysing its full implications as social practice.

The novel offers two sub-plots underlining the importance of place to the novel's reading of popular culture. Clare has been excluded from her convent for becoming too close to one of her pupils, Hilda. Even though the matter progresses no further physically than a regular peck on the cheek, she describes the relationship to Mark as 'a love affair really' (*Picturegoers* 152). Following this confession, Clare is unexpectedly invited by the girl's parents to see if she can help with her strange behaviour following her own expulsion from the school. Hilda's family lives in a suburban district at the end of the underground line, crossing a boundary that is marked by the incongruity of the tube trains in the sidings 'looking lost and blind above ground, like worms' (*Picturegoers* 187). What she encounters is Hilda's new obsession with the not-long-dead James Dean, amusingly misnamed 'Dreme'; a substitute symbolically wed Christ that further emphasizes the religion/cinema analogy. Like Mark, Hilda's desires are ultimately selfish, leading to her withdrawal from her family and friends except for one single fellow worshipper. Clearly her sexual desires are being sublimated and yet it takes Hilda to point out the similarity between her own actions and the fetishization of the suffering Christ in the convent which Clare maintained as a novice. Even then Clare struggles to make the connection:

> This cult of James Dreme.... I'd hate to think it was because of what happened at the convent. I know you suffered a lot. So did I. I'm sorry, because it was mainly my fault for letting things go that far. But if that was unhealthy, this is ... diseased. You must see that it isn't natural. Your parents are desperately worried, and no wonder. You've got to shake yourself out of this dream. (*Picturegoers* 192; ellipsis original)

Hilda's sexual displacement has much to do with place and class. She is middle class and has been brought up in the 'no-man's-land between London and "the country"' (*Picturegoers* 39). Her reaction is to make of popular culture – as she has from religion beforehand – what she brings to it; a habit of withdrawal, egotism and sublimated sexuality.

The second example is more challenging. Harry is one of the ensemble of characters we are introduced to at the beginning of the novel winding through the south London streets with the shared goal of the cinema. Yet he is totally estranged from those around him, consumed by pent-up hate, fantasies of violence against those he feels slight him and a raging sexual frustration. Rather than conceal this turmoil of feelings, he openly displays them to the street and in the cinema, or at least imagines he does: 'You could read in his face that Harry was different from them; he didn't wear flash clothes and take cheap little tarts to the pictures, not Harry. He wore black, all black, except for the white, soft-collared shirt, and he took his pleasures alone' (*Picturegoers* 20). Such a distinctive uniform for the late 1950s leads to mockery, which further feeds into his alienated self-image: ''Oo's 'e think 'e is – Robert Mitchum?' (*Picturegoers* 21). The film reference is interesting here, pointing to the celluloid 'style' Harry has modelled himself after, no doubt borrowing Mitchum's hard-boiled 'bad boy' screen persona. Yet the cinema is not the cathartic experiential space for Harry as it is for others, and in fact stokes his psychological lust for sex and violence rather than providing a release for forbidden desires. On leaving the cinema he 'prowled on through the dark, deserted streets, hands plunged into the black depths of his raincoat, his crêpe soles sliding occasionally on the damp film of mud that coated the pavement' (*Picturegoers* 83–4). On returning home there are clear indicators of an unpleasant home life and unsatisfying masturbatory writhing in his bed. Later in the novel, Harry is seen to stalk Bridget, another patron of the cinema and one of the prota-gonists of the multiple sub-plots of the narrative. Finally deciding to attack her on a deserted bomb-site short cut to her home, he is fur-ther humiliated by her resistance when she easily fends him off and he retreats in panic. In many respects, Harry's character recalls Walter Benjamin's urban prowler, the *flâneur.*

> The crowd is not only the newest asylum of outlaws; it is also the latest narcotic for those abandoned in the crowd. In this he shares the situation of the commodity. He is not aware of this special situation, but this does not diminish its effect on him and it permeates him blissfully like a narcotic that can compensate him for many humilia-tions. The intoxication to which the *flâneur* surrenders is the intox-ication of the commodity around which surges the stream of customers. (Benjamin 1997 55)

This is a rather different version of the *flâneur* than that most fre-quently cited from Benjamin's work – the middle-class voyeur, aloof and penetrating but sealed and protected from the contamination of the crowd. Clearly the strong response Harry doggedly provokes by his attitude and the sense of alienation is sought and cultivated. By despising the crowd he creates a cause for the humiliations that each sally into the city streets and the cinema provides for him. Yet his equally deliberate uniform also translates him into a commodity to be decoded and catalogued as part of an urban typology. While we have seen an initial identification to the stage personal of a film actor, it is the 'crêpe soles' of Harry's shoes that positively identifies the youth fashion he wishes to associate himself with: the Teddy Boys.

The crêpe-soled 'brothel creeper' shoe was closely associated with

Ted fashion, and they are intermittently mentioned throughout the novel to provoke the sort of reaction that Harry cultivates. The link is underlined when the damage Harry has caused to his cinema seat with a knife – another symbol of his sexual frustration – is directly identified as the likely behaviour of Teddy Boys: 'It's them young Teds, sir, you mark my words. A lot of 'ooligans what's got nothink better to do' (*Picturegoers* 118). The Ted's style of clothing was initially an upper-class phenomenon signalling nostalgia for the Edwardian Indian summer of the Victorian class system, although this was rapidly abandoned to aspirational working-class mimics 'initially from south London, a group with some money but not much status, now trying to arrogantly assert itself'. Sinfield argues that: 'Subcultures are not founded always, or even particularly, in opposition and resistance; more mundanely, they are ways of coping. They afford to those who live them stories of their own identities and significance' (Sinfield 153). It is already evident from Harry's character that his internal narrative is a strategy for coping with alienation, sexual frustration, lack of status and a failed, if not actively humiliating, family environment. He does so by deliberately turning himself into an urban commodity by a strongly visual dress code and behaviour copied from the gangster films he loves. Popular culture is again a displacement in the novel, but one that is consciously mapped out as a means of self-defence. The problem comes of course when that fantasy is carried by Harry onto the city streets in the form of attempted sexual violence.

Initially part of the same misogynistic strategy of empowerment – 'He closed his eyes and went through in detail what he would like to do to the curly-haired tart. And then he began to think, why not do it, why not? It was time' – his attempted assault merely brings his inadequacies into undeniable reality when he fails. Yet the wreck of his personality is tied to the disappearing post-war wreck of London, his chosen ground: 'He had played here as a kid just after the war, when it *was* a bomb-site, with tottering, gutted houses, uncovered cellars, bits of furniture, twisted pipes, water tanks. They'd had a good time. And tonight he was going to have a good time. A bloody good time' (*Picturegoers* 159). This fragmented and tormented London, like Harry's fragmented and tormented psyche, needs a unifying principle for a new generation of Londoners. Once more it is the cinema that provides it, although not through film but music, recalling the picture house's former glory as a focus for working-class popular entertainment as a music hall. The 1950s version is a trans-Atlantic import forged from various musical styles – rock 'n' roll:

> It didn't really matter. He just swivelled around in the middle, while she danced. He champed on his gum in time to the music, and kept a poker-faced expression. She pushed him into the right positions. She jerked up his arm, and spun round under it. Her skirt rose to her

thighs. She had good legs. The whole cinema seemed to be dancing now. There was a terrific din, everybody was singing and dancing. It was great. The lights went on, but the music and dancing continued. The blonde was good-looking in a cheeky sort of way. Her hard little breasts poked out under her sweater; they didn't wobble, they clung to her twisting body. It was surprising how strong she was. She pulled him past her, and as he went he let his hand float out casually behind him, as he had seen it done, and was overjoyed to feel her small, damp hand fall solidly into his palm. He turned, and they laughed. (*Picturegoers* 229–30)

It is the blonde – Jean – who offers the promise of a place to which he can belong. Moulding him to the dance steps, she is the guide that he has never had before. She also gestures to the way out from the 1950s. Her slight figure and assertive manner contrasts with the opulent figure and heavy sensuality of film stars like Amber Lush, taken to be the paragon of sexual desirability earlier in the novel. All the signs are that this new era will suit Harry, no longer burdened by his paranoia and crushing sense of inadequacy. It is this working-class London misfit who achieves the only real promise of change and happiness in the novel. Mark returns to his middle-class suburb and withdrawal from the world into religion; Clare is left confused; Hilda remains obsessed and withdrawn; even the working-class couple Len and Bridget seem condemned to a future of toil and hardship in their new marriage. Only Harry seems to achieve the promise of unfettered happiness in the music and the new world to which he opens up socially. His experience looks forward while other characters remain moribund, face an uncertain future, or even regress, as Jerry White observes: 'The Ted's uniform, their cult of toughness and their attachment to a particular strand of musical culture combined to make them the first real youth movement of the century. For good or ill, the history of youth on London's streets over the next fifty years could in part be viewed as the chain reaction triggered by this metropolitan innovation' (J. White 325).

If *The Picturegoers* shares some structural similarities with the male picaresque tradition, how do the shifting cultural and social trajectories of the city affect representations of female experiences in the city? While Lodge offers us Hilda, Clare and Bridget, none of them seeks self-revelation in the locality in which she grew up. Hilda is middle class, but does not journey to the city. Doreen, another minor character from the novel, hints at such a progression, but it is away from not towards London. After an affair with the cinema manager, she is forced to mature rather quickly when she becomes pregnant. The end of the novel sees her travelling by train to Newcastle to discreetly have her child. This promises another story, but London is Doreen's home town and it is another city that will witness her self-development. Further, as a working-class woman, her story does not raise the range of questions initiated by a class tourist like Mark.

Published in the same year as *The Picturegoers* – 1960 – Lynne Reid Banks's *The L-Shaped Room* approaches London from exactly the same class-based trajectory as Lodge, but with a female protagonist. Jane Graham is another middle-class refugee from a rather staid London commuter suburb. While the actual locale is unnamed, it is clear it is in the leafy south-west suburbs. Like Mark, Jane also has a bohemian past having spent time in her youth as a member of an acting collective touring the north – perhaps echoing Jean Rhys's earlier *Voyage in the Dark* (1934), although that novel ends in prostitution and worse. Attacked by and chased from the company by a male homosexual colleague interested in the same man, we meet Jane some years later, pregnant and moving into a less than salubrious studio flat in Fulham. Like Mark's experience of his parents, Jane's home life with her father, a workaholic civil servant (her mother died some years before) is distant and formal. Her relocation is not some undergraduate desire to 'rediscover' the people and a family life she has not enjoyed, but a self-inflicted punishment having been banished from the family home by her father once he learns of her condition. The differing motivations behind these two different middle-class forays into alien London are striking in their basic similarity in structural terms but, of course, utterly different in their enactment and consequences. One cannot but be struck by the voluntary voyeurism of Mark's sojourn with the Mallorys and lack of real ties, compared with the enforced anonymity of Jane's resettlement and the very real fact of her pregnancy. If Mark echoes the picaresque male protagonist who is more or less a free agent in the city, so Jane internalizes her father's 'Victorian' reaction to her predicament, casting herself as a modern archetype of the fallen woman. Indeed, the Fulham Jane discovers is an updating of many Victorian novelists' description of working-class urban slums:

> The neighbourhood was completely strange to me. If I'd been in any mood to make judgements I'd have judged it to be pretty grim. The shabby houses fronted almost right onto the pavement, though some of them had front yards stuck with a few sooty bushes. Most of the windows lacked curtains and that gave the houses a blind look, or rather a dead look, like open-eyed corpses. They were decaying like corpses, too. Some of the front yards had dustbins instead of bushes, which would have smelt if it hadn't been drizzling. But the drizzle didn't do anything to reduce the dog-smell, which was foul. You had to watch where you walked. It hadn't been raining long and the pavement had that sweaty look. (*Room* 8)

This macabre corpse-like city of the dead clearly matches Jane's mood as she consciously buries her old life and self-respect. The dog-muck, too, clearly expresses some deep-seated sense of contamination and worthlessness.

These contrasting cities are created by protagonists whose family backgrounds differ, fundamentally, only on the question of the gender. Class tourism for the male protagonist does not carry with it the same social stigma. While Mark flirts with the idea of marrying Clare, there is no suggestion that it would damage his own class status; instead Clare would be 'raised'. The initial impression we gain from Jane's paternal and self-imposed exile is that she has lost status for good. The sexual double standard is marked, but not unexpected even in 1960. However, it does invite questions of the way city is imagined and experienced from a gendered and sexualized perspective, as Stephen Frosh argues: ' "women" here is a product of the imagination, literally the imaginary; a fantasy that holds masculinity in place. Moreover, she is a *spatial* fantasy, a kind of boundary around a safe terrain' (Frosh 293). The spatial terminology of this observation – place, boundary, terrain – suggests an explanation for Mark's interest in Clare. While she looks upon their increasing closeness as representative of real commitment, Mark is using her to work through his own psychological and social issues. The city and the home space of the Mallory family offer a space/place of difference from his own background allowing him to view himself with a feeling of detachment. Of course the motivation for his actions is profoundly selfish and narcissistic – he cares little for whom he might hurt in this drama of self-realization. Jane in *The L-Shaped Room* does provide definition for some of the male characters, but not so that she becomes dominated by their needs. Indeed, Jane is notable for the real investment in place which is a key aspect of her character. One of her friends observes when visiting her in hospital after a miscarriage scare:

> 'But why? You'll die of depression in that bug-run ...'
> That hit home. I felt an unwonted defensiveness rising. 'It's not all that bad,' I protested.
> Dottie stopped short, frowning. 'Do you love it?'
> 'Well I do in a way. It's seen me through a lot.'
> 'You and your places!' (*Room* 155; ellipsis original)

Once attached to a place it is not within Jane's nature to give it up easily. Her psychological map of London is dominated by three locations: her family home in the suburbs, the house in Fulham and her former place of employment – a luxury hotel in the West End called Drummonds. Each location represents strong personal attachments. Home is of course her father, with whom she shares a stronger attachment than his actions at the beginning of the novel might suggest; the flat in Fulham represents strong newly formed relationships with the black Jazz player John and the Jewish aspirant writer Toby, as well as functioning increasingly as a surrogate family or at least a close-knit community; and Drummonds represents the close friendship with her mercurial boss, James. While obscured at first glance by the intimate and ironic first-person narrative, these relationships are socially and politically radical. Jane's relationship with her father is shocked out of its traditionalism by her pregnancy, revealing a man with both a strong conscience and high emotional dependency on his daughter – in her absence he turns to drink and neglects that bastion of middle-class sensibility, the suburban garden. James her boss hides behind exterior bluster that reveals a man of considerable sympathy towards Jane and her condition, although it is the gentle supportive actions of the owner of the hotel that are most intriguing. Recognizing early that Jane's mysterious illness is pregnancy, he asks her to take time away from work, but does not sack her outright by keeping the door open to return to the job she loves. He even directs the dense James to look her up when she doesn't keep in touch. Most significant is Jane's relationship with John and Toby. John is both black and gay. The latter detail is carefully revealed to the reader through several clues in the narrative, although Jane only becomes conscious of this towards the end of the novel. As a positive representation of a gay black man this must have been unique in 1960; such characters are pretty thin on the ground even today. Crucially, it enables Jane and the reader to work through their prejudice of both gay and black men. Malcolm, the gay actor who attacks Jane when she is with the theatrical company, reflects several stereotypes of gay men – highly camp, unsympathetic, potentially vicious, hysterical – and Jane's first encounter with the extremely racist newsagent near her new flat – 'Live an let live, I say, all except the bobos, you have to keep them their place' (*Room* 10) – set the early benchmarks of prejudice away from which the narrative progressively draws the reader.

Then there is Toby, a sensitive aspirant writer with whom Jane falls in love. He is a vehicle through which various male preconceptions are explored. Firstly Toby comes to terms with Jane's pregnancy and then, although less surely, the social presumption that he should be the breadwinner. Their separation comes from his own fear of a loss of creativity which he attempts to blame on Jane, although she identifies his essential fear of failure before the break: 'if by succeeding you mean in your own eyes . . . it's as important as self-respect – it's *part* of self-respect. Without self-respect and a sense of satisfaction in his work, a man's nothing, and if he's nothing, he's not worth loving' (*Room* 184). On the face of it, this seems to be a stereotypical restatement of the importance of work in defining masculine identity, and yet it is significantly prefaced by 'in your own eyes'. Toby is not being assessed as a potential provider, but for his ability to become a rounded person. Then there is the question of his Jewishness. Both Jane and Toby are subconsciously sensitive to this issue. As Jane observes when they first meet: 'I privately thought [his name] was probably Cohen and chalked it up against him that he should have changed it' (*Room* 38), and after they have become lovers Toby attempts to paint Jane as racist in a farewell letter: 'By the way, I'm a Jew. So you probably wouldn't have wanted to marry me anyway' (*Room* 217). Given that the owner of Drummonds is Jewish as well, there is a definite attempt to overcome anti-Semitic prejudice in the novel. The city spaces/places that the novel creates reveal not only prejudice but also the possibility of confronting it in the intimacy of the city. To recall Raban's observation, 'The modern city, of small apartments and densely occupied communications routes ... makes us live hugger-mugger, cheek to cheek' (Raban 13). And yet as Banks demonstrates in this novel, such intimate spaces have real potential for political and social development, a point made more recently by bell hooks: 'As a radical standpoint, perspective, position, "the politics of location" necessarily calls those of us who would participate in the formation of counter-hegemonic practice to identify the spaces where we begin the process of re-vision' (Keith and Pile 6). The narrative space created from London in *The L-Shaped Room* is just such a location that challenges – 're-visions' – racial and social prejudices.

Yet Jane has her own journey to take before she realizes the cathartic potential of the space she creates in Fulham. In this respect her attitude towards both Toby and the unborn child are tied to the resolution of her vision of both the apartment and the London streets as a psychological space. Lodge's Mark expresses his sense of bewilderment as a writer by looking out over the misty vista of the city which expresses his lack of personal vision: 'out there is London; beyond is the world. I can't see it because of this fog' (*Picturegoers* 79). Using a similar fog image, Jane sees her own confusion and irresolution in the London streets. After spending her first night with Toby, Jane is confronted by John's disgust at the sounds of lovemaking overheard through the thin partition between their rooms. Clear to the reader by this point that John is gay, there is an added poignancy to his anger that leads him to scare off the sensitive Toby by revealing that Jane is pregnant and calling her a whore. This touches on her own barely suppressed view of herself that she has internalized from her father. Indeed, on first arriving in Fulham, it is the double-meanings of prostitutes' advertisements that her eye settles upon in the newsagent's window: 'French girl gives lessons, phone after 6 p.m.' and 'Photographer's Model free evenings. Special poses' (*Room* 8). She then chooses a lodging house with two prostitutes living and working from the basement flat, a fact that 'the landlady had been quite open about' (*Room* 7). Having potentially lost Toby and openly been called a whore, Jane is drawn to the prostitutes: 'I had some dim idea that I should see what sort of creatures these whores were, so that I might find out what *I* was' (*Room* 110). Of course what she finds is a rather ordinary woman with a very matter-of-fact attitude to her occupation and a rather pitying attitude towards men. In short, rather than the 'painted whore' of middle-class preconception, Jane's personal encounter with the woman humanizes her without sensation:

> 'I've enjoyed meeting you,' I said.
>   She looked at me for a moment, measuringly, as if wondering whether I meant it. 'Have you?' she said at last, curiously. Then, briskly: 'What a lousy night! I hate this bloody mist, it gets into everything and makes your hair straight.' It was the first time she'd sworn, except the one perfectly correct use of a word more generally used in any but its proper context. My language was considerably worse than hers.
>   'Good-bye,' I said, and shook hands with her. I went up the stone steps into the street, and let myself into the house. I didn't quite close the door, and after a few moments I could hear her footsteps walking briskly past. Looking after her, I saw her reach up and tuck a strand of hair into place before the dark mist swallowed her up. I suddenly remembered her name was Jane. (*Room* 115)

The 'London particular' is, as Peter Ackroyd notes, 'the greatest character in nineteenth-century fiction', but the smogs of the 1950s and early 1960s were also a serious matter (Ackroyd 2001 434). In 1962 some 60 people were killed over three days by lethal smog. It has long been an expressive tool in the hands of artists of both menace and beauty. As Burton Pike observes, the city-image 'brings into the text a power of its own; it might be more accurate to say that a writer harnesses the image rather than he creates it' (Pike 13). For Monet 'the London fog became a token, or revelation, of mystery' (Ackroyd 2001 436). There is an element of both mystery and revelation in this passage from *The L-Shaped Room*, but also ambivalence. Their shared name points to their shared humanity, but while the narrative is confronting the dehumanization of prostitutes, this is not automatically a two-way process. Jane gets her answer and is satisfied that she is not a prostitute, while broadening her own social horizons, although her liberalism remains rather naive. In this respect it is significant that she does not close the door, although it seems rather trite to note that prostitute Jane's language is polite. There is an essential analytical distance to this comment as there is in the hesitation over the genuineness of Jane's commonplace remark 'I have enjoyed meeting you'. Indeed, Jane the prostitute has assumed that she has some sociological interest in her rather than as a neighbour due, no doubt, to her middle-class accent.

The issue of class creates further separations in the fog imagery. The prostitute is enveloped by the fog as if she belongs to it and the city, whereas Jane retreats inside and looks out onto the street. This leads to the second occasion where fog gains symbolic weight in the novel around another internalized crisis – Jane's attitude to her baby. Again, the impetus is the missing Toby. In her confusion, Jane resolves that it is her pregnancy keeping them apart. Telephoning the doctor who offered her an abortion earlier in the novel, she is overheard by Mavis, another tenant in the house, who offers to achieve the same end with a bottle of gin and some mysterious pills. With these two options before her, Jane gets a sudden craving for curry that draws her into the early evening street into which the prostitute Jane had disappeared: 'A glance outside told me it was still foggy – getting worse, if anything. Naturally, I knotted a headscarf round my throat so savagely I nearly choked myself, and crept – I had to creep, because of Mavis – downstairs and out into the fog' (*Room* 142). As the night streets lose their definition in the fog the journey assumes the structure of an ordeal, a journey towards decision recalling the multiple uses of fog in John Bunyan's quest allegory *The Pilgrim's Progress*. Certainly the 'grey fog of doubt' is an appropriate image here, as is the 'slough of despair': 'Passing a street-light came to seem quite an event; one watched their brave little sulphurous smudges receding with a feeling akin to despair, as if we might never find another' (*Room* 143). The commonplace nature of the London streets – the bus, the 'grinding sounds of traffic – but muffled' (*Room* 144) – have been transformed into a threatening 'jungle' of dread. Stumbling down her own street she slides down a lamp-post, only to be rescued by Jane the prostitute: 'The fog had made her eye-black run and it lay in ridges in the lines under her eyes; her hair was hanging in strands from under her hat. I could smell her scent, very sharp and close, through the fog and dog smells at the foot of the lamp-post where I was sitting on the ground' (*Room* 144–5). Hitting rock-bottom and finding dog piss and a ragged prostitute is a rather troubling image. The effect of humanizing Jane the prostitute seems further diminished even though she is Jane's rescuer.

This symbolic landscape demonstrates to Jane that she is only a fleeting visitor to these 'mean streets'. Indeed, this is a turning point in the novel. Rushed to hospital, she narrowly averts a miscarriage (rather implausibly brought on by the curry) and returns to her flat determined to have the baby. Despite the liberal credentials of this novel, it is clear that there are elements of Mark's patronizing attitude towards the working-class Mallorys in Jane's attitude towards the characters she has arranged on her stage – it is as well not to overlook that the first chapter of the novel recounts Jane's experiences as an actress. She has also 'staged' her room as the first step of that transformation. The remainder of the novel is a reversal of many of Jane's negative experiences. She confronts the father of her child, reconnects with Toby and the death of her aunt means she becomes financially independent. She is finally reconciled with her father. The latter reconciliation enables her to escape the L-shaped room and return to the parental home that has been newly liberalized. Toby and John are of course the godparents to this transformation and the new baby. The *staged* nature of this very contingent transformation only leads to a return to the middle-class suburbs although with a broader circle of potential visitors. As Zukin observes, 'stage-sets evoke the social production of visual consumption.... In this land-scape, socio-spatial identity is derived purely from what we consume' (Zukin 243). Jane, like Mark Underwood, has created and consumed a particular image of London to resolve her crisis of identity. They both return to their middle-class origins, although it is only fair to observe that *The L-Shaped Room* doesn't burn its social bridges quite as finally as Mark's experience in *The Picturegoers*. After all, the novel does gesture at a broader attitude towards race and sexuality, but not towards the overtly working-class characters such as Doris the landlady and the prostitutes. They remain in a specific, class-based, locale that doesn't travel with Jane to her new-found happiness. Her adventure has been transformed into nostalgia: 'To have been wrenched away from it so suddenly made me feel like a snail with a broken shell. I was sucked back irresistibly for one last look' (*Room* 265). Nostalgia is not social transformation, but a fantasy that points to a false sense of community existing safely in the past. Jane has been the star of her own, largely deliberate, narrative. While this self-conscious design is certainly a trajectory through the city, it is not quite the lived experience for which de Certeau argues. Both *The Picturegoers* and *The L-Shaped Room* explore this essentially class-based distancing strategy through their central characters, Jane and Mark. Nearly everyone else is left where they were found or facing a very real crisis.

Much the same self-consciousness can be identified in Rodney Garland's *The Heart in Exile* (1953). The central protagonist of the novel, Anthony Page, explains his experience of investigating a for-mer lover's suicide in and occasionally around London as 'I felt I was *living* a novel now' (*Heart* 134). He also concedes that his knowledge of people from outside London and from a different social class is something 'I knew only from novels' (*Heart* 114). While Page's ordering of experience is closely associated with the form of fiction, he often associates those he examines with the cinema. When he first interviews his dead friend's fiancée he observes: 'I was thinking of the young woman facing me. I found myself wondering how people could have behaved in a crisis before cinema-going became a habit' (*Heart* 21). Later when he contemplates the photograph of his friend's unnamed final male lover, he again reflects: 'At first glance, he could have been any variation of Atlantic Youth – American, French, Eng-lish, the prototype being Guy Madison or Burt Lancaster. Clearly, either he or the photographer had tried to give him the look of the popular young film star of the day' (*Heart* 53). While Ann, the former fiancée, is wealthier than Page and her former lover, Julian Leclerc, her origins are 'vulgar' – the offspring of a provincial commercial family, whereas the male lover is working class. This characterization by media clearly marks off the distance between the upper-middle-class, university educated, old money (or at least old family) world of

Page and Leclerc, and those who do not belong to this class strata. The division grants the novel an intriguing tension since it concerns the gay 'underground' – as it is referred to in the novel – of London. Most of Page's and Julian's circle are upper class, yet the lovers they desire are entirely working class. Indeed, the novel is replete with quite astonishing generalizations, seldom contradicted, about both women and the working class. This tends to bring to the fore an obvious ignorance of both. Moreover, the former are almost despised while the latter are romanticized:

> I mean, look at the West End today. The war years were exceptional. What a harvest ... but compare the years before the war with the present. You went out on a Saturday and between Leicester Square and Marble Arch you usually found something. Young men from the suburbs, from the provinces. They were yours for the asking. Sometimes it cost money, but not much. Boys accepted us because we were class; and not only that: they liked us because, unlike women, we didn't cost them money. I suppose we made a fuss of them, which their girls didn't. Anyhow, today they can afford women, and if they don't want women they have plenty of money for other amusements.... And what's more tantalising is that the young worker today is so good looking, so well-built, well-dressed ... (*Heart* 99–100)

For a novel that is ostensibly a daring, extremely frank and sympathetic representation of 1950s Gay London, it is, ultimately, a representation of shifting post-war social relations between the classes and a commentary on the new popular culture. Before the war, working-class men were a commodity that the homosexual upper-class man could 'harvest' from the London streets for sexual gratification. They were both deferential and, it seems, flattered by the attention. Above all it was a conspiracy based on masculinity that excluded 'expensive' and 'fussy' women. The better-paid, better-dressed worker can now 'afford' to have a relationship with a woman or pay for 'other amusements'. These 'other amusements' range through motor cars, the cinema, clothes, a bedsit away from the oppressive and crowded family home, fashionable haircuts, education in the form of evening classes, even the hint of rock 'n' roll implicit in some of the fashions described. The working-class male has become a consumer and thus empowered (although women of all classes remain marginalized, if not trivialized, in the novel).

This situation recalls Harry from *The Picturegoers*. His sexual and social frustration takes the form of a violent misogyny which is eventually tempered and resolved in rock 'n' roll, although this could equally be read as the gaining of status. He is an unexpectedly good dancer and his manner of dressing seems now to have gained a popularity, which retains a sense of rebellion while providing a large group of peers. In a different context, perhaps, Harry would have been one of the working-class men flattered by the attentions of an upper-class man. Yet it is the 'feminization' of the new fashions that is a component of the puzzle in *The Heart in Exile*. According to Page, one of the reasons working-class men are attractive to the upper-class homosexual men of the novel is their masculinity; a masculinity not available among the refinements of their own class. And yet Page notices a certain contradiction in both this desire and its mode of expression: 'We would not be able to draw attention to ourselves in such blatant if successful ways... As so often, I began to wonder whether these young, metropolitan working-class males effect this remarkable self-dramatisation for their women. Maybe, I thought, but it was doubtful. They wanted to assert their personality and wanted to be admired by both sexes' (*Heart* 54). Like Teddy Boy fashion, the combination of flamboyant clothing, narcissistic grooming, combined with a tough if not outright violent reputation has a particular resonance with this attitude of attraction and patronization. The new fashions have been copied from the upper classes and can be recognized as fake, but the working-class butchness they signal is irresistibly attractive – both dangerous and inferior.

This tension between, or the desire to bridge, the effete world of the middle classes and the butch world of the working classes is reproduced in Page's urban trajectory. By constructing his own consciousness as novelistic and aristocratic, and characterizing the more down-to-earth social practicalities and visual roles offered by the cinema as 'vulgar', whether associated with working class or new money middle class. The former is introverted and individualized (books are 'consumed' alone) while the latter is extrovert and communal. Ann and many of the working-class males who attract Page and Leclerc take their cues from cinema, either to structure the expression of their feelings or to make a visual statement on the street. A novelistic vision is seen as less desirable or alienated from the 'life' of this new urban code. Indeed, Theodore Adorno could observe as late as 1967 that 'the stereotype of the artist remains the introvert, the egocentric idiot, frequently the homosexual' (Adorno 129). Yet this is the very point that the novel wishes to stress in presenting a sympathetic representation of homosexuality in anticipation of a hostile audience. Those gay men who make an 'exhibition' of themselves by visually dramatizing themselves and their sexuality on the streets are frowned upon in this novel. Visibility on the streets or in pubs and other public spaces means that the 'underground' is no longer submerged, leading to an openness that is a matter of disgust to Page: 'Then one of them gave a nod to the group of pansies who stood around the fireplace ... Theirs was the least interesting group. It may be that I am too severe in my judgement of them. I try hard to be understanding, but I shudder from them. It is not only that they give the game away, but it is my experience that such people are usually unintelligent, verbose, neurotic and generally tiresome' (*Heart*

62). This was not an uncommon attitude in the 1950s. Peter Wilde-blood, in the book he published after his own trial and conviction as a homosexual in 1954, sought 'tolerance' for homosexuals but not for 'the effeminate creatures who love to make an exhibition of themselves' (Wildeblood 7). So exhibitionism in the middle-class 'hunter' is a negative attribute, but a certain butch exhibitionism in the working-class 'prey' is highly desired. The novel, therefore, constructs the following male attributes as desirable in the middle-class hunter: refined but physically tough, intelligent, succinct rather than verbose, restrained rather than exhibitionist, calm and self-possessed rather than neurotic. This is, in effect, the identity that both Julian and Page project and insofar as middle-class culture is seen as effete, the focus of desire passes to the working-class male. Even Ann is admired for a certain masculinity in her appearance. While working-class men might now seek to draw attention to their physical attractiveness, this is deemed acceptable since it fails to mask, if not enhances, the 'essential' masculinity lent by their class and the physical nature of their employment.

Page's psychological detective plot maps these identifications onto London. This is not a tracing, or accurate reflection of physical London, but an enactment, a creation of lived space from the social structures of the city. As Deleuze and Guattari observe, there is a key distinction between mapping and mere tracing: 'The map has to do with performance, whereas the tracing always involves an alleged "competence"'' (Deleuze and Guattari 12). The map in this context is exploratory rather than prescriptive; a matter of personality and identity and involving not a little fantasy and desire – 'a presence and not merely a setting' (Pike 8). The climax of the novel is therefore not the resolution of the detective plot concerning the question of Julian's suicide (the cause of this was never hard to guess), but Page's identification and location of Julian's lover whose photograph he finds hidden behind Ann's in Julian's flat. The physical locale is Islington:

> As I drove up to the Angel, it never for a moment occurred to me that I might perhaps draw another blank, as in the case of Ginger. Perhaps this was because Ron lived in Islington, which was for me a special significance. It was a district that had always spelt mystery and magic for me ever since I'd walked through it one summer evening when I was very young, years before I met Julian, when London was still new to me. I never really came to know the place well, but in my imagination I had invested it with a strange sense of romance. It certainly had life and a good deal of colour. There were secrets about Islington, some of which in the ensuing years I had solved, but many of which I dared not touch for fear that the magic would vanish. For one thing it had a past, and its past, as in the case of many poor districts in London, was exciting and noble. In the early nineteenth century it was still smart and some of its

good architecture had survived; Regency grandeur mixed with the gaudy vitality of working-class life in the twentieth century was an exciting contrast.

People south of the river were indifferent. They still had the warmth and naïvety of provincials. The men of Islington were metropolitan, tough and seasoned, in contrast to their environment of gentle squares, quiet parks, old cemeteries, deserted railway stations and vistas of a canal which could look incredibly romantic. But perhaps I was investing the place with a glamour that didn't really exist outside my imagination. (*Heart* 228–9)

This passage is a variation on middle-class romanticism of the working classes and the areas of the city they are seen to inhabit. The 'mystery and magic' is a reformulation of nineteenth- and early twentieth-century middle-class fascination with the 'abyss' or 'dark heart' of London that can be traced through the writing of Dickens, Meyhew, Gissing, Conrad and Morrison, as well as a whole host of social observers and missionary groups active in the East End whose writings were avidly consumed by middle-class readers. Indeed, Julian spent time at the University Settlement in Mile End that was one outcome of the social movement. Yet rather than the titillation of tales of depravation and crime, the 'mystery' of Islington means something rather different here, an association with youth and childhood romance hints at adventure; a boy's own realm of quests and *rite de passage*.

It is no coincidence that later nineteenth-century writers – for example, Conrad in *Heart of Darkness* (1899) and Conan Doyle in his Sherlock Holmes stories – established a connection between the 'dark places' of Empire and the urban jungle of the metropolis. That these in turn drew upon a tradition of masculine adventure writing that was ambivalent about women to say the least – for example, Rider Haggards's *King Solomon's Mines* (1886) or Kipling's *Kim* (1901) – is significant. Much the same turn towards adventure can be seen in Greene's wartime novel *The Ministry of Fear*. Islington, however, represents the nostalgia for middle-class adventure exclusively constructed as a space of masculine desire with only young, vigorous, working-class men lingering in the street who are intimidating and exciting. Even the physical attributes of the area symbolize an intermingling between middle-class Regency grandeur and the 'gaudy vitality of working class life'. This scene spatializes both components of Page's identity and desires. The promise of the vigour of the working class has accreted around a fabric, or structure, erected by *his* middle class, while the resulting disunity between elegance and energy is 'an exciting contrast'. This union but not resolution of difference has significant symbolic import in the novel. In one sense it signifies the increasing influence and affluence of the working classes after the war. Yet social fluidity is discouraged. Julian loses interest in his working-class partners insofar as they begin to resemble him: 'Dighton had actually lost some of that masculinity which originally may have sprung partly from his working-class background and culture' (*Heart* 150). The social import of this is interesting. Julian is attracted to working-class men so long as they retain their working-class identity. Such desires are irreconcilable in a social context that is encouraging greater class mobility, and perhaps points to an element of conservatism in his sexual liaisons.

The replication of these class issues through romantic and sexual relationships is also present in both *The Picturegoers* and *The L-Shaped Room*. Any crossing of class boundaries is revealed to be superficial at best: Mark Underwood retreats into the certainties of the Church and returns to his suburb; Jane also returns home after her adventure, suggesting only temporary social interaction; while Julian faces an ultimatum from his father. A father who doesn't relent like Jane's and pressures his son into suicide. But what of Anthony Page? While tempted by Ron and those like him and sharing the same basic desire for working-class masculinity, he realizes instead he is in love with his housekeeper/assistant – a male former nurse called Terry. It is this relationship that develops throughout the novel providing a contrast to the vagaries and dangers of gay – underground – London. There is a further contrast in Terry's character: 'he was a delightful freak of Nature. He loved housework as much as any woman' (*Heart* 179). The gender stereotyping inherent in this statement is disturbing, but even more so is Terry's servility and the erotic stimulation with which it provides Page: 'One saw the servant's humility in the attitude. But one also saw the broad shoulders, the arched back with the freckled skin under the rebellious hair, and he would look up as I entered and give me a beautiful smile of his brown dog eyes and white teeth' (*Heart* 179). Terry is working class, but significantly from outside London, unlike the 'seasoned' men of Islington. Terry is also interested in popular and high culture. He has a fashion sense, likes the cinema, listens to music, is a keen cyclist and attends a gym, but also reads novels and attends plays. Ostensibly he offers the promise of an eroticized combination of both middle- and working-class interests but with none of the angst, aggression, or danger involved in seeking sexual partners on the streets and public places of the city. In this respect he represents a quiescent working class and a tamed popular youth culture. Like Lodge's Mark and Reid Banks's Jane, the middle-class Page maintains class superiority through a romantic relationship projected onto the fabric of the city. Significantly, however, all three characters withdraw from central London to realize these fantasies leaving as the true representatives of the flux and energy of London identities – Teddy Boy Harry, the Jewish writer Toby, the black homosexual John and the some time working-class homosexual Ron.

4

Stress Fractures

The city is not ruinous, although
  Great ruins of an unremembered past,
With others of a few short years ago
  More sad, are found within its precincts vast.
The street-lamps always burn; but scarce a casement
In house or palace front from roof to basement
  Doth glow or glean athwart the murk air cast.
            James Thompson, *The City of Dreadful Night* (1882)

The immediate post-war cultural history of London bears witness to the persisting scars of war damage that would linger into the 1970s, contrasted by the energy of reconstruction that would be both celebrated in reformulated locations like the South Bank, and rued with the rise of buildings produced by an unholy alliance between greedy property speculators and town planners desperate for a quick-fix traffic or housing solution. Yet this combination of Blitz damage and often ill-planned and ill-designed redevelopment fanned the gentle flames of a new fascination with London's history, visible in an urban fabric that was increasingly being remoulded by redevelopment. The publication of John Summerson's *Georgian London* in 1945 is an important landmark of this emerging consciousness charting what had survived, what had been lost and what was at risk of one era of London's fabric. This was not an entirely unique phenomenon for London but it had never stimulated interest on the same scale, nor had it been accompanied by specific social developments like gentrification. As the term 'gentrification' suggests, this resurgent fascination was a class-specific phenomenon:

What had been the burning obsession of a few gradually became a lifetime investment for many. This was not so much apparent in the study of London's old buildings for study's sake, although there was to be more of that than ever before. Rather it was the conscious decision by a substantial part of the London middle classes to seek the good life, not in the suburbs as their parents and grandparents had done, but in the very areas that had been abandoned in that first suburbanizing process. (J. White 63)

This suggests a new confidence among London's middle classes to counter the sense of a passing of the old order and a diminishment in civility identified by many amid the improving economic and social prospects available to the working classes. For many among the well-to-do middle classes, the social hierarchy of London and the country had no less than capsized. As David Hughes observed: 'Before the war, the upper crust, still residential, attended functions in full drag; now, patriotic to the last clothing-coupon, they dressed dowdily and the spivs had assumed their plumage as well as their habitat' (Sissons and French 89). The Teddy Boy phenomenon, too, had initially been an upper-middle-class movement attempting to evoke a cultural late flowering of Victorian certainties in the early twentieth century, subsequently appropriated by working-class youths.

Property, however, had long been the middle classes' chosen ground, despite the historical tendency for smart and fashionable developments to give way to atomization as houses gave way to flats, then rooms, and increasingly suffered neglect as the middle classes moved on to the latest bastion of civility and the working classes moved in – an inexorable process that would eventually lead the better-off to the outer suburbs. The rediscovery of the fine Georgian buildings of inner London is both a reverse of those earlier impulses of fashion, and a desire to reclaim and reassert the influence that habitation in such buildings and estates originally conveyed in a radically changed social and economic milieu. The publication of Summerson's *Georgian London* also points to the post-war resurgence of the conservation movement which can be identified as a middle-class ideology in its conservative attachment to the physical fabric of the city, recalling earlier – and desired – social hierarchies. Yet there is also a more suggestive politics of place in evidence within post-war fiction that engages with these issues. Frederick Jameson observes that the condition of the post-war era is distinguishable from the earlier twentieth century by the logic of spatial organization rather than time: 'I think that it is at least empirically arguable that our daily life, our psychic experience, our cultural languages, are today dominated by categories of space rather than categories of time, as in the preceding period of high modernism' (Jameson 16). The post-war conservationist movement and inner-city gentrification are early indications of this cultural and experiential shift.

The reassertion of middle-class influence on the cultural and physical capital of the nation – London – appears simultaneously with the loss of ground in traditional expressions of servility and the exclusivity of university education. This reappropriation is quite literal as formerly evacuated districts are 'reclaimed' by class migration, but also discursive in that the impetus for the phenomenon is expressed in aesthetic terms. In this respect, Rodney Garland's *The Heart in Exile* (1953) provides an image of Islington as historically middle class, currently working class, but also on the cusp of reclamation for the middle-class imagination that had never deserted it. The late Regency architecture was 'first rate' but it was now (early 1950s) 'entirely proletarian and neglected' (*Heart* 229). Even though the streets are occupied by examples of assertive, well-dressed, relatively well-paid, young working-class men, Garland's protagonist Anthony Page unconsciously assesses the street as a potential reclamation project, noting the physical neglect of the fine architecture. This ability to interpret, assess and read/decode the environment distinguishes his outlook from the working-class inhabitants of this faded architectural glory which recalls, and of course anticipates, a gentrified Islington that was never really absent. The spatialization of discursive codes based on wealth, education and tradition still hold sway over the practical occupation of place. The implication is that the working-class inhabitants of Islington are the equivalent of the Vandals living among the ruins of Rome – they did not conceive nor realize this space, and thence will remain disempowered and excluded from the powerful social codes that it elaborates.

Unusually, it is the reactivated middle-class reading of the architecture of London that represents a 'radical' political position. When bell hooks argues that:

> Our living depends upon our ability to conceptualize alternatives, often impoverished. Theorising about this experience aesthetically and critically is an agenda for radical cultural practice. For me this space of radical openness is a margin – a profound edge. Locating oneself there is difficult yet necessary. It is not a 'safe' place. One is always at risk. One needs a community of resistance. (hooks 149)

It also evokes the radicalization of a beleaguered middle-class identity regrouping and, in an urban context, reoccupying both the physical sites and the discursive codes of an earlier form of its hegemony, even where such sites will only be marginal among the great sea of inner-city life around them. In effect, it is taking two steps backward to take another branch of the road to wealth and influence. This ability to persevere, at risk, is to form a powerfully symbolic 'community of resistance' in post-war middle-class society still 'traumatized' by the ascendancy of a Labour government. Such pressures would be felt throughout the second half of the twentieth century, and as Philip Tew observes, it represents no less than a 'crisis of identity [for the middle classes], its enculturation and the species of peculiarly liminal urban ontological existence that they at least imagine that they particularly have to endure' (Tew 2004 86). Yet the material success of this migration is at odds with the internalization of a sense of cultural marginalization, since those areas that were seen as up-and-coming in the immediate post-war years – parts of Westminster (including Pimlico), Marylebone, Hampstead, Chelsea and later Islington and the Docklands (J. White 63) – are now synonymous with wealth and exclusivity.

The literary representation of this new 'old' London suggests three forms of middle-class re-engagement with the city that can equally be read as post-war realignment of social and political conservatism in line with the political and cultural dimensions of space and place noted by Jameson and hooks. The first, as already discussed, is gentrification. It is not insignificant that both major phases of the return of the middle classes to inner London are distinguished by the reassertion of conservative politics – in 1951 with the return of Churchill and in 1979 with the election of Margaret Thatcher. In both instances, the elections were won on the basis of holding back the tide of Labour mismanagement and a radical socialist agenda. The social and cultural implications of the residence of the middle classes in central London are explored with considerable subtlety in Stella Gibbons's *A Pink Front Door* (1959). Indeed, the very title evokes 1951, the moment of Labour triumph in the Festival of Britain but also political defeat: 'the first improved houses were marked out in the public consciousness by brightly painted front doors in Festival of Britain colours' (J. White 63). Secondly, gentrification also offers a model that is aspirational in both cultural and social terms. The protagonist of B. S. Johnson's *Albert Angelo* (1964) is a supply teacher of working-class origins who desires to enter the quintessential middle-class profession, architecture. His fixation on largely Georgian architecture is an attempt at alignment with the middle-class imaginary that Garland explored in *The Heart in Exile*. It is clear from Johnson's novel that architecture is a thin disguise for writing, which demonstrates the slippage between the aspirational nature of cultural capital vested in the bricks and mortar of a revalued Georgian London and the equally exclusive middle-class realm of letters. Yet the novel studiously works to ensure that the experiential and material fabric of 'real' London exposes the risks of such a cultural alignment in the contemporary city. Finally, Doris Lessing's *The Four-Gated City* (1969) offers a speculation on the fate of an upper-middle-class family who hold on to their fine Georgian terrace through the post-war period and into the latter decades of the century. As a caricature of English values, they are seen as variously respectable, then communist and then reactionary, leading to travails that take a terrible toll on the female members of the family. The implication is that it is the world and London that changes around them while the house provides a bastion of values, of order and proportion. The novel takes its most radical fictional turn just as the family is about to be evicted so that the building can be expropriated as government offices, presumably

so it too can lay a claim to the order and stability the Palladian design
of the house expresses. These three novels collectively represent a
complex negotiation between the fictional representations of London
grounded in the physical elaboration of earlier discourses embedded
in the city's fabric.

The opening description of Bottle Court in *A Pink Front Door*, the
fictional home of James and Daisy Muir in Old Hampstead, north
London, emphasizes the sacrifice of modern convenience, but also
middle-class realignment:

> In those days, the Muir's cottage had been the only one so transformed
> and painted; now, the tenants who had lived there for many years were
> gradually dying off or being tempted by speculators to sell their
> charming inconvenient houses for large sums, and tenants of another
> type were eagerly buying and moving in; young prosperous artists, dress
> designers, advertising executives, rising Television personalities and a
> few bright young business men and their families...
>
> Space was not one of the amenities offered to prospective tenants in
> Bottle Court. Big cars belonging to its residents had to be garaged in
> wider streets lying immediately below it or wherever they could find
> room nearby to park, for there was no way of approaching it directly
> save by thirty or so shallow eighteenth-century stone steps leading up
> from the High Street, or by a kind of lane between the houses too
> narrow for any but the smallest vehicles to pass. Oh, a madly incon-
> venient, unbelievably picturesque, passionately sought-after residential
> quarter was Bottle Court, N.W.3. (*Pink* 21)

The social change being wrought here is not only the gradual elision
of the former tenants who clearly do not fit in with the new wave of
occupants. There is a change in the composition of the traditionally
prosperous middle-class occupations which are being renewed by the
professionalization of the new media industries – advertising, television, art (presumably 'modern') – and a few 'bright young business
men'. Indeed, 'bright' and 'young' seems to span the general tenor of
these new tenants, as well as the inconvenience that such people will
'endure' for the right address with the right architectural style. This is
the staged city manufactured through the new vision of newly
respectable advertising and the popular media that finds its official
counterpart in the Festival of Britain. Perhaps surprisingly, given the
span of almost twenty years between the two texts, this particular
mixture of occupations is similar to those we find in the exclusive
tower block of Ballard's *High-Rise*. Laing in Ballard's text moves from
a gentrification hot-spot in Chelsea 'forward fifty years in time' (*High-
Rise* 9), whereas Bottle Court is a journey back in time with access
symbolically restricted by 'eighteenth-century stone steps'. The professional composition of this new London middle class remains
consistent between these two novels, but their aspirations shift from a
recherché return to London's past to an aspirational ultra-modernity.

Bottle Court, like Ballard's tower block, is the expression of a desire for exclusivity and detachment from London as a whole. Cut off from the usual traffic of the city in both instances, height is a factor contributing to the self-consciousness of occupation. Bottle Court is significantly 'up' from the High Street, and later it is clear that it offers a dominating view of the city since it is possible for James Muir to walk 'to the window and [look] down at London lying spread out under the sunset' (*Pink* 24), and later, 'London displayed itself as a pattern of light, glittering away behind the dark crooked chimneys of the houses lower down the hill' (*Pink* 27). Equally, Ballard's tower block provides a panoramic view of the city that occludes direct contact with life within it. Yet herein lies the very real difference between Ballard's and Gibbons's protagonists: Laing revels in his detachment from the city and the inward-looking, incestuous and ultimately destructive 'community' of the tower block, whereas Bottle Court through Daisy Muir is still very much engaged with the life of the city. There is also some similarity to Mark Underwood's overview of night-time London in Lodge's *The Picturegoers*, but there is little of his overtly melodramatic identity confusion in Gibbons's novel although the formation of identity within the city is certainly significant. It is consistently suggested that such detachment *is* desired by her husband James, but it is a more traditional class exclusivity than that suggested by the new post-war middle-class professions: 'The roots, the framework, of that life he so much liked – and rather envied – went back further still; deep into the Oxford of the sixties' (*Pink* 25). This directs the reader to associate the reassuring age of Bottle Court with James and not Daisy. The issue is reinforced towards the conclusion of the novel. Before Daisy is reclaimed by James from her preoccupation with London's lower-middle-class waifs and strays to the traditional duties of marriage and motherhood, one of her 'hopeless cases', Molly, compares Bottle Court to a new town house she is viewing with several of Daisy's other 'projects'. Since Molly has conceived a passion for James, the articulation of her desires are rather pointed: 'Yes, *very* bleak, Molly was thinking ... and no *atmosphere*. Give her Hampstead every time, and for preference Bottle Court, so quaint and historical' (*Pink* 226).

While James is one of the new professionals drawn to places like Bottle Court – he works in advertising – his tastes are strictly traditional, pointing towards a more suburban identity. Indeed, while their house reflects James's preferences, Daisy's constant engagement with London leads to an estrangement from the home he has chosen when James attempts to exclude those she tries to help. His attitude strikes a cord with Daisy's own very upper-middle-class family, the two old cousins Ella and Marcia and her father, Colonel Furnivall. James goes so far as to attempt to shield the Colonel from the lower-middle-class acquaintances she tries to help:

The ones whom he had actually met at the house with the pink front door had all been carefully screened by the prosaic James, and such rumours of Delia Huxtable, Tibbs and the rest of the Soft-Core that had reached him were, so to speak, muffled – both by distance, and by his lack of personal experience of the post-war London jungle. (*Pink* 55)

Note how these people are 'Soft-Core' implicitly to be contrasted to the 'hardness' of the pre-war middle classes. The phrase recalls Jonathan Raban's observation: 'For at moments like this, the city goes soft; it awaits the imprint of an identity. For better or worse, it invites you to remake it, to consolidate it into a shape you can live in' (Raban 9). The traditional middle classes represented by James and Daisy's family are engaged in such a process; to imprint an identity on the city and remake it on terms they can live with. By contrast, Daisy's waifs – the central-European refugee Tibbs, Molly, and Don and Katy – are unable to impose their identity on the metropolitan landscape. Indeed, one of Daisy's chief tasks for her 'projects' is to find them somewhere to live. Here identities can also be 'soft', suggesting that Raban's observation has unacknowledged limitations based on social class.

Yet the struggle between James's backward-looking and socially conservative instincts and Daisy's outward-looking, liberal feelings is the leitmotif of the novel. The narrative is closely attuned to the changing social relations in London. For James, this means an increasing sense of alienation from the very 'traditional' home he has tried to create in Bottle Court. This is evident whenever the narrative point of view shifts to him. Evidence of his gradual alienation from the house and its urban location as increasingly 'unhomely' serves to reinforce the desire for a traditional family home and social relations that no longer seem possible in London. As Anthony Vidler suggests: 'Tinged with late nineteenth-century nostalgia … the uncanny became an equally powerful trope for imagining the "lost" birth-place, against the deracinated home of post-industrial society' (Vidler xi). The house in Bottle Court, despite its Georgian origins, pink front door and traditional family organization, is ultimately unable to accommodate the desires of someone like James who betrays the 'late nineteenth-century nostalgia' identified by Vidler. Indeed, the entire notion of gentrification is arguably tinged with this sense of nostalgia which inserts uncanniness at the heart of middle-class urban life – the family home.

This is explored in the novel by engineering several points of comparison between Colonel Furnivall's, Marcia's and Ella's homes and lives in London, but most strikingly in the conflict between the aristocratic Mrs Cavendish and Daisy's university friends, Don and Katy. Mrs Cavendish is the owner of a particularly grand London town house with rather too much silver to clean, who faces, as a consequence, severe difficulties finding and keeping a servant. This reference to social changes that had been in process since the end of the First World War points to 'Old Cavendish' as something of an anachronism in the 1950s. The disjunction from contemporary social conditions after another world war is acutely apparent when Daisy visits the house after many years' absence:

> It did seem low, when you faced it squarely, to practically drop some-one because they were a snob and a bore and then pick them up again because they might have a couple of rooms to let ... but then Daisy remembered the Hultons. Heavens, Old Cavendish had had her life, hadn't she, and not too bad a life either, with a house and a prosperous husband and a pretty daughter ...? 'The older generation may take such blessings for granted, but *our* generation,' thought Daisy, 'the generation that has grown up alongside refugee camps and the bomb and overcrowding – we know just how lucky Old Cavendish's genera-tion was. Why *shouldn't* they "do their bit", as they would say, towards helping ours?' (*Pink* 102–3)

The 'they' of that final sentence is revealing. Daisy enunciates a popularist post-war socialist position that reveals a great deal about her political outlook that is caught between the conservatism of her husband's desire for a traditional family environment and Daisy's sense of social justice. Mrs Cavendish herself is a Miss Havisham figure with a pretty daughter whose sole 'career' aspiration is to marry into the financial security of the aristocracy. Yet the outmoded way of life that they represent is signalled by their house. Not only through their inability to retain a charwoman under a pre-First World War social contract, but also its physical dilapidation and the increasingly empty void within as her possessions are gradually sold off, to meet living expenses and to maintain the status of her daughter in the marriage market. This way of life is being literally and socially dismantled piecemeal in the face of a refusal to adjust and adapt. There are echoes here of Edgar Allan Poe's *House of Usher* as well as Dickens's Satis House in the uncanny atmosphere created by Mrs Cavendish's socially disjunct class obsessions: 'The ceiling was frankly black. And there was something desperate, secret, starving, in the cold air. Daisy suddenly longed for the house with the pink front door' (*Pink* 106). Yet Daisy also feels that she 'had known them, it seemed to her, ever since she could remember, and, suddenly and quite unexpectedly she felt fond of Old Cavendish just for having remained the same' (*Pink* 105). These contrary emotions, nostalgia for what Mrs Cavendish represents socially in a rapidly changing society, and her aversion to the oppressiveness of the house, again recalls Vidler's association of nostalgia with the uncanny: 'For Freud, "unhomeliness" was more than a simple sense of not belonging; it was the fundamental pro-pensity of the familiar to turn on its owners, suddenly to become defamiliarized, derealized, as if in dream', or perhaps a nightmare (Vidler 7).

Daisy's confused nostalgia and alienation is partially resolved within the narrative via a proleptic anticipation of the future, as her mind turns back to Bottle Court and thence the security and conformity of the life offered by James: 'Daisy did not know, yet, how strongly and deeply she cared for old friends, familiar places, family traditions. In twenty years' time, a group of young relatives was to say of her: Daisy's a great *family* girl' (*Pink* 105). The brief visitation of Daisy's university friends Don and Katy and their young family on Old Cavendish as tenants engineers a clash between a socially mobile family of working-class origins and a downwardly mobile family with aristocratic pretensions. Gibbons resolutely refuses to allow the resolution of this conflict within London by enabling both families to succeed on their own terms. Don and Katy eventually move out of London to a new town in Essex to be near the industrial complex where Don has found employment, and Mrs Cavendish retreats to the country estate of her new son-in-law who has improbably become the Earl of Devonhurst. This brief coming-together of radically different social classes, if not the old and the new, is possible in London but does not lead to permanent settlement in the city.

This is the final failure of the social reconciliation that Daisy strives for throughout the novel. Taking the socially mobile but tenuously middle class and financially disadvantaged and bringing them together with her upper-middle-class and aristocratic family and its wider connections, is a symbolic attempt to merge the old middle-class order with the new that is staged in London, but is ultimately shown to be impossible. In response, Daisy finally accedes to the 'traditional' family life for which James has pressed. His ultimatum is founded on the insistence that they leave London and Britain altogether by taking up a new job in Canada. His declaration is a very deliberate rejection of the reconciliation that Daisy has attempted to establish in the city:

> 'I said, "I want you, not bloody telephoning and meals",' said James, and he raised his voice more than a little. 'I happen to love you, and I'm damned sick of sharing you with half the hard-luck cases and neurotics in London. I married *you* – not old Miss Parsons and Susan and all the – the – the – and don't *come* at me' – twisting away from her outstretched arms – 'I've had enough of it. That's why I'm accepting. I shall enjoy it – I've always felt half-stifled in London anyway – and if you – you can come too, if you want to. But we're – we're going to have a very different way of living, if you do ... no, I don't want to kiss you.'
> (*Pink* 243; ellipsis original)

James's wish is to take Daisy away from London to prevent her interaction with 'half the hard-luck cases and neurotics in London' by whom he feels threatened. In a very real sense this is a fear of the new, of social change. And while the sentiment of the novel is largely on his side – those hard-luck cases and neurotics are all mildly repellent characters – it does point to a profound retraction from the process of social cohesion promised by the war years. James's tactics here are a rejection of such egalitarian values, as Alan Sinfield observes: 'Since the late eighteenth century, when enclosures, the factory system and urbanisation helped to provoke the Romantic movement, the middle class has thrown up a dissident faction partly hostile to the hegemony of that class' (Sinfield 41). That hostility is at work in James as much as it is in Mrs Cavendish. In many senses, the novel is a rejection of the sentiment expressed by the Labour politician Herbert Read in his 1941 pamphlet entitled *To Hell with Culture*: 'The whole of our capitalist culture is one immense veneer. ... When Hitler has finished bombing our cities', let's build good new ones (Read 49). However, the novel does not end with James and Daisy.

Ella Furnivall and her cousin Marcia are two elderly spinsters who belong to the same generation as Daisy's father and Mrs Cavendish, and share many of the same class-based presumptions. They keep a servant, Annie, who has been in the family since the late 1890s when she was 14. The family has prevented her from having a life of her own by discouraging at least one serious suitor. Yet Marcia seems largely unconscious of the oppressiveness of this action when she comes to reflect upon it, even though she has in her own day been a pioneer for women's rights, exemplified by her university education in chemistry, distinguished overseas duty during the First World War, and G.B.E. (Order of the British Empire). Marcia is in every way the image of upper-middle-class liberation represented by and envisioned by the suffragettes. She even prefers to ride atop double-decker London buses in an echo of Mrs Dalloway's daughter Elizabeth, who anticipated the sort of freedoms that Marcia has enjoyed. Her companion, Ella, is shy, delicate, artistic, and by contrast to Marcia, intimidated by servants like Annie whom Marcia found tyrannizing her when she returned to London in the 1920s. The two women harbour an unspoken passion for each other, but it is their close tie to London that distinguishes them in the text, especially Ella, whose hobby is painting the city's streets to which her response is notably elegiac:

> The little pictures were nearly all landscapes – streetscapes, rather: rows of the crumbling brown or white houses which, with their curtained secretive windows and their flight of grey stone steps leading up to a dark and heavy door, belong typically and unmistakably to an older London. But there were other subjects too: lengths of ancient wall, expanses of grey paving stones wet with rain whose every crack was depicted, great aspen trees whose myriad silver leaves almost covered the paper from edge to edge, gutters where orange peel glowed, roads paved with damp cobbles. Sometimes Ella painted sparrows or a stray cat; sometimes a dog; very rarely people. Her tiny landscapes were

usually as bare of human life as if everybody were indoors and fast asleep. (*Pink* 67–8)

While this passage denotes a deeply felt affiliation to London, it has an affinity to James's enjoyment of the view over the city from Bottle Court. Devoid of inhabitants, Ella's city is another valorization and aestheticization that privileges a middle-class gaze recalling de Certeau's contrast between the sterile, imposing grid of the mapped city – an uninhabited abstraction – and the 'spatial stories' of the city as lived place (de Certeau 115–30). Ella's painting is another form of mapping that elides the life of the city streets and resembles in a different form Marcia's failure to think of her servant Annie in human terms. Even after 50 years of service and a radically changed social landscape, social progression is only available to women of the correct class. Ironically, it is a final encounter between Ella and Annie that precipitates the release of the antagonism seen in other relationships throughout the novel. Abroad in the city on another painting trip, Ella alights on Campion Street as her subject:

> The railings above the basements were a pale and ghostly red. Not a soul was in sight. It was late afternoon; the light blue and silver spring sky dreamed and floated overhead, sometimes a woman's drawn face looked up from a basement or out of an upper window. 'The children are having their tea,' Ella thought. 'That's a good thing, they won't bother me.' The air smelt of soot, and spring. (*Pink* 250)

The 'woman's drawn face' reminds the reader that this must be a poorer area than Ella is used to, but it elicits no recognition; it is just another street and subject. This is rudely interrupted by her servant Annie, who has friends living in one of the basement flats. She bullies Ella to accede to a moment of social equality by inviting her to tea with her friend, to which Ella is drawn by a sudden sense of Annie's attractiveness. Annie in turn gives in to a moment of irresistible spite born of years of social repression and pulls Ella down the basement steps. Recalling Vidler's observation, the familiar certainly does turn on Ella. The city that is emptied of life in her paintings becomes 'defamiliarized, derealized, as if in a dream'. The failure to achieve social interaction recalls Forster's 'only connect' and parallels the withdrawal from London of Mrs Cavendish and her daughter, Daisy and James, as well as Katy and Don. London promises to become a social catalyst, but social interaction fails to be established across class divides. The politics of 'place' in Merleau-Ponty's sense of a closed, homogenous spatiality is triumphing here, and the promise of his 'anthropological space', of social interaction and interchange, is present but not ideologically an option (de Certeau 117). The novel suitably ends in an amorphous mist. The city, the lived streets increasingly indistinct to the narrative gaze, derealized, defamiliarized, uncanny: 'It was all just the same; the shadows already gathered into the railway cutting before they had completely invaded the trees on the other side of the bank, the terrace floating in the pale orange afterglow, the hint of London smoke veiling the white towers and blocks of new flats still just visible beyond the houses to the south' (*Pink* 254).

B. S. Johnson's *Albert Angelo* (1964) continues many of the same themes identified in Gibbons's novel but in a far more radical fashion. Barely five years separate the publication of these two texts, and yet stylistically you would be hard pressed to find two more superficially dissimilar novels. Gibbons's realism belongs to a fictional lineage that stretches back through Arnold Bennett, while Johnson's writing owes more to the experiments in consciousness familiar to readers of Virginia Woolf and other modernists. Yet both texts share common preoccupations, not least the material, figurative and psychological centrality of London to both texts. In each, estrangement from the city based on class is a significant theme. Albert is of working-class origins, working as a supply teacher in London while harbouring aspirations to become an architect. This class mobility, even if largely aspirational rather than realized, is enough to estrange him from the working-class children he attempts to teach. Moreover, the novel is increasingly a meditation on place and identity, and latterly on writing, narrative structure and art in which London as a social matrix, cultural nexus and physical presence becomes increasingly uncanny. As Tew observes: 'The sense of geographic reality he draws highlights at certain points its contrast to the distortions of perception, and by this kind of literal exactitude concerning building and elevation above sea level elicits a series of contradictions with the personal domain of socialized and inner spaces' (Tew 2001184). Indeed, such 'distortions of perception' form the middle-class accommodation with modern London in Gibbons's narrative, and in much the same way a denial of the experiential city is present in *Albert Angelo*. Albert represents a desire for social and cultural conformity in his preference for Georgian architecture that resembles the physical and ideological manifestation of middle-class consciousness in *A Pink Front Door*. When the novel becomes a reflection upon literary creation, the choice of the architectural metaphor represents a stifling of both positive engagement with the flux and flow of the city and creativity.

The experiential certainty suggested by the concrete London Albert attempts to evoke momentarily disguises the subjective London produced by his responses to, and interaction with, the city. This is strengthened by the material-focused discourse of architectural analysis that emerges in the early stages of the novel. On one level, the use of this discourse would seem to respond to the artist's desire for 'truth', and yet the London 'constructed' in this way does not suggest an artistic truth with any more success than Ella's painting of artificially empty London streets and houses. In both instances an attempt to evoke a material London in words or paint can only be an illusive project and produce the 'distortions of perception' suggested by Tew. This is, perhaps, the source of Johnson's dissatisfaction with the correlation between architecture and poetry as a narrative gambit:

> – look, I'm trying to tell you something of what I feel about being a poet in a world where only poets care anything real about poetry, through the objective correlative of an architect who has to earn his living as a teacher. this device you cannot have failed to see creaking, ill-fitting at many places, many places, for architects *manqués* can earn livings very nearly connected with their art, and no poet has ever lived by his poetry, and architecture has a functional aspect quite lacking in poetry, and, simply, architecture is just not poetry. (*Angelo* 168)

The 'objective correlative' here is not really the equation between architect and poet (although this does have a certain resonance), but between the practical activity and discourse of the architect countered by the subjectivity and impressionism of the poet. It is ill-fitting for the practical reasons Johnson's textual persona identifies, but this does lead to the question, why should an architect substitute for a poet? The anxiety here is disingenuous, for both discursively and figuratively the comparison/substitution this intervention forces the reader to consider is a resonant issue, particularly in relation to the means by which the fictional text evokes the 'material' spaces and places of London. When Henri Lefebvre considers the literary contribution to the construction of social space, he too points to the 'creaking, ill-fitting' continuum between literature and architecture:

> Clearly literary authors have written much of relevance, especially descriptions of places and sites. But what criteria would make certain texts more relevant than others? ... The problem is that any search for space in literary texts will find it everywhere and in every guise: enclosed, described, projected, dreamt of, speculated about. What texts can be considered special enough to provide the basis for a 'textual' analysis? Inasmuch as they deal with socially 'real' space, one might suppose on first consideration that architecture and texts relating to architecture would be a better choice than literary texts proper. (Lefebvre 14–15)

Both Johnson and Lefebvre share a common concern that textual space is an unreliable model for analysing material space. For Lefebvre this is merely a step along the way to offering his preferred solution to a methodological dilemma which largely ignores literature, but for Albert (and later Johnson's textual persona) it represents both an existential and latterly a representational crisis.

His architectural flights are attempts to assert meaning and order on a world, or more specifically a city, that has become threateningly mutable. This befits his chosen middle-class self-identification as an architect, artist and intellectual which replicates much the same representational crisis that was irreconcilable in *A Pink Front Door.* What is presented in the novel as an artistic dilemma is a displacement of more class-based anxieties. Rather than the attractions of traditional structured middle-class certainties of Gibbons's novel most easily seen in James, the desire for structure is manifest in the comparison between Albert's architectural narrative of London related as he traverses the city between jobs as a supply teacher, and attempts to assert discursive structure through lessons given to largely indifferent London schoolchildren. It is suggestive that he has a marked preference for the Georgian architecture that dominates the homes of the established middle classes in *A Pink Front Door.* As Jerry White notes: 'it is notable that Georgian property, rather than anything more recent, was the special object of the [gentrifying] pioneers' (J. White 63–4). Albert may not be in the same income bracket as the Muirs, but he shares the same awareness of what was catching a revitalized middle-class eye in the 1950s and 1960s. For example: 'Georgian second ratings with mansard roofs; the pitch of the mansards is particularly well chosen, subtle. It pleases you' (*Angelo* 28); or later, during a night out in Stepney: 'Visually, architecturally, Cable Street, Cablestrasse, The Strasse, at night excites us: everywhere we go in this part of Stepney there are Georgian façades in all stages of repair' (*Angelo* 51). This preference is most clearly seen early in the novel when Albert compares King's Cross and St Pancras railway stations. While both Victorian in date, the exterior of the former has a Palladian austerity that contrasts dramatically with the Gothic revivalist excesses of the latter:

> I walk down the hill from Percy Circus, along Kings Cross Road, into Pentonville Road, towards Kings Cross. The station has two great squat stock-brick arches, their yellow uncommonly unblackened; Cubitt, the youngest, Lewis. Then there are the pseudo-Gothic excrescences of Scott's St Pancras. I wonder shall I ever come to accept St Pancras station, living so near? Or even like it? Perhaps it is fatal to live so near to St Pancras for an architect? Certainly it would be to bring up children here: their aesthetic would be blighted. (*Angelo* 20)

Through this ostensibly simple expression of aesthetic discrimination, the reader learns a great deal about Albert's character and the thematic preoccupations of the novel. Perhaps the most obvious point to make about Georgian or, more broadly, Palladian architecture is its decorative understatement and the use of classical orders, which is evident in King's Cross Station despite its Victorian date. It has traditionally indicated educated taste and discrimination. More significantly still, such architecture follows rigid design rules that allow little outward variation achieving a high degree of visual conformity. If we accept at face value the assertion of Johnson's textual persona at the end of the novel that Albert, as aspirant architect, stands in for Johnson as aspirant poet, then the architect poet is actively seeking order, form, understatement and, perhaps, conformity. If this analogy is allowed for the moment, it suggests a preference for the way Georgian poets married a close attention to classical form with biting satire, contrasted with the baggy digressive form of Victorian realism that is both present and challenged by the experimental form of this novel.

This figurative preoccupation with architecture is also revealing in another way. The Germanization of Cable Street as 'Cablestrasse' hints at stereotypical constructions of Germans as methodical and ordered, as well as the possibility for such a value system to mutate into political fascism – a resonant connection to a 1960s London still pock-marked by bomb-sites – and perhaps anticipating Albert's own predilection for beating more troublesome students into submission. Further, given the association the novel maps between architectural structure and literary narrative, the transmutation into 'Cablestrasse' also associates his aesthetic predilections with the structural, political and social concerns of modernist poets like T. S. Eliot and Ezra Pound. Indeed, Cable Street is also no neutral location to link with fascism since it was the principal locale for the notorious Cable Street riots of 1936, when a coalition of numerous anti-fascist groups prevented a march by Sir Oswald Mosley's British Union of Fascists. The battle was, however, largely fought between the anti-fascist groups and the police who strove to clear a path for the blackshirts whom they saw as a 'legitimate' political march: 'The police, treating the crowds as ruffians, were intent on dispersing what they saw as a mere mob ... police horses charged along Cable Street and elsewhere the crowd surged and swayed and lapped around them' (C. Bloom 332). These associations reveal in Albert's character a certain predilection for authoritarianism in both his character and his work, thence increasing the tension within the novel between the extreme experimentation of traditional (realist) narrative order contrasted with a central protagonist who leans towards formal architectural styles and repressive classroom tactics. The London of the novel is equally conflicted as Albert strives to impose order through a fascination with buildings and space while completely misunderstanding the city as lived place.

However, it must be remembered that Albert's designs never make it off the drawing board, and the latter sections of the novel point towards an inability to express himself through the formal and structural constraints that the design demands. He reveals both a paradoxical lack of interest in having his designs realized – 'Ought really to go in for more competitions. It's the only way to become known, to break out of this destructive teaching' (*Angelo* 103) – and latterly a complete block:

Hell! What time is it? Seven! You bloody fool! Guilt.
  Guilt.
  Close the window. Specks of smut on my drawing, hell, London smut. Smuts. Still.
  Another day just frittered, as far as ever, farther because nearer death, from success, whatever that is, whatever that may mean, frittered, the worst crime, against myself, guilt.
  Smuts, flecks of soot, coal. Damn. Won't clean off, ruined drawing, not that there was much to ruin, three lines of a...
  Three lines. It's not nothing, exactly. Not exactly nothing.
  (*Angelo* 119; ellipsis original)

Note how it is London – 'London smut' – that breaks Albert's attempt to inscribe order and form on the page. Yet three lines don't make a building, so the disruption, the block, was in Albert's mind before material London intruded in the form of a smut. Indeed, the day starts for Albert full of enthusiasm for work at the drawing board, but he finds the draw of London and its pubs irresistible, leading to the reverie which brings him to seven in the evening with no work done beyond three lines. Despite Albert's architectural interest in London, it is clearly the plurality of the city itself that is a major distraction and disruption, if not anxiety. That plurality is best symbolized in the excesses of the Victorian Gothic rather than the classical order of Palladian architecture, and it is significant in contrast to his professed aversion towards St Pancras that he develops a strong desire to work in that style himself: 'Of course, I would really like to be designing a Gothic cathedral, all crockets and finials and flying buttresses, but I must be of my time, ahead of my time, rather, using the materials of my time, the unacknowledged legislators, and so on, in accord with, of, my age, my time, my generation, my life' (*Angelo* 107). At this moment Albert is working on the design for a modern theatre and it is the three lines of this design that will a little later become obscured by the London smut. The project recalls Lewis Mumford's observation: 'The city fosters art and is art; the city creates the theatre and is the theatre. It is in the city, the city as theatre, that man's more purposive activities are focused' (Mumford 94). Albert's desire for the order of Palladian architecture or the austerity of post-war modernist architecture is actually his stage, but it is false and contrary to his experience of the city. Both forms represent an idealization, an ideology, a theatrical staging of control and order with which he attempts to displace the chaos of his personal life – the loss of his lover Jenny.

This return of the repressed is increasingly apparent in the narrative through Albert's ever more frequent turn towards the city's past, even though modernization was very much on the agenda in the 1960s with many a new-hatched carbuncle looming over the metropolitan skyline. Indeed, the use of London's past as a trope for the repressed underbelly of modern life and identity looks forward to the work of Peter Ackroyd and Iain Sinclair from the 1980s, where it returns in a markedly uncanny register (see Chapter 6). Here it can be most obviously seen through the mutations of Albert's architectural stream of consciousness, but also emerges in his classroom teaching where lessons become disquisitions on London as an elaboration of his psychological struggle: 'You begin a geography lesson which turns into a lesson on London then into a lesson on architecture' (*Angelo* 43). The slippage between the geographical determinants of the city and its physical appearance externalizes the struggle in Albert's own mind between the deep and surface structures of his own dilemma. Unable to physically remake the landscape, the city becomes an ideological concept as Albert focuses on the expression of its social order in its architectural features. The geological foundations of the city are less susceptible to human order unlike the artificial, manufactured social space formed by London's buildings.

Later at the Wormwood Street School, where the rest of Albert's teaching experiences in the novel are located, he is interrupted reading a standard text on Gothic architecture (Paul Frankl's *Gothic Architecture* of 1962), which then seamlessly mutates into another lesson on London geology (*Angelo* 62). All this is very far from the grace, simplicity and repetitive order of Palladian stock architecture which was, by the 1960s, far from the dominant architectural style of London. What the quotation from Frankl's text brings to the novel is the very absence of a guiding philosophy. Instead the passage identifies a disjunction between the necessities of erecting a secure structure and the aesthetics of the building; between the pragmatic, the material and the symbolic: 'The changes had nothing to do with the Crusades, which began only later, or with the liturgy, or with philosophy. The architects were intent simply on making necessary improvements. As far as can be reconstructed, this was a process of trial and error ...' (*Angelo* 66–7). The city embodies this ethic of trial and error over a guiding philosophy, the Gothic over the Palladian. London is an unlovely city that has always favoured the pragmatic – and the profitable – in pursuit of a solution rather than the grand symbolic gesture. Yet it is also a space that challenges any uncomplicated desire for order. Indeed, it is significant that for all the mediation of class present in *A Pink Front Door* resolution, or rather the deferment of resolution has to be sought beyond the city itself. As Jonathan Raban argues: 'the city as we imagine it, the soft city of illusion, myth, aspiration, nightmare, is as real, maybe more real, than the hard city one can locate on maps, in statistics, in monographs on urban sociology and demography and architecture' (Raban 10). The apparent solidity and materiality of the city ebbs away by travelling through it, both physically and psychologically. Albert's attempt to give his existence in the city the material foundation of architectural order is doomed to fail. This is exemplified by his need to dig further into the literal foundations of the city – its geography and geology – in search of solid ground. It is highly significant that such attempts are disrupted by his pupils, the inhabitants of that very same city who are absent from maps, architectural drawings, or geological surveys, just as they are absent from Ella's paintings. The symbolism of Ella's death at the hands of her servant is repeated in *Albert Angelo* since it is the city that turns on Albert when those elided Londoners drown him at the conclusion of the novel.

The novel, the individual and the city are, as the penultimate self-referential sections remind us, in a process of perpetual dis/integration. Moving from a more or less realistic mode structured by Albert's architectural discourse, and a more or less integrated protagonist, the narrative gives way to textual disintegration as his past and present increasingly come to represent disorder, confusion and frustration, if not despair. The interjections of historical London move along a continuum that underpins this progression. Initially they are comprehensible either as part of Albert's architectural discourse, like the mention of Scott and Cubitt, architects of St Pancras and King's Cross respectively, or the search for existential bedrock through geology. Later, they appear random and more threatening, such as the interjection of Christopher Marlowe's death in Deptford. This peers through into earlier sections of the narrative via several windows cut into the preceding pages, anticipating Albert's own death. Indeed, the reader is unsure whether this is in fact Albert's death until the full page is reached. While evident by the conclusion of the novel, this physical fracturing of narrative continuity on textual and extra-textual levels was present figuratively from the very beginning. Percy Circus, Albert's fictional residence, combines all these elements:

> The first thing you see about Percy Circus is that it stands most of the way up a hill, sideways, leaning upright against the slope like a practiced seaman. And then the next thing is that half of it is not there. There are trees in the circular railinged area in the middle: planes mostly, but one or two oaks and a long hanging willow, oddly twisted like a one-legged circus tumbler. There is a little grass there, too, and rubbish of various kinds littered around – bicycle wheels, bottomless enamel buckets, tins, rotting cardboard. Some of the houses have patches where new London stocks show up yellow against the older blackened ones; then you know what happened to the rest of the circus. New flats at an angle, awkwardly. A blue plaque tells you that Lenin once lived at number sixteen. (*Angelo* 13–14)

The symbolism of Percy Circus is emphasized by Johnson's textual persona in the penultimate section of the novel, and connects London, England and Albert's psychological struggle: 'between built-on-the-skew, tatty, half-complete, comically called Percy Circus, and Albert, and London, and England' (*Angelo* 176). Yet a reading direction of this sort cannot be wholly prescriptive. Taken as a symbol of 'London, and England, and the human condition' it is hard to overlook the crookedness of the Circus's state of repair, the rubbish and of course the bomb damage that has been patched-up. The Circus is in this respect emblematic of post-war London and a declining Britain. Further, the Circus provides the counterpart to Albert's scruffiness, his barely begun architectural drawing and perhaps hints of impending middle age; his emotional distress and physical decline patched-up much like the buildings. The traditional architecture that Albert favours is contrasted with the awkward modern flats abutting the Circus, suggesting both the intrusion of the modern and a lack of accommodation with it. The motif echoes the final view of London in *A Pink Front Door*: 'the terrace floating in the pale orange afterglow, the hint of London smoke veiling the white towers and blocks of new flats still just visible beyond the houses to the south' (*Pink* 254). Here the modern flats loom, whereas in *Albert Angelo* they abut and intrude, confirming the asymmetry that the bomb damage has given to the square. Ella's fall is a consequence of her lack of sympathy for the lived city as a consequence of her class *immobility*; for Albert that estrangement is a consequence of his class *mobility*. Both characters seek refuge in a representation of the city that precludes the lived experience of its inhabitants. Both are killed by those very same inhabitants in a manner that is emblematic of the failure of the form by which they seek to contain the social space of the city. As Tew notes: 'Space inscribes social and historical forms, but these convey a sense of quite how and through what forms the world is constituted' (Tew 2001 171). In these instances, an immobile space is constructed – synchronous rather than chronological – which has been invested with the characters' inability to come to terms with aspects of their own identities, displaced into an artificially ordered, idealized, urban landscape. The historicization of the spaces created by both Ella and Albert precludes an accommodation with contemporary experience of space and place, and their experience and sense of self become dangerously disjunct from a comprehension of 'quite how and through what forms the world is constituted'.

Yet occluded by Johnson's autobiographical intervention is, paradoxically, what cannot be articulated even through this overt attempt to pre-empt the reader. The novel becomes a disquisition on form and order, which are taken to be essential in the construction of meaning, be it of the city, of the individual, or the literary text. Yet the more the text seeks to bring experience to the fore through formal innovation, the more the coherence of the text is challenged, leading finally to the reciprocal collapse of the protagonist. The intrusion of Johnson's textual persona in the 'Disintegration' section of the novel is a last attempt to shore up the narrative against the conclusion that there is, quite pointedly, no sense in the city, the individual, or the desired realist narrative. Percy Circus is emblematic of all three. The invitation to seek meaning in the symbolism of the Circus is a residual attempt to encourage the reader to impose an order that is not there. The reader is discursively drawn into the text, becoming a replacement for the protagonist, and is invited to attempt what Ella and Albert have failed to achieve within their narratives. The hodgepodge conglomeration of discontinuous architectural styles, decay and randomized bomb destruction has no real narrative other than the passage of time and the more or less random events that have made it what it is. The dilemma of the city as image in such narrative contexts is identified by Burton Pike:

> On the one hand there is the visible city of streets and buildings, frozen forms of energy fixed at different times in the past and around which busy kinetic energy of the present swirls. On the other hand there are the subconscious currents arising in the minds of the city's living inhabitants from this combination of past and present. (Pike 4)

By denying the latter, the text comes into conflict with the 'kinetic energy' of the present, of social change and reformulation which is ultimately destructive despite the elegiac tone ascribed to the false 'solidity' of the past. Indeed, both *Albert Angelo* and *A Pink Front Door* suggest that meaning in the city, as in the text, comes down to an act of individual will, in contradiction to Pike's 'subconscious currents'. In turn both texts point to the contingent nature of such 'mental mapping' (Werth 7) in its necessary and unavoidable abstraction from lived experience. The text/city/individual is caught in an oscillation between the desire to articulate the 'truth' and the foregone failure to do so.

The first sentence of the 'Disintegration' section is simultaneously amusing and painful: '– fuck all this lying look what im really trying to write about is writing not all this stuff about architecture trying to say something about my writing'; an 'almighty aposiopesis' (*Angelo* 167). Writing about writing is never going to deliver the existential 'truth' which literally cannot be uttered, only experienced. The attempt must inevitably be broken off, like this novel. Thence the 'space' of the city, of the text, or of the individual is reduced to the abstraction of writing in *Albert Angelo*, or of painting in *A Pink Front Door*. As Henri Lefebvre argues: 'The quasi-logical presupposition of an identity between mental space (the space of the philosophers and epistemologists) and real space creates an abyss between the mental sphere on the one side and the physical and social spheres on the other' (Lefebvre 6). Lefebvre's formulation of 'mental space' can usefully be extended to include ideologically constructed spaces and places. In *A Pink Front Door*, Daisy's attempt to engage with the lived city through her 'projects' comes into conflict with the ideology of the traditional middle-class family, and her role within that formulation as mother and wife. For Albert, however, and indeed Ella, the inability to acknowledge the denial of their own natures – for Ella it is her homosexuality, for Albert his failure as an architect, as a lover with Jenny and perhaps homosexuality in his borderline misogyny and friendship with Terry as surrogate partner – is expressed through a denial of lived experience in the city. Whereas James can retreat from London altogether and thence flee the contradiction between his ideological construction of the family home and the lived experience of the city, Ella and Albert are unable to reject the city, but are equally unable to achieve reconciliation between their commitment to place and the denial of their own natures. As Edward Soja observes: 'we must be insistently aware of how space can be made to hide consequences from us' (Soja 6), and for both Ella and Albert the attempt to hide behind a spatialized, dehumanized city leaves them dangerously exposed to the life within it, which takes the form of class conflict. To recall hooks, 'It is not a safe place. One is always at risk. One needs a community of resistance' (hooks 149).

Doris Lessing's *The Four-Gated City* (1969) explores both the need for community in the city as well as the attractions of anonymity, a rather different form of hiding 'consequences'. The culminating novel in a five-volume series, *Children of Violence*, the central character is Martha Hesse, a South African émigré who has fled the confining experience of racism, marriage and motherhood in her homeland. Her initial response to London is an intoxication of freedom:

> Coming to a big city for those who have never known one means first of all, before anything else, and the more surprising if one has not expected it, that freedom: all the pressures are off, no one cares, no need for the mask. For weeks then, without boundaries, without definition, like a balloon drifting and bobbing, nothing had been expected of her. (*City* 14)

Yet her experience reverses the conventional expectation of the city as 'a community of people who are strangers to each other' (Raban 15). Alienated from her previous existence in South Africa, the greater alienation of the city provides self-effacement and a desired loss of identity. In this there is a very different shift in emphasis from *A Pink Front Door* and *Albert Angelo*. The two earlier novels represent attempts to retain a specific self-conception, a particular form of life from which the individual cannot bear to part but the modern city can no longer accommodate. Yet there is a question over Martha's belief that she does not need a 'mask'. Raban argues that in the city 'you become a walking legible code, to be read, and as often misinterpreted, by strangers. You are frighteningly exposed' (Raban 50). Martha's response to the city is an act of wilful ignorance rather than social invisibility. She is constantly being evaluated and categorized by the people in the street, even more so as the young woman she is at the beginning of the novel. This act becomes comparable to both Ella's and Albert's elision of the people from their imagined city. Here Martha populates the city with teeming crowds, and chooses to believe in her own freedom from boundaries and definition as a form of armoured self.

This belief does not survive her experience of the city for very long. As de Certeau argues, even the restless movement of the mass contributes to the meaning of place: 'The swarming mass is an innumerable collection of singularities. Their intertwined paths give their shape to spaces' (de Certeau 97). Her own self-realization of this is the true beginning of the novel: 'Martha had never before seen soil that was dead, that had no roots. How long had this street been built? Iris thought about two hundred years, but she didn't know. For two hundred years this soil had held no life at all? How long did roots live under a crust of air-excluding tarmac?' (*City* 18). In contemplating this London street, Martha's desire for an absence of roots is self-evidently barren, 'no life at all'. Yet the imagery is disturbing. Two hundred years again takes us back to the Georgian period; a period that celebrated architectural order and uniformity, the very kind of definition Martha wishes to escape. Moreover, the airless seal of the tarmac also points to the stifling of growth and life.

The image is, however, contradictory. On the one hand Martha feels the lack of roots, a history, a definition in this place – but at the same time, that very insertion and participation in a personal history in the city is suffocation, restriction, death. Frederick R. Karl argues that *The Four-Gated City* is an example of a literature of enclosure akin to Kafka and Proust. The 'four gates' of the city 'all lead to houses of constriction, nightmare, impotence' (Karl 78):

> Space exists not as an extension but only as a volume to be enclosed in a room, or a house, or even a city. Joyce's Dublin had this quality – as though the city were not open to the sky but were a series of enclosures of houses and bars and meeting places. Such a city conveys not the sense of something unfolding, but of something accruing, like an internal growth which invisibly expands to tremendous size under cover of the flesh. (Karl 82)

Karl's argument is compelling. The remainder of the novel does see Martha move between four houses; the working-class café run by Iris and Jimmy at the beginning of the novel; to Jack's house, a casual lover who later becomes a procurer for a brothel; to Mark Coldridge's family home (her employer for much of the novel); and, finally, to the house of waifs and strays owned by Paul, Mark's nephew, where she explores the limits of her own sanity. Yet when he suggests that the four houses are 'various circles of Dante's *Inferno*', the metaphor restricts rather that explicates the complexities of the mediation between place and identity that the novel is exploring. This does, however, provide an intriguing connection with *A Pink Front Door* and Ella, since while all her own paintings of London remain unframed on the floor, 'The only picture on her wall was Henry Holiday's famous one of Dante's meeting with Beatrice' (*Pink* 68). *The Divine Comedy* is Ella's sublimation of her attraction to Marcia, reading the entire cycle three or four times a year. This is different to Karl's far narrower focus on *Inferno*, but he is right to point towards the correlation between the multi-layered city structure of *The Divine Comedy* from the heavenly city, through purgatory, to hell that has inscribed over the entrance: '*Per me se va ne la città dolente*' (*Inferno*, canto III). As Lefebvre observes:

> The poets in their noble expatiations have neglected neither chasms and abysses nor their corollaries, summits and peaks. At the dawn of Western culture, Dante dealt in an incomparably powerful manner with the themes of the depths (Inferno) and the heights (Paradise), although in doing so he displayed a measure of disdain for surfaces ... (Lefebvre 241–2)

Cosmologically, hell has been imagined as a place below the earth just as heaven has been above it, which suggests a stratified reading in which the earthly city equates to purgatory. This fits better with all three novels. Ella turns to Dante's stratified cities to sublimate her feelings for Marcia and paints an idealized empty city, Albert suffers under failure and the loss of Jenny creates an equally ideal city in his architectural drawings, geology and geography devoid of people, and for Martha too, London is a testing place rather than simple enclosure of her attitudes to class, politics, self and sanity. With Ella and Albert, the empty city is a hiatus or more accurately, an aporia, a conceptual space into which doubt and perplexity are projected. The tension that results is, of course, the challenge presented by the material and psychological city.

Martha's sense of freedom as a newcomer to the city is her equivalent to Ella's and Albert's sublimation. Yet she chooses to reengage with life in the city which has similarities to the project that Daisy attempts and fails. Mark Coldridge's house is another Palladian town house which in its surface order is attractive to Martha:

> The house was not on one of the famous squares, but nearly so: from the front door, it seemed as if the trees and plants of the square claimed the house. Tall, narrow, formal, it was like the houses of the squares; and the whole neighbourhood, now that the different shades of 'white' chosen by their owners before the war had dimmed into an unremarkable but uniform grey, had the unity of its original design: houses, terraces, grassy squares full of old trees. Here, in short, one thought of the beauty of London, not of its ugliness. (*City* 99)

The words 'formal', 'uniform', 'unity' define both the design criteria of the house and the location dominated by near identical terraces and squares. The place does not oppress Martha, even though she fears this. When she enters the interior there is none of the uncanny atmosphere prevalent in both *A Pink Front Door* and *Albert Angelo*. Her encounter with the Coldridge family is, however, another matter, and it is here that she recognizes all the family and social pressures that she has fled. Noting that the house would dictate a certain mode of behaviour, 'She felt attacked by the house – claimed', even though she 'was out of place' (*City* 99), being 'out of place' reflects her resistance to the traditionalism that the house embodies, the counter to its 'attack'. Yet choosing to stay, and choosing to stay for years even though she always seems to be about to leave, points to a commitment and sense of belonging that belies her constructed sense of the temporary. There is a prevalent implication that, 'Places are known through ... sensibility, but places also, in turn, constitute the sentient individual' (Keith and Pile 9). Martha soon finds herself in effective control of the house and despite her ongoing reservations, the life within provides a creative tension for her between belonging and alienation that had not been possible in *A Pink Front Door* and *Albert Angelo*. She survives. And more than that, she is able to grow.

The novel's opening chapters create a city space in which being outside provides Martha with psychological release from the limitations of social integration and interaction even if her freedom is, in fact, rather contingent. Karl's suggestion that the Coldridge house should be viewed negatively as entrapment, oppression and a bastion of all the values and roles that have led Martha to feel enclosed and stifled in the past is not entirely borne out by her experience. That she does not feel so negatively raises questions about her interpretation of her own feeling and desires. Martha resembles one of Daisy's waifs or strays, but we are given a view from the waif's perspective rather than the helper, and in this Mark Coldridge's tolerance, willingness to help and ownership of an iconic house suggests comparisons to Daisy. The difference is, of course, that Mark is not overtly creating a social statement by dressing and presenting his house as the cutting edge of a particular lifestyle and a social resurgence for his class. Both he and the house do of course represent an upper-middle-class lifestyle and tradition, but it is not the static entity worn like a badge or a mask as James's carefully staged cottage in Bottle Court. Martha's reconciliation with the house is therefore less surprising. The mask it presents to the world is lightly worn and open to dramatic change and accommodation with that world. Thence Martha feels less pressure herself to obscure her identity by hiding behind a social mask of her own. The house, despite her ongoing reservations and confusion, retains something of the freedom that she found as a stranger on the streets of the city. Waking in her room becomes 'the moment of her greatest pleasure' and it is now more broadly the city that cannot accommodate her:

> A terrible pang – real pain. Oh no, she must go, and fast. Christmas or no Christmas, particularly as a good part of her fear of going was that London had no more space in it for her now, as it had had months ago, when she had arrived. She did have some money now though, thanks to Mark – over two hundred pounds. She never seemed to have anything to spend her salary on. She would leave – in the next days, take a room, or small flat, and risk her chances with all the other waifs and strays of London who had no family at Christmas. (*City* 116)

There are echoes of Virginia Woolf's *A Room of One's Own* (1929) in this passage, but more significantly uneasiness about the attractions of homelessness, which as Heidegger observed in his 1947 'Letter on Humanism', 'is coming to be the destiny of the world' (Vidler 8). In the modern city, a city of strangers, everyone is a potential 'waif and stray' which, as Martha increasingly recognizes, robs the experience of its illusion of freedom. Belonging, having a community, as hooks argues, is important since 'one is always at risk' (hooks 149). Indeed, one can only allow oneself to be at risk within a community, as Martha realizes later in the novel when she is free to experiment with her own consciousness with the awareness of the safety-net her community provides. Moreover, Lynda, Mark's psychologically unstable wife, returns to the family home even while the social conventions and pressures that had led to her illness persist. *The Four-Gated City* is a parable of community. The community focused around Mark's house, but particularly the closer unity of the family, persists through social and political ostracism. When Mark's brother, a scientist, defects leading to the suicide of his wife, Mark assumes responsibility for his nephew but it is a difficult relationship, to the global meltdown of the world as Lessing speculates on the consequences of humanity's disregard for the environment. Symbolically this is emphasized further when it is apparent that Lynda, and to lesser degree Martha, are not ill but have the psychic ability to 'hear' other people's thoughts and emotions. After the catastrophe, such people hold various pockets of humanity together.

This would seem to leave the city behind, and in a respect it does since references to physical London are considerably diminished after the intensity of the first four chapters. But the symbolism of the city and community becomes increasingly significant throughout the novel. Mark's first major success as a writer comes from a modern-day utopian city fiction, but the germ for the novel is founded in a response to Martha's restlessness which is still located in London:

> 'Well,' he said, and again with the unfair reproach: 'You're going off. You're right.'
> 'I'm not what's needed here!'

'Yes, but what is! Oh very well – I don't want to . . . so you're going off to find . . . do you know what it is you're really wanting, Martha?'

And he proceeded to tell her. She was seeking, without knowing it for the mythical city, the one which appeared in legends and in fables and fairy stories, and (here he laughed at her, but affectionately) it was a hierarchic city, which is why she refused to even consider it. He proceeded to describe it, as clearly as if he had lived there; and she, laughing affectionately at him, who knew this archetypal city so well yet said he believed in nothing but a recurring destruction and disorder joined him in a long, detailed, fantastic reconstruction which, by the time they had finished, was as good as a blueprint to build. (*City* 150; ellipsis original)

Towards the end of the novel when the looming global catastrophe is becoming all too apparent to people like Mark, an American offers to build the city in North Africa. Construction begins and Mark devotes himself to settling people in what is hoped will be safety. As Britain and the world edge towards dystopia with increasingly authoritarian governments, this literalization of Mark's utopian city becomes one of two dominating symbols of the novel, alongside the community formed by those who can psychically overhear. Among the political uncertainties of the 1960s, these two metaphors restate the value of belonging, sociability and community as Lessing anticipates the conservative backlash towards 'swinging London', as Jerry White observes: 'Much of the optimism of Swinging London turned to dust in the authoritarian reaction, the economic difficulties and the racial tensions of the 1970s, and in the social disturbances and unemployment crises of the early 1980s' (J. White 350). Lessing achieves to some degree the reintegration between classes, races and political positions that are impossible in *A Pink Front Door* and *Albert Angelo*. Yet she is only able to do so against the background of an apocalyptic vision of the near future. But like the earlier two novels, resolution of sorts is only reached by leaving the city, or staying and dying. The desired continuation of community and city is projected to another location as London falls and its inhabitants either die, find refuge, or are scattered to the margins of Europe. The centre still fails to hold; it is displaced and dissipated.

5

The New Londoners

I conclude that it is my need for anonymity. . . . I have grown up with just an urban identity and come to treasure that. In Picktown I am trapped – in my family identity, the identity of my community and the identity of my opportunity. In London I had lived another life, grown other feelings, got to know myself as 'Tyrone.' . . . I do not want the involvement of 'belonging' without the choice of 'not belonging.' I feel unhappy outside my harsh urban skin, unable to site myself in time and space.

Beryl Gilroy, *Boy-Sandwich* (1989)

In his recent study of 'postcolonial' London, John Clement Ball observes that 'the prevalence of London-based novels in Commonwealth literatures undoubtedly provides evidence of the continuing hold of London, and the empire it spatially concentrates, on the postcolonial imagination' (Ball 13). The 'postcolonial imagination' is a problematic concept, and not just in relation to London. In fact, it would be more accurate to refer to the construction of London as space and place to be seen in Commonwealth literatures as a representation and continuation of colonial or imperial discourse. Nalbantoğlu and Wong's definition of 'postcolonial space' captures this discursive continuity: 'The term "postcolonial space" is both a reminder of a colonial past and a salutary gesture towards the future' (Nalbantoğlu and Wong 7). That future in the novels to be considered in this chapter is, of course, London. Yet this enactment of and continuity with the past is qualitatively different from the work of British authors born to immigrant parents (e.g. Hanif Kureishi or Zadie Smith) that have a different, exclusively British focus that should be understood as part of contemporary British fiction rather than a separate category. This contrasts with the work of Commonwealth-born writers for whom the experience of coming to Britain and London is a prevalent motif in their fiction. While Britain's empire was waning and actively being disassembled, the discourses that had sustained its symbolic significance would prove more durable. Though referring to London at the turn of the twentieth century, Jonathan Schneer's observation that 'London was the empire's capital, and the imperial metropolis of the world' (Schneer 4) still held considerable sway in the minds of British citizens resident in both the British Isles and its former – or soon to be former – colonies. Terminology aside, post-war migration to London was a, if not the, major factor in the development of contemporary London, its society and cultures. As Jerry White observes: 'Of all the changes to London and Londoners in the twentieth century this was the greatest' (J. White 131). This remaking of the Londoner not only radically altered the capital's demographic, but was also crucial to the development of post-war youth cultures and the exuberance of the 1960s, and also racial tensions, jealousies and ghettoization.

Ball's study (2004) is just one among three major recent studies of post-imperial London that appeared within 12 months of each other. Ball (2004), McLeod (2004) and Sandhu (2003) collectively seem to point to a new hold of London over the imagination of postcolonial critics. The surprise, perhaps, is the belatedness of this sustained attention from literary critics. As Sandhu in particular demonstrates, the presence of colonial 'others' among the legions of London's writers has a far longer history than the post-*Windrush* focus of McLeod's and Ball's studies, as they would readily acknowledge. Indeed, the vast majority of Sandhu's material is also located in this period. Yet the particular coordinates of the post-*Windrush* generation of writers hailing from the Caribbean, Africa, the Indian sub-continent and the Far East is certainly resonant. V. S. Naipaul sums up the enigma of London for this generation in *An Area of Darkness* (1964): 'It had become the centre of my world and I had worked hard to come to it. And I was lost. London was not the centre of my world. I had been misled; but there was nowhere else to go' (Naipaul 42). The London that was the centre of Naipaul's imagination is the symbolic centre of empire that coalesces around buildings, spaces, and institutions – London Bridge, the Houses of Parliament, Trafalgar Square, Buckingham Palace, etc. – and the literary representation of London imparted via a thorough British colonial education. In disappointment, he repeats Conrad's *Heart of Darkness* trope – 'an area of darkness' – in relation to the city.

While lacking experience of the place itself, many writers who came to London from former British colonies shared the same literary tradition of the city as other contemporary British writers, as Sinfield notes: 'Commonwealth immigrants were in fact British citizens' already, with all that implies of shared cultural traditions (Sinfield 126). The disappointment that Naipaul expresses is an acute failure to correlate the expectation created by the literary and cultural significance of the metropolis, and the material reality of the city. Indeed, his reaction serves to emphasize the extent to which metropolitan spaces are creations of cultural imagination. In Burton Pike's terminology, imperial London had been 'mythicized', and as 'the cultural conventions of a historical period' even if rapidly passing, they 'are usually slow to change' (Pike xi). Lacking experience, the reading of the city can only be partial and disorientating, as Kevin Lynch observed in 1960: 'Every citizen has had long associations with some part of his city, and his image is soaked in memories and meanings' (Lynch 1). The newcomer to the city might have shared textual and cultural memories and meanings, but profoundly lacks the close association with any part of the physical city as lived space. Once the imperial image of London had been rejected to some degree as 'unrealistic', the task is to gain a knowledge of place and remake the city anew.

The literary representation of the city contributes to, creates and records memories and meanings of the city, but cannot provide that materiality. Any attempt to assume that literary texts represent that reality needs to be treated with caution (although there is a tendency to 'read through' postcolonial writing in this manner). While the historical, cultural and social subject matter of the writing of Commonwealth arrivals to the city obviously differs from the experience of British-born writers who were inevitably external observers of many aspects of a rapidly developing post-war multicultural city, it would be wrong to assume that the *form* of their textual engagement with the city is so far removed from their contemporaries. The identification of this newest tradition of London writing as variously 'postcolonial' (McLeod), 'transnational' (Ball), or as simply 'black and Asian' writing (Sandhu) provides valuable critical insight, but such categories unintentionally isolate this writing from the tradition of writing post-war London that is the subject of this study. This chapter will resist this temptation by placing a selection of 'arrival' fictions within the context that previous chapters have identified: post-war trauma and physical devastation; a loss of middle-class confidence in the city; the rebuilding of the city both socially and materially; and, not least, the struggle to formulate a cogent identity during a period of painful and rapid change. But above all, I will trace contiguities and innovations in the representation of London through literary examples from the 1950s to the 1970s, focusing on Sam Selvon's *The Lonely Londoners* (1956), Colin MacInnes's *City of Spades* (1957), V. S. Naipaul's *The Mimic Men* (1967) and Buchi Emecheta's *Second-Class Citizen* (1974).

Colin MacInnes holds something of an anomalous position among post-war writers, inexplicably never quite attaining the stature of some of his peers. Although born in the city, MacInnes was an immigrant to London, returning after having migrated to Australia with his parents in 1918. The social upheaval he witnessed around him after his return is certainly that of an outsider in terms of age, class, sexual orientation and ethnicity – London identities that have been the subject of earlier chapters. As neither a 'real' Londoner, of the colonies but not

colonized (as a white Australian), excited by the new, strongly masculine and heterosexual culture of West Indians and Africans newly
arrived in London, but excluded on grounds of his homosexuality,
MacInnes's literary engagement with the city is a complex nexus of
enthusiasms and uncertainties. While welcoming the shake-up of a
moribund London still traumatized by the war, his writing never
achieves the detachment nor, conversely, an insider's view of the city
in the 1950s. As Sinfield notes: 'Colin MacInnes's enthusiasm for
(male) black immigrants was partly sexual, partly humanistic, and
partly a refreshing excitement at the new cultural opportunities
offered by blacks in a stodgy and boring English scene' (Sinfield 127).
The problematic result of this positive, liberal enthusiasm when
coupled with desire, is the (re)creation, at best, of an updated version
of the noble savage, and at worst stereotyping. This was a dilemma
prevalent among white intellectuals of the period in response to the
changing city. As Sheila Patterson summarized the argument in her
1960s book *Dark Strangers* (1963):

> A coloured skin, especially when combined with Negroid features, is
> associated with alienness, and with the lowest social status. Primitiveness,
> savagery, violence, sexuality, general lack of control, sloth, irresponsi-
> bility – all these are part of the image. On the more favourable side,
> Negroid peoples are often credited with athletic, artistic and musical
> gifts, and with an appealing and childlike simplicity which is in no way
> incompatible with the remainder of the image. (Patterson 212–3)

This effectively maps the assumptions of the feckless Montgomery
Pew, newly appointed Assistant Welfare Officer of the colonial
department in MacInnes's *City of Spades*. While not accepting the
judgement of the older man he replaces that 'the Negro's still, deep
down inside, a savage' (*Spades* 14), Pew argues how he likes blacks for
their 'sleek, loose-limbed appearance' and flamboyant dress. On the
other hand he objects to spirituals and 'idiotic calypso'. Note how
Pew's admiration settles on the physical while he rejects as 'idiotic'
black culture. This initial image suggests blacks are childlike in their
culture but attractive in their athletic posture and sartorial exuberance. His evaluation is not unlike Anthony Page's appreciative eye for
the young working-class men of Islington in Garland's *The Heart in
Exile* – another idealization fuelled by physical desire exaggerated by
the risk of violence. There is certainly a commonality of class attitude
between the two texts. Both construct social inferiors from a white,
middle-class, liberal position, and like Garland's working-class beaux
who occupy but do not culturally possess the faded glory of the
Regency architecture of their streets, the black immigrant in London
represents a physical disturbance of Pew's image of the city. Like
Page, the physical change through occupation is an improvement
focused, in this instance, on a traditional London pub, 'that

gloomiest of English institutions' occupied by regulars 'belching, back-slapping beside the counter or, as is more often, sitting morosely eyeing one another in private silence' (*Spades* 48). This London scene is transformed into a meeting place for the new black London:

> Within, where dark skins outnumbered white by something like twenty to one, there was a prodigious bubble and clatter of sound, and what is rare in purely English gatherings – a constant movement of person to person, and group to group, as though some great invisible spoon were perpetually stirring a hot human soup. Struggling, then propelled, towards the bar, I won myself a large whisky, and moved, with the instinct of minorities, to the only other white face I could see who was not either serving behind the bar, or a whore, of whom there were a great many there, or a person of appearance as macabre as scarcely to be believed. The man whom I addressed was one of those vanishing London characters, the elderly music-hall comical, modelled perhaps on Wilkie Bard, all nose, bear eyes, greased clothes and tufts of hair. (*Spades* 49)

Not surprisingly given the thrust of the passage, the 'elderly music hall character' standing in for working-class London of the previous generation, dislikes the new black clientele 'and all their rubbish' and is waiting for the day when the pub is returned to hands of the gloomy regulars. This is a very different use of the music-hall motif compared with Archie Prest in Hamilton's *The Slaves of Solitude*. In Hamilton's novel, Prest represents a return to the warm embrace of London's humanity after the oppression of the suburbs. Here instead it is the cold hostility of the working classes towards newcomers. Only ten years separate these two novels, but there seems to be a world of difference between the two London scenes they represent. Jerry White argues that for 'a generation from 1914 to 1940 … London had become less foreign and more British' (J. White 131), so that for MacInnes's vestigial music-hall character, an influx of physically different migrants represent the ruin of his 'traditional' London. However, Nigel Thrift observes of the construction of London as an 'English space' that, 'this sense of Englishness was necessarily ambivalent, since the history of the City's success was in part based upon a constant infusion of foreign immigrants' (Thrift 239). Yet hostility in both novels is directed towards the foreigner. Miss Roach's triumph over the German Vikki and the fascist sympathizer Thwaites represents a threatening foreign infection in the English suburbs balanced by the reassertion of a fundamental English/London institution – the Music Hall. MacInnes's Wilkie Bard lookalike yearns for a return to the spirit of Miss Roach's wartime London.

What both novels point to is the investment of personal identity in particular places and popular institutions. For Pew, the traditional English public house is stultified, stale, if not oppressive, but that does not override the significance of the institution to constructions of

London, Englishness and Britishness. His dislike is strongly class-biased, since it is clearly a working-class hostelry and shares something of Winston's bewilderment when he visits the Prole pub in *Nineteen Eighty-Four*. Reoccupation and adaptation of 'traditional' spaces is a key strategy in *City of Spades* that is not, ultimately, necessarily positive. This largely ascribes racial hostility to the working classes, leaving Pew as an opened-minded middle-class voyeur. From a postcolonial perspective, one might point to how such reformulations 'by inhabiting and "using" metropolitan spaces in new ways, begin to detach them from traditional meanings and associations' (Ball 10), but MacInnes avoids such a simple narrative of transformation – Little England is willing to wait out the newcomers. He is there to voice resistance in the form of racism, 'darkies and like what's here and all their rubbish' (*Spades* 49), which is a sentiment also expressed by the shopkeeper in Reid Banks's *The L-Shaped Room*; both 'traditional' and 'new' working-class London struggle over the same space/place. The significance of such tension cannot be underestimated. Keith and Pile observe that 'the social and spatial are inextricably realized one in the other' (Keith and Pile 6), which leaves the door open for competing visions of social space coexisting or, as here, in potential or actual conflict. MacInnes prefigures conflict rather than the progressiveness favoured by postcolonial politics to the point that the 'weight' of London increasingly becomes threatening.

It is a confrontation that MacInnes's text faces directly if not provocatively. The chapter 'Idyll of miscegenation on the river' is designed to provoke the fears of this conservative sensibility. Johnny Fortune, the young Nigerian student who is Pew's narrative counterpart and erstwhile guide to black London, enjoys a guided cruise along the Thames with his white girlfriend, Muriel. Johnny's father, a student in his turn, had a relationship with Muriel's mother, leaving a son who is half-brother to both Johnny and Muriel. He is violent, unpredictable and a petty thief. Caught between the two worlds of the novel, his character is either the product of abandonment by his father or the flawed result of a mixed-ethnicity relationship that is less than the sum of both contributors to his heritage. The novel raises both possibilities while refusing to provide a resolution. Indeed, the chapter that explicitly raises the spectre of miscegenation does so in a flippant, ironic manner – 'idyll' and 'miscegenation' are hardly comfortable words in such a context. Beyond the ironic language, the threat of crossing this 'colour line' is projected onto an unsympathetic London landscape:

> The boat passed underneath the bridge, and faces suddenly grew darker. Muriel watched her native city as the boat chugged on between Venetian façades of eyeless warehouses, dropping into ancient Roman mud, where barges lay scattered derelicts under lattices of insect

cranes. This was her first sight of Dockland, shut off from inquisitive view on the land by Brobdignagian brick walls. Missing familiar pavements and shop windows, Muriel saw her city as a place quite unfamiliar, and wondered what it might do to her, and Johnny Fortune. (*Spades* 116)

There is a clear echo of Conrad's *Heart of Darkness* in this passage. Marlow's tale of colonial rapine in the Congo is also recounted from a boat on the Thames which concludes with a contemplation of the Docklands, savagery, and violence – 'the heart of an immense darkness' (*Darkness* 124). The equivocation of Marlow's observation that 'London too had been a place of darkness' is confirmed in Muriel's reflections. The city is explicitly threatening and, even to a native Londoner, unfamiliar. The city of this novel is increasingly alien and multifaceted, able to turn upon its inhabitants at a moment's notice. From the lived space of houses and shops, there is a hidden London obscured by the Swiftean 'Brobdignagian' barriers that are out of all proportion to the proportions of domestic life. Barriers have other figurative meanings; representative of the scale of the social barriers erected between her and Johnny, as well as the class-based barrier between Muriel's London and the wealth and power represented by the docks of which she shares no part. The passage suggests both racial and class-based opposition to her happiness. Indeed, the weight of London's history also bears down on Muriel's mood as the 'resourceful guide still bludgeoned the passengers' defenceless ears' (*Spades* 117) with facts and events invariably from the underbelly of the city's history – pirates, opium dens, bloodthirsty judges, stews and Billingsgate. The overall effect is both to overawe by wealth of history but also to instigate fear of sordid violence that is, in many respects, the future of their relationship. A pattern exemplified by her sister who is both beaten and prostituted by her pimp/boyfriend, the Gambian Billy Whispers.

By the end of the novel, all the major characters are cowed by their experience of London. Johnny, his allowance spent on gambling, drifts into small-time drug dealing, living with a now-pregnant Muriel in the East End. When the relationship collapses he is persecuted by the police. Firstly for living off the immoral earnings of her sister's prostitution (a false charge) which he defeats in court, and then more accurately for his cannabis dealing for which he is convicted. He eventually decides to return home by working his passage on a ship, too proud to ask for money from his parents. Montgomery Pew is jobless and has subsumed his own interests to the vagaries of Johnny's fate. When he says farewell to his friend at the dockside he receives an invitation to visit Johnny's family in Lagos, but he is to be kept apart from Johnny's sister who has arrived in London to study nursing. This is an interesting, if unspoken rebuff. Muriel is of course left with a baby and condemned to repeat her mother's experience as Johnny has his father's. Theodora, Montgomery's friend who has become another of Johnny's lovers, loses her job at the BBC by testifying in Johnny's favour and publicly revealing that she is also carrying his child. It is hard to look sympathetically on Johnny's protectiveness of his sister in light of his relationship with Theodora who, if not Pew's lover, certainly had some sort of relationship with him that extended beyond normal friendship.

Oddly, though, London remains a force of attraction: Theodora, recuperating in the countryside, writes: 'I'd forgotten, Montgomery, how ghastly the country is until I came here to recoup. The colours are green and grey, invariably, and in the village nothing happens: nothing. I'll be glad to get back to London ...' (*Spades* 269). London retains a fierce energy by contrast to the countryside as it did for Hamilton's Miss Prest in *The Slaves of Solitude*, but not necessarily to the benefit of those who chose to live there. It is a place to survive, an ordeal rather than an unvarnished pleasure, and it is in this vein that Johnny responds to the concerns of his friend at the dockside: 'This is my city, look at it now! Look at it there – it has not killed me!' (*Spades* 287). The city has offered both scope to indulge in behaviour impossible at home – Johnny's excesses in London are very much part of a coming-of-age drama, as his father acknowledges on his departure for England: 'Of course, I know you'll drink, have fun with girls, and gamble, like I did myself. ... But mind you don't do these enjoyments too excessively' (*Spades* 17; ellipsis original) – but also increased visibility, disappointment and oppression. As Sinfield observes: 'The culminating event is the framing of Johnny Fortune by the police – an audacious move by MacInnes, at that date, and owing something to his experience as a homosexual' (Sinfield 128). This correlation between Johnny's experience of London's black community and what Garland's Anthony Page refers to as the gay 'underground', is a significant motif of the novel. Indeed, this might also explain Pew's excessive attraction to Johnny which the novel displaces into a sexual relationship with Theodora rather than confront directly.

In both novels we are told a succession of pubs become temporary, unofficial, meeting places and clearing houses while the police keep the community in check by regular raids and framing individuals. Many of the middle-class homosexual men of *The Heart in Exile* are attracted to working-class men, while in *City of Spades* it is suggested that there exists a strong mutual attraction between black men and working-class women. Indeed, to reinforce the association, MacInnes includes a gay character attracted to the black London scene, Alfy Bongo: 'The spades trust me, see? They trust the little queer boy because we're both minorities ... I was brought up by the Spades – did you know that?' (*Spades* 188), raising further questions that are not resolved in the text. Does this simply point to common cause between London's minorities, or suggest that Alfy's sexuality is the consequence of the cultural confusion of his upbringing? Indeed, it is scarcely credible among Afro-Caribbean London which has a strong tradition of homophobia. Yet MacInnes is not the only writer to make the association between gay and black London in the period. Lynne Reid Banks's 1960 novel *The L-Shaped Room* combined the two groups in one character, the gay black jazz musician John, and offers a limited exploration of middle-class prejudice – although the racism of the shopkeeper at the beginning of the novel goes unremarked. But MacInnes goes much further by suggesting that black culture is a persecuted, underground, almost illicit activity. Harassed by the police simply for who they are, the marginal criminality that underground cultures are forced into appears to enhance their attractiveness to white working-class women and young middle-class men. The parallel, however, remains awkward. Homosexuality was still a criminal activity in the 1950s, which is a much stronger form of persecution than just harassment by the police. Some tenor of the police response to homosexuality can be gathered from the popular memoirs of former Vice Squad officer Bob Fabian first published in 1954 and reprinted throughout the latter 1950s: '[homosexuality] is an offence against decency and is punishable by heavy imprisonment' (Fabian 66). This contrasts with his attitude towards black Londoners: 'I had a great deal to do with the African and West Indian boys in the West End, and got along with them very well. You cannot tell me that they are an inferior race' (Fabian 15). The blurring of these two minority experiences of London is a white, middle-class framework for understanding black London culture. As a consequence, the black London experience in *City of Spades* undoubtedly exaggerates the positive aspects of life in London for the immigrant.

Indeed, Johnny Fortune is not an immigrant at all but a visitor who returns home after sowing his wild oats in London like his father before him, presumably wiser and more seasoned for responsibility in his very respectable middle-class home in Nigeria. It is a picaresque narrative and, as such, he is no more a Londoner than Mark Underwood of Lodge's *The Picturegoers*. The retreat and return home of both these middle-class characters from close engagement with the city is suggestive. Those who remain and intend to settle in London are tacitly ignored, if not implicitly dismissed as inferior. It is an epiphany for Johnny when the ubiquitous Alfy Bongo warns him, 'You're turning sour, Johnny ... It's bad in London, when a spade turns sour' (*Spades* 275). Johnny is at risk of being ruined by the city of which Sinfield observes: 'In MacInnes's view, England spoils the utopian possibilities of black culture' (Sinfield 128). *City of Spades* is not then a paean to a new black London but, again following a traditional picaresque pattern, the great corrupter of youth and culture.

A better sense of the formation of a permanent black London is provided by Sam Selvon's *The Lonely Londoners*. Often grim in its representation of life in the city, Selvon's text is less a novel than a series of vignettes of 1950s London, seen through the eyes of recent West Indian immigrants. While more solidly discernable as the establishment of modern black London culture personified in the most authoritative and longest-resident character Moses, most of the West Indians still harbour intentions to return home having made their fortune and enjoyed an adventure in the imperial metropolis. The novel initially therefore creates a sense of both settlement but also impermanence, although the latter is gradually eroded through the narrative as it is more and more evident to the characters and thence the reader that they are in London to stay. Yet London is far from the Promised Land implied by Moses' name and the role we first see him in, an unofficial 'liaison officer' for new arrivals (*Lonely* 8). The city is cold, fog bound and unwelcoming:

> One grim winter evening, when it had a kind of unrealness about London, with a fog sleeping restlessly over the city and the lights showing in the blur as if it is not London at all but some strange place on another planet, Moses Aloetta hop on a number 46 bus at the corner of Chepstow Road and Westbourne Grove to go to Waterloo to meet a fellar who was coming from Trinidad on the boat-train. (*Lonely* 7)

The echo of the central organizing metaphor from Eliot's *The Waste Land*, 'unreal city', establishes a less than propitious atmosphere for the novel. The defamiliarized landscape created from the fog and the bleeding street lamps enacts a familiar enough literary image of London. Yet the expectation of the new arrivals at Waterloo is of an imperial city of light so the conditions for disappointment are established early and develop the negative promise of the title. As Pike suggests of *The Waste Land*, London the 'unreal city' is the 'centre of imaginative and mythic power in an exhausted culture. The denizens of this city lead encapsulated, enervated lives' (Pike 104). Moses is the equivalent of Eliot's Tiresius, a prophet of doom: 'We can't get no place to live, and we only getting the worse jobs it have' (*Lonely* 13). As Sandhu observes, 'Estrangement is the dominant emotion' (Sandhu 166).

Yet even this atmosphere is not enough to dampen the enthusiasm of the newcomers. When a whole family arrives on the boat train, their relative is left in an impossible situation with 'all these people on his hands, in London, in the grim winter, and no place to stay' (*Lonely* 14). The essential truth of economic betterment is spelt out by his mother, Tanty: 'But they say that it have more work in England and better pay. And to tell you the truth, when I hear that Tolroy getting five pound a week, I had to agree' (*Lonely* 15). Alongside Moses' nostalgia for the tropics, sparked by seeing so many arrivals from the

Caribbean – 'Still, the station is that sort of place where you have a soft feeling. It was here that Moses did land when he come to London, and he have no doubt that when the time come, if it ever come, it would be here he would say goodbye to the big city' (*Lonely* 10) – the arrival of Tanty and her extended family suggests settlement and permanence that her character will later impart to her environment as she actively moulds London to her needs by making it local to her identity: 'Everybody in the district get to know Tanty so well that she doing as she like' (*Lonely* 63). The significance of this sense of belonging cannot be underemphasized. Yet the illusiveness of the city, its unreality, remains part of Tanty's experience. Never venturing beyond her local district – 'Like how some people live in a small village and never go to the city, so Tanty settle down in the Harrow Road in the Working Class area' (*Lonely* 64) – the one time she does so her journey into the city is marked by an indistinctness. Great Portland Street contracts into 'Greatport Street', much to the confusion of a local policeman. Her journey is marked by tube stations and bus routes but the details of the city recede, unnoticed: 'She was so frighten that she didn't bother to look out the window and see anything, and when she got off at the Prince of Wales she feel relieved. Now nobody could tell she ain't travel by bus and tube in London' (*Lonely* 67). While able to mould and influence her immediate locality, Tanty's grip on London as a whole is weaker. It is *the* city rather than her city. To her, the district abutting Harrow Road is a 'practised place' in de Certeau's terms (de Certeau 117), but this outlook is local rather than metropolitan. Her travel story is the exception to her usual practice and fails to establish the 'spatial syntax' that is the positive spatial practice of the everyday city-dweller (de Certeau 115). In short, Tanty's experience of the city and her ability to alter it to her needs is limited, if not ghettoized.

This is tied to her gender. Male migrants to the city do not face such hesitations in roving about the city. Galahad, the man Moses meets from the boat train at Waterloo, is initially boastful and overconfident about the ease by which he will master London, much to Moses's mixed amusement and disgust. Yet as the novel progresses, he regains his original confidence. 'Galahad feel like a king living in London':

> He had a way, whenever he talking with the boys, he using the names of the places like they mean big romance, as if to say 'I was in Oxford Street' have more prestige than if he just say 'I was up the road.' And once he had a date with a frauline, and he make a big point of saying he was meeting she by Charring Cross, because just to say 'Charring Cross' have a lot of romance in it. ... Jesus Christ, when he say 'Charring Cross,' when he realize that he, Sir Galahad, who going there, near that place that everybody in the world know about (it even have the name in the dictionary) he feel like a new man. It didn't

matter about the woman he going to meet, just to say he was going there made him feel big and important, and even if he was just going to coast a lime, to stand up and watch the white people, still it would have been something. (*Lonely* 67–8)

Undoubtedly excited by the stage of London that he sees himself upon, Galahad's ability to casually name famous London locations would certainly seem to suggest a certain degree of appropriation. Especially when it becomes a place for him to meet a woman who matters less than the scene he can create for himself. But this is still the 'unreal' city, a place in the 'dictionary' rather than a lived, 'practised place'. This verbal mapping of proper names again recalls Deleuze and Guattari's observation that 'the map has to do with performance, whereas the tracing always involves an alleged "competence"' (Deleuze and Guattari 12). Galahad's engagement with tourist London is certainly performative in a literal sense, yet his mapping lacks the greater intimacy of the tracing, even if that competency is only 'alleged' over a polymorphous space like London. He is still a visitor, a tourist, rather than de Certeau's 'practitioner'. Yet Galahad slips easily into what might appear to be the empowered perspective of the *flâneur*. Benjamin's observation that 'the street becomes a dwelling for the *flâneur*' (Benjamin 1997 37) closely aligns with Galahad's positioning of himself in the city 'like a king' with the specular power of the observer 'watch[ing] the white people'. This echoes Baudelaire's comment that 'an observer is a *prince* who is everywhere in possession of his incognito' (Benjamin 1997 40). Yet this fiction of empowerment is shattered by his very visibility as a black man in London when a child observes, 'Mummy, look at that black man!' and recoils in terror (*Lonely* 71). The scene is almost identical to an episode from Frantz Fanon's *Black Skin, White Masks* (1952) when he recalls encountering a white girl and her mother – 'Mama, see the Negro! I'm frightened. Frightened! Frightened!' (Fanon 112). Galahad becomes the object rather than the subject, the other rather than the self, the colonized rather than the colonizer. The child's terror forces him to acknowledge a construction of himself as the fearful and the uncivilized black man in the white man's city. His *place* in London is immediately robbed from him. As Steve Pile and Nigel Thrift observe: 'the black man's visibility has a double effect: his skin allows him to be seen and marked as different (from whites), but it also separates him (from whites) in a way that makes him unknowable (to whites)' (Pile and Thrift 42–3). It is his experience, though, that restores his composure. Reflecting later over the alarm the episode would have caused him if he had been a new arrival, he can now nonchalantly shrug the episode off 'like duck back when rain fall – everything running off' (*Lonely* 72). It does, however, provoke the key observation of the novel:

Colour, is you that causing all this, you know. Why the hell you can't be blue, or red or green, if you can't be white? You know, is you that cause a lot of misery in the world. Is not me, you know, is you! I ain't do anything to infuriate the people and them, is you. Look at you, you so black and innocent, and this time you causing misery all over the world. (*Lonely* 72)

Galahad's reduction of prejudice, domination and violence to a simple aversion to the shade of his skin is remarkably charitable since it enables him to displace the discourse of fear and hate that colonialism has bred. This of course enables him to function in the city and even after his 'theory' receives short shrift from Moses, he soon regains his buoyant mood on the way to a date with a white woman, Daisy. Later they make love, his first time with a white woman, but even this, when Moses is told later, is met with a 'knowing smile' (*Lonely* 77).

A key theme in both *City of Spades* and *The Lonely Londoners* is the presumed attraction that white women hold for black men, and vice versa. This tramples on a number of colonial taboos focused around anxieties of loss of caste and miscegenation that London seems to break down. On the one hand, this confirms middle-class prejudice that working-class women would become irresistibly attracted to black men given the opportunity. But both novels also feature middle-class women equally besotted. It is difficult to overlook elements of misogyny in this proposition. *City of Spades* attempts some balance by showing Pew attracted to Johnny's sister, Peach, at the end of the novel, but in *The Lonely Londoners* Selvon maps quite different experiences of the city around gender when Tanty's limited engagement with the city is compared to the roving Galahad. It is hard not to conclude that Galahad's theatricalized experience and the numerous tales of sexual exploits in the novel effectively commodifies him, and others like him. This is linked to the elements of the *flâneur* in his characterization that was also evident in Harry from Lodge's *The Picturegoers*:

The *flâneur* is someone abandoned in the crowd. In this he shares the situation of the commodity. He is not aware of this special situation, but this does not diminish its effect on him and it permeates him blissfully like a narcotic that can compensate him for many humiliations. The intoxication to which the *flâneur* surrenders is the intoxication of the commodity around which surges the stream of customers. (Benjamin 1997 55)

Galahad's unbounded joy simply at his presence in London shares such a sense of narcotic intoxication and lack of awareness through humiliations like the little girl: 'people sitting and standing and walking and talking and laughing and busses and cars and Galahad Esquire, in all this, standing there in the big city, in London. Oh Lord'. (*Lonely* 74)

His commodification is more disturbing, because equally unconscious. His friend Frank tells him, 'Boy it have bags of white pussy in London, and you will eat until you tired' (*Lonely* 74), which depicts Galahad as a consumer of what London has to offer. Moses tells a different tale of being picked up and taken to a club in Knightsbridge by a wealthy woman whom in the heat of passion cries out 'black bastard' (*Lonely* 93). Offended, Moses leaves. Both black men and white women seem prostituted in these stories, while the motif repeats the sexual anxiety of colonial racism with the figure of the white male physically absent but ideologically present – misogyny and miscegenation. As Pile and Thrift note, 'the exchanges between the colonizer and colonized involve the ambivalence of desire and fear' (Pile and Thrift 43). When Moses reflects 'everybody look like they frustrated in the big city the sex life gone wild' (*Lonely* 93), and while it is white men that are the source of that frustration they remain the keepers of the old colonial and gender order much as Caryl Churchill would suggest in her play *Cloud Nine* (1979).

By contrast to *City of Spades* and *The Lonely Londoners*, V. S. Naipaul's *The Mimic Men* (1967) represents London not as a place of migration but of exile. The novel recounts the story of Ralph Singh, a successful businessman turned colonial politician from the fictional Caribbean island of Isabella (based on Naipaul's own Trinidad). While much of the first-person narrative is set in Isabella as Singh retrospectively tells the tale of his childhood and career, it is permeated with the presence of London. Indeed, Singh recounts his story from a suburban London hotel where he has become a long-term resident. His exile echoes some aspects of Miss Roach's exile from central London at the Rosamund Tea Rooms – another 'slave of solitude' – yet the novel opens by alternating between the memory of his first residence in London in post-war Kensington as a student living 'narrowly', and his present life as an exile living in a suburban hotel. London frames his past and present and the shape of the narrative to follow. Singh's experience of contemporary 1960s London registers major changes in its fabric and population: 'sitting in the train, going past the backs of tall sooty houses, tumbledown sheds, Victorian working-class tenements whose gardens, long abandoned, had for stretches been turned into Caribbean backyards' (*Mimic* 12). This is a permanent Caribbean London made good from Selvon's *The Lonely Londoners*. Following the promise of Tanty and those like her, the fabric of this district has changed to meet the material needs of these new Londoners. Yet Singh, though from the Caribbean, is clearly alienated and excluded. His London is not a space/place of settlement and community. While lyrically powerful, his ambivalence towards London is evident from his student days as he recalls his first winter in the city – possibly the great freeze of 1947 – in a passage that resonates thematically throughout the novel:

Standing before the window – crooked sashes, peeling paint-work: so fragile the structure up here which lower down appeared so solid – I felt the dead light on my face. The flakes didn't only float; they also spun. They touched the glass and turned to a film of melting ice. Below the livid grey sky roofs were white and shining black in patches. The bombsite was wholly white; every shrub, every discarded bottle, box and tin was defined. I had seen. Yet what was I to do with so complete a beauty? And looking out from that room to the thin lines of brown smoke rising from ugly chimneypots, the plastered wall of the house next door to the bombsite tremendously braced and buttressed, looking out from that empty room with the mattress on the floor, I felt all the magic of the city go away and had an intimation of the forlornness of the city and of the people who lived in it. (*Mimic* 9)

The passage establishes an image of London covered by a flimsy façade of misleading solidity, concealing the essential weakness and decay of the structure below. The 'fragile structure' of his boarding house built on the appearance of solid foundations; the beauty of the blanket of snow barely concealing the 'ugly chimneypots' belching 'brown smoke'; the plastered wall of the neighbouring house concealing the drabness of London's prevailing brickwork and 'tremendously braced and buttressed' war damage. The false façade of the temporary beauty brought to the city by the snowfall resonates back into Singh's room, emphasizing its emptiness and desolation with only a mattress on the floor. London, 'the heart of empire', loses its magic for this colonial visitor repeating early much of the pessimism that Moses represented in *The Lonely Londoners*. By contrast to the indistinctness of London fog suggesting the immigrant's uncertain status in the city, Naipaul's snow suggests a huge funeral pall over both the future of the imperial metropolis and his own. Selvon's loneliness finds its counterpart in Naipaul's 'forlornness' precipitated by the loss of imperial 'magic', but whereas Selvon refers to the loneliness of the migrant, Naipaul repeats the urban anomie that has echoed throughout several of the novels in this study, but perhaps most significantly in Bowen's *The Heat of the Day*.

For Stella, Bowen's protagonist, the deadening silence of the blackout resonates from the street into her home, just as here the desolation of the same war-torn landscape is visible but concealed beneath the fresh snow, removing the distinction between interior and exterior to the extent that the city becomes an extended image for Ralph's future – a uniform surface giving the appearance of solidity while concealing fragility, weakness and an essential malaise. Ralph, as we come to learn, never engages, never truly commits, drifting through life without conviction. A similar hiatus faces Stella in the reality-defying wartime social whirl that has to be confronted and moved beyond so that her life can advance. For Ralph Singh that never happens. His place *is* the suburbs, defying the usual accepted cosmopolitan attractions of the city. The pall of solidity he finds there, false and contrived, contrasts with 'the great city, so solid in its light, which gave colour even to unrendered concrete – to me as colourless as rotting wooden fences and new corrugated-iron roofs – in this solid city life was two-dimensional' (*Mimic* 23). The imperial metropole is inextricably tied to its colonial hinterland, both developments of the same essential disorder. Singh's point of comparison in this passage is the 'wooden fences' and 'corrugated-iron roofs' of his Caribbean homeland from which he has been exiled, while not escaping the disorder which he also finds among the concrete façades of London: 'The great city, centre of the world, in which fleeing disorder, I had hoped to find the beginning of order' (*Mimic* 22).

Like Selvon, Naipaul finds his inspiration in modernist representations of London like *The Waste Land*, or Eliot's other great creation, Prufrock, who observes: 'lonely men in shirt-sleeves, leaning out of windows?' (Eliot 14). Prufrock is as devoid of energy as Singh's narrative voice, which comes to share elements of Eliot's vision of the city: 'its centre had become the urban apocalypse, the great City dissolved into a desert where voices sung from exhausted wells' (Kenner 46). Just as Eliot's later verse sought spiritual redemption and order in the suburbs – see *The Four Quartets* – Singh retreats to the suburb, but the result is mere vacuity. His post-exile sexual adventures have this quality and are spatialized in London suburbia. Walking with one partner Beatrice – another echo of Dante, perhaps – through the streets of St John's Wood, the sexual energy of the day is drained away when she announces they are just going to be friends (*Mimic* 28). On another occasion Singh finds himself again slipping into immobility, retreating from the promise of a sexual encounter: 'it was the moment I dreaded. Both of us adrift in London, the great city, I with my past, my own darkness, she no doubt with hers' (*Mimic* 29–30). This further echo of Conrad's 'dark heart' of London's past contrasted with the bustle, order and enterprise of the imperial city is subtly realigned, emphasizing an oft-ignored element of Conrad's complex imagery in *Heart of Darkness*, the microcosm of the imperial adventure – the ship adrift on the Thames tide anticipating Kurtz's wayward imperial vision and Ralph's own colonial confusion.

London is also the framework for Singh's recollections of his upbringing and later career on Isabella. While still a student he drifts into a marriage with an English student, Sandra, 'though of the city, her position in it was like my own. She had no community, no group, and had rejected her family' (*Mimic* 53). Becoming a touchstone for London contrasts, in Isabellan society she regales island socialites with her 'North London tongue' (*Mimic* 76) and Ralph takes especial delight in seeing exposed on Isabella what was hidden in London: 'The stockings and shoes of London had concealed those feet. They were nervous without being too bony; they were feet one could caress;

I frequently did' (*Mimic* 74). The pleasure Ralph takes in the shock value of his wife among their social circle and the delight with the unravelling of parts of her anatomy is linked to the way she confounds the myth of London prevalent in his homeland. Here was a 'real' Londoner, not some upper-middle-class colonial fabrication of British identity. Her London accent and unself-conscious accommodation to the tropics in matters of attire equally serve to dismantle the colonial myth.

Ralph's enjoyment of this stage-managed confrontation between myth and actuality becomes ever more sadistic as he simply steps back and observes Sandra's directness gradually provoke hostility. She begins to personify the disorder that he later seeks to counter in the imperial capital. She is labelled as 'common' and déclassée as society gossip reduces her to 'a girl from the East End of London, without breeding or education, who had been rescued by myself, besotted by the glamour of her race' (*Mimic* 79). As we saw in both *City of Spades* and *The Lonely Londoners*, the working-class woman is seen to be the trophy for the colonial adventurer in London. It is common enough knowledge in Isabella to be offered as a powerful insult. By her challenge to the vestigial image of the colonizer, by representing a London as lived place rather than imperial myth, Sandra is reduced by gossip to little more than the expected working-class sexual adventure of a curious colonial man enamoured of her white skin. The slander is devastating to both Sandra and Ralph, but only seems to wear down the former. The sexual connection between the two ebbs out of their relationship, which becomes increasingly focused on public displays of leg and feet caressing while they both enjoy sexual adventures outside their marriage. Ralph's odd fetishes for parts of her body fragments Sandra, who ceases to be a living woman for him but a symbol of his own suppressed dissolution: 'Those ill tempered eyes! That bony face with its jut of jaw. Those feet, as nervous and expressive as hands, but much more subtle and complex' (*Mimic* 83). She finally leaves him just as their newly built facsimile of a Roman villa is completed and he realizes that she is one of the principle anchors holding his life together; a grounding that he later seeks in London, Sandra's original home:

> It was fear of the unreality around me; it was the fear of the man who feels the veils coming down one by one, muffling his deepest respon-ses, and panics at not being able to tear down the unreality about him to get at the hard, the concrete, where everything becomes simple and ordinary and easy to seize. It was my London fear; and now in addition I feared for the luck I attributed to Sandra, this luck to which I thought mine was linked. It was then I began to will everything away: the gift, ambition, everything; and consoled myself consciously with thoughts of extinction, as a vague general fate, as once, in London, I could get into sleep only with the thought of the Luger at my head. (*Mimic* 85–6)

'Unreality', a lack of concreteness, the London fear. Ralph simply wishes to dissipate. It is not, however, strictly a *London* fear, but lack of a concrete identity as an East Indian West Indian of a colonized Caribbean island. In fragmenting his luck, Sandra, representative of London, England, and the colonizer, he seeks both to comprehend multiple and confusing identifications, and to exert a measure of specular control as he observes Sandra struggle with, disrupt and ultimately become the victim of Isabellan society. This too can be read as a manifestation of the *flâneur* seeking an integrity and wholeness from the position of a detached observer which obscures the fragility of that identity. In Salman Rushdie's terms, his colonial history means Ralph is a 'translated man' (Rushdie 1992 10), but unlike Stuart Hall's optimistic assessment that the people in such a subject position 'inhabit more than one identity, have more than one home; who have learned to "negotiate and translate" between cultures ... and thus finding ways of being both the same as and different from the others amongst which they live' (Hall 47), he can find no stable plateau on which to anchor himself. Not even in London, the symbolic heart of imperial order.

Ralph desires anonymity. To be invisible, withdrawn and simplified; to abdicate his life for the routines and banalities of suburbia, and the functional order and certainties of a residential hotel surrounded by symbols of stolid British national identity. This identity is criticized in *City of Spades* as being 'of glum clothes and shut in faces' and 'morose' silences, and becomes the final fragmentation that provides the inertia that he needs: 'For here [in the hotel] is order of a sort. But it is not mine. It goes beyond my dream. In a city already simplified to individual cells this order is a further simplification. It is rooted in nothing' (*Mimic* 42–3). For Ralph the city replicates the rootlessness of colonial identity atomized beyond contradiction, just as he revelled in breaking down Sandra's body into fragments of fetishistic desire. Self-excluded from all communities, he makes his home in artificiality. He finds peace of a sort only by stripping the world of any meaningful connectedness leaving only its most banal components, anticipating Stephen Barber's observation that 'the banal supports the city and gives it life' (Barber 7). His final comfort is the sense of imagined community among those whom, scattered around London, form no community:

> We are people who for one reason or another have withdrawn, from our respective countries, from the city where we find ourselves, from our families. We have withdrawn from unnecessary responsibility and attachment. We have simplified our lives. I cannot believe that our establishment is unique. It comforts me to think that in this city alone there must be hundreds and thousands like ourselves. (*Mimic* 296)

The association of family with 'responsibility and attachment', and from there with national identity and culture is not, on the face of it, a remarkable observation. Yet it is the significant structuring principle of all the novels examined in this chapter. In *City of Spades* a contrast is made between the stability provided by Johnny's Nigerian family and the behaviour of both himself and his father before him in London, fathering children and abdicating responsibility for them. This certainly fits in with the picaresque aspects of the novel, but it is also a strong challenge to the presumptions of colonial subservience. Johnny's awe at London is strictly limited to the tourist who is going to take full advantage of the anonymity of the city to behave badly, unlike Naipaul's Ralph for whom anonymity is all that he seeks. Johnny is, of course, soon enmeshed in compromising complexities, in a similar way to the men in *The Lonely Londoners*. There are comparisons to be made between Johnny's initial enthusiasm for London and Galahad's unwillingness to shrug off the novelty of 'staging' himself in London, even when his status as an outsider is underlined by the fear of the little girl in the street. Johnny ultimately approaches Moses's level of cynicism, although the novel ends on a potential lighter note by his return to Nigeria and family stability. This is a prospect not even realistically considered by Moses, even though he occasionally feels nostalgia for the Caribbean. This contrast is a consequence of his middle-class origins that explains his attractiveness to both Montgomery and Theodora – he may not be of the same ethnicity but is of a comparable class. In this respect, Johnny resembles Ralph. Yet Johnny the aspirant playboy actively seeks the disorder promised by the city and finally learns sobriety, even if he does not live up to the responsibilities he leaves behind in the form of two children. For Ralph it is the false promise of order that leads to profound disappointment and eventual withdrawal into the banal routines of the suburban middle classes after fleeing the chaos – or rather the inner chaos – that he displaces onto his own country.

By contrast to these male trajectories in the city, the burden placed on female characters is significantly different. The counterpart to Johnny is his socially conservative and studious sister, Peach. For Ralph there is Sandra, a fragment of 'North London tongue' he uses to counter the pretensions of the upper classes of his homeland. Ralph would rather hide behind another than confront social convention himself – 'I sought accommodation where I ought to have imposed authority' (*Mimic* 76) – as his later retreat into suburban hotels demonstrates. By contrast there is Tanty. Significantly she enjoys a limited triumph, bending local London shopkeepers to the system of credit she is familiar with in Jamaica, while having no interest in London as a whole. The emphasis is on family and community: 'Like how some people live in small village and never go to the city, so Tanty settle down in the Harrow Road in the Working

Class area' (*Lonely* 64). Her minor role in the novel belies the significance of her narrative. Order and settlement rely on an association with place, with belonging. To grasp London, to accommodate it, one must have a strong sense of the local. As Diana Fuss argues: 'what is *essential* to social constructionism is precisely this notion of "where I stand", or of what has come to be called, appropriately enough, "subject position"' (Fuss 29). None of the male characters examined so far in this chapter establish a 'subject position' in the city and many, like Galahad or Johnny, do not wish to, preferring instead to indulge in various forms of machismo in a less than convincing metropolitan will to power. Thence Johnny's observation as he boards the ship to return home: 'This is my city, look at it now! Look at it there – it has not killed me!' (*Spades* 287). The figure who comes closest to Tanty is Moses, but in contrast to her positive action on the city, his pessimism and fear for the future fails to inspire either hope or warmth: 'the boys laughing, but they only laughing because they fraid to cry, they only laughing because to think so much about everything would be a big calamity' (*Lonely* 126).

Buchi Emecheta's *Second-Class Citizen* provides an important corrective to male-focused narratives of settlement in London. The novel's protagonist, Adah, is a woman of determination and ambition. Even as a child, she ensures that she receives the best education available to her in her home town in Nigeria, first by pressuring her parents and, later, after her father's death and her mother's remarriage, by winning a national scholarship with no help from her extended family. Yet when adulthood approaches she realizes that there is only so much she can accomplish as a single woman in Nigerian society, so she has to marry. Once married and in possession of a well-paid job at the American embassy, she decides to act upon her ambition to migrate to England, and specifically London. Although never explicitly articulated, Adah's subconscious need is not just economic betterment for her children, but an escape from the patriarchal strictures of Nigerian society. Facing further opposition from family, this time her husband's side of the family, only he goes to England to study while Adah remains at home with her good job and young family: 'Why lose your good job just to go and see London? They say it is just like Lagos' (*Citizen* 24). This comparison discursively diminishes the imperial capital in a manner that reveals the limitations of her husband and his parents. As Gaston Bachelard observes, 'the cleverer I am at miniaturising the world the better I possess it' (Bachelard 150). In defensiveness as well as persuasiveness, London is dismissed in local terms. Likewise, the highly educated, independently minded, daughter-in-law is, by association, put in her place.

Yet as a child, Adah was warned away from Lagos. Although born in the Nigerian capital she was brought up in another city, Iburza, and taught that Lagos was a place contrary to the values of her own home city: 'Her parents said that Lagos was a bad place, bad for bringing up children because here they picked up the Yoruba-Ngbati accent. It was bad because it was a town with laws, a town where Law ruled supreme. In Iburza, they said, you took the law into your own hands' (*Citizen* 2). Adah's own character shares a dislike of restraints on her own actions. The restrictive traditions of the patriarchal Nigerian family must be resisted, and 'the law' taken into her own hands. Yet if Lagos is a city of laws, so is the London with which it is later compared. As a city of laws London would seem to be inimical to Adah's early values and ambitions, yet she has already learnt that even if Iburza lacked a system of externally regulated law, the law of the family could be equally powerful. Adah finally achieves her goal and departs for London, but finds that she miscalculates. While gaining liberation from family tradition, so does her husband: 'He was free at last from his parents, he was free to do what he liked, and not even hundreds of Adahs were going to curtail that new freedom' (*Citizen* 36–7). Adah learns too late that it was only Francis's parents who restrained his sexism, to petty despotism, low self-esteem and violence. Adrift in an unfamiliar city, she finds that disorder follows the absence of social structure which brings her initial experience of the city close to that experienced by Ralph Singh.

The physical reality of London is also forbidding and is resonant of the cold 'unreal' city of the opening section of *The Lonely Londoners*. On her journey from Liverpool to London Adah is reassured by the beauty of the snow-covered countryside and a glimpse of the factory where Ovaltine is made, comforting in its familiar imperial associations. Yet the beauty of the snow is only a prelude to the underlying meanness of London itself. For Ralph, the snow resembles a funeral pall communicating the forlornness of the city and its people. For Adah, London is a culture shock of another type, although equally as bleak:

> Francis had told her in his letter that he had accommodation for them in London. He did not warn Adah what it was like. The shock of it all nearly drove her crazy.
>
> The house was grey with green windows. She could not tell where the house began and where it ended, because it was joined to other houses in the street. She had never seen houses like that before, joined together like that. In Lagos houses were usually completely detached with the yards on both sides, the compound at the back and verandas in front. These ones had none of these things. They were long solid blocks, with doors opening into the street. The windows were arranged in straight rows along the streets. On looking round, Adah noticed that one could tell which windows belonged to which door by the colour the frames were painted. Most of the houses seemed to have the same curtains for their windows. (*Citizen* 34–5)

The class disorientation of this passage offers a very different London than the shared class coordinates of the relationship between Johnny Fortune and Montgomery Pew. Here interracial relationships based on class identification are not possible: black people are 'low class'. Francis revels in bringing his wife down as a form of vicarious power over her, which betrays his innate sense of inadequacy: 'We are all blacks, all coloureds, and the only houses we can get are horrors like these' (*Citizen* 35). Free from family pressure to excel and justify his expensive education, Francis is keen to embrace the mediocrity and anonymity offered by London and an easier, if meaner, life. While clearly different from Naipaul's Ralph Singh, he is also quick to see the possibilities in London for hiding from one's culture and responsibilities. The lack of distinguishing features among the working-class terraces to which he brings Adah signals both his relish for meanness and a desire for the lowest possible denominator to measure his life in the city.

Yet it is not so simple to suggest that Francis's downward mobility is the negative to Adah's class standards. Frequently allowing snobbery to triumph over national and racial solidarity, Adah is horrified to observe that 'she had to share the house with such Nigerians who called her madam at home; some of them were of the same educational background as her paid servants' (*Citizen* 36). Sensing this hostility, they make life hard for Adah and continually pressure the easily led Francis to bring her down a peg or two. Indeed, the title of the novel does not, as one might at first suspect, refer only to the inferior status conferred on Commonwealth migrants to the city, but also to Adah's class presumptions. Disturbingly it is Francis who embraces both downward class mobility and racial prejudice. A black man or woman cannot be a first-class citizen. He is happy to be absolved from the responsibility for maintaining status on the grounds of race, that he is not strong enough to maintain on ability. Adah's life in London, on the other hand, is predicated on maintaining a middle-class identity rather than struggling against racial prejudice. She certainly encounters the latter, particularly when trying to achieve a stable home in the face of the unwillingness of white landlords to admit black tenants, and she is aware of the compromises that she has to make because of her ethnicity: 'She, who only a few months previously would have accepted nothing but the best, had by now been conditioned to expect inferior things. She was now learning to suspect anything beautiful and pure. Those things were for the whites, not the blacks' (*Citizen* 71). Yet the search for a home is the only significant occasion in the novel where Adah dwells upon racial prejudice as a barrier for achieving her aims. The issue certainly emerges elsewhere, but Adah is rarely confounded by it other than through Francis's deteriorating behaviour.

More troubling is that she is not averse to adopting the worst kind of racial slur when she compares Francis to a gorilla. The reference is clearly intended to indicate his bestial nature as a husband, but is far from a neutral metaphor in the context of 1960s race relations in London. Moreover, the image is highly sexualized, uncomfortably linking bestiality, sexual desire and black men: 'How like animals we all look when we are consumed by our basic desires, thought Adah standing there by the sink, like a wicked temptress luring her male to destruction. All that Francis needed to be taken for a gorilla was simply to bend his knees' (*Citizen* 89). The image is all too potent because Francis is black. While it is possible to imagine the metaphor being used in relation to a white man's sexual aggression, it would scarcely have quite the same negative resonance. The pointed inference of Francis's 'savagery' recalls the characterization of the black Jazz musician in Lynne Reid Bank's *The L-Shaped Room*. That novel is punctuated by comments on John's 'warm, animal smell' (*Room* 51), or his inquisitiveness – 'He's just naturally inquisitive. Like a chimp, you know, he can't help it' (*Room* 46). While Reid Banks's novel strives to reach beyond these stereotypes, Adah is introducing them. By doing so she is enacting a middle-class discourse that would not be remiss among a previous generation of colonialists, but is of particular significance in an age of decolonization. On the one hand Adah's '*we* all look' seems inclusive, yet it is Francis who attracts the bestial comparison. As Alan Sinfield argues:

> The myth of universal savagery is the final, desperate throw of a humiliated and exhausted European humanism. It is informed by both an anxiety about and a continuing embroilment in imperialist ideology. It works like this: when it was just the natives who were brutal, the British were enlightened and necessary rulers. But if the British are (have been) brutal, that's human nature. (Sinfield 141)

While Adah starts with a universalizing 'we', she excludes herself from the 'gorilla' metaphor and thence follows the discursive strategy of the post-imperialist British middle classes. These attitudes would presumably have provided the foundation of her education in what would have still been colonial Nigeria.

What becomes increasingly clear in her narrative is that Francis is the brutal, uncivilized, if not decultured, colonial subject. But rather than allow that this is a legacy of colonialism, it is Nigerian culture that has made him so. Adah's own predilection for the culture and lifestyle of the colonizer is emphasized in her hallucinations under the influence of gas while in labour with her third child. Conjuring a fantasy of future prosperity and happiness with Francis remembering 'their terrible time in London', she imagines 'Titi ... in a convent school in England and Vicky was at Eton' (*Citizen* 112). Adah desperately aspires to British upper-middle-class society and resents it when her racial difference becomes visible through loss of status, such as when she writhes in embarrassment as the only woman in the maternity ward without her own nightdress: 'Adah did not so much mind wearing the shirt-like nightdress, with the blood-coloured stripes. What she minded most was that she was the only woman wearing one' (*Citizen* 122). Moreover, she imagines other people's thoughts through a racially charged lens: '*Look at that nigger woman with no flowers, no cards, no visitors, except her husband ... Look at her, she doesn't have a nightdress of her own*' (*Citizen* 124; italics original).

Adah's behaviour indicates that she believes that class status elides the inequalities of race she encounters in London, contrary to the biracial class solidarity found in *City of Spades*. To some degree her experiences at work support this. The library at Chalk Farm is the epitome of positive middle-class liberalism within a supportive, multi-ethnic, multinational environment. This is Adah's community in London and contrasts with Francis's disapproval of friends. It is Bill, the white Canadian, who introduces her to new 'postcolonial' fiction, beyond the few Nigerian writers like Chinua Achebe and Flora Nwapa of whom she was already aware. Through James Baldwin she learns that 'black was beautiful', and even starts to read Marx (*Citizen* 161). Both would provide a counter discourse to the oppressive self-loathing of Francis, and encourage her to become a writer herself which is, of course, opposed by her husband. Yet the irony of being introduced to this heritage by a white man from a former British colony is difficult to ignore. It is also to Bill that she turns for confirmation that her writing is worthwhile. This realization of Adah as a creative force, nurturing her children, forging friendships and creating novels is, on the face of it, a little too glib. Her sense of potential achievement and success ostensibly creates a very different city:

> But Adah was deep in thought as they crossed Haverstock Hill into Prince of Wales Road, pushing the pram with Vicky trotting by her side, the sun shining in the sky, the day hot and merry like any day in Africa. People were passing her this way and that, all in colourful, sleeveless summer dresses, one or two old people sitting on the benches by the side of the Crescent in front of the pub smiling, showing their stiff dentures, their crooked hats pulled down to shade their tired heads from the unusual sun. She walked into the Crescent where the smell of ripe tomatoes mingled with the odour from the butcher's. But she saw none of this, her mind was turning over so fast. Could Peggy and Bill be right? Could she be a writer, a real one? Did she not feel totally fulfilled when she had completed the manuscript, just as if it was another baby she had had? (*Citizen* 176)

In the first flush of achievement, London becomes a reminiscence of Africa; an 'unusual sun', fragrances from 'ripe tomatoes' and 'the butcher's shop' evoking a sensuous African streetscape. Yet behind Adah's euphoria, London-proper peeks through. While the passers-by in colourful summer clothing do little to disturb these associations, the elderly people's 'stiff dentures', 'crooked hats' and 'tired heads' are all London, signalling that the 'unusual sun' is something alien to Adah's prevailing experience of the city. Her attempt to make an unfamiliar and largely hostile London safe and evocative of Nigeria is closely tied to the potential for success as a writer. What Adah recalls here is her success and status in Nigeria, through a burst of metropolitan nostalgia that mirrors Moses from *The Lonely Londoners*, and his feeling of homesickness as he approaches Waterloo to meet the boat train and the latest arrivals from the Caribbean: 'When he get to Waterloo he hop off and went in the station, and right away in that big station he had a feeling of homesickness that he never felt in the nine-ten years he in this country' (*Lonely* 9). For Moses, such nostalgia is weakness, although even he harbours a vague expectation to return home to Trinidad, and this too lies behind many of Adah's desires – the return to Nigeria and her old life of middle-class respectability.

But for both Moses and Adah, London retains a hold. By the end of *The Lonely Londoners* it is clear that Moses loves the city. His narrative concludes with an epiphany that turns his own thoughts towards writing. The background is the Thames, where storytelling is inextricably tied to the fluctuations and energy of the city as he watches a tugboat drift on the river and meditates on laughter, tears, vastness and greatness (*Lonely* 126), a positive reworking – reversal – of Marlow's boat in Conrad's *Heart of Darkness*. For Adah, the destruction of her first novel at the hands of Francis finally precipitates her final separation and divorce. The aggression directed against her words is matched by violence against her person. These events conclude the final few pages of the novel and leave her stranded and confused outside another butcher's shop in Clerkenwell. Unexpectedly meeting a childhood friend, she finds her status still defined by her awful marriage and the patriarchy she has always resisted: 'This old friend of Adah's paid for the taxi that took her home from Camden Town because he thought she was still with her husband' (*Citizen* 186). Reclaimed from the London streets by another man acting as her husband's social proxy, the final summation of the city for Adah might be read as one of entrapment and a continuing patriarchal restriction.

The syntheses of London and Africa, founded on her new-found power of writing is tied, rather mawkishly, to her identity as a mother. Christine Sizemore suggests of Adah's London that 'although Adah goes to work every day, there is very little description of her public life. The public "space" of the city and even the freedom to work are less important to Adah than the security of a "place" both for herself and her children' (Sizemore 371). This observation has similarities to Selvon's Tanty. For her, 'public' London also warrants little attention and curiosity, by contrast to the endless fascination of the men with the stage they find themselves upon. But Tanty's ability to mould her locality into an accommodation with her values and as credible family 'place' points towards the conflict in Adah's character. She desires public recognition as an educated, middle-class woman, but also the security and happiness of belonging. In this respect, Adah is a considerable advance over the motherly Tanty, whom Francis would most likely respect for her domestic powers and lack of ambition beyond that sphere. The point of synthesis, as it may be for Moses, is in writing. As Michel de Certeau observes, 'Stories thus carry out a labour that constantly transforms places into spaces and spaces into places' (de Certeau 118). London may still provide security of place.

The narrator of *The Lonely Londoners* poses the question: 'What is it that a city have, that any place in the world have, that you get so much to like it you wouldn't leave it for anywhere else?' (*Lonely* 121). While the novels examined in this chapter demonstrate that there is no single literary experience of migration to the city, they share structural and thematic similarities. Each combines elements of the picaresque and *bildungsroman* that has a considerable history in representations of the city. Each journey is predicated on the allures of a mythic London of empire and colonial education, met by various forms of disappointment. Johnny Fortune's London provides a foil for him to test the limits of his freedom. Yet he is the only major character who leaves, a true picaresque figure that retreats back to status, family and responsibility, having sown his wild oats. Yet many of his compatriots remain, having achieved some form of accommodation with the city. But why does London, with all its meanness, cold weather, cold inhabitants, violence and racial prejudice, retain its allure? One could argue that it is purely economic, a better job, a better education, a better standard of living, even better status. But through literary narrative the image of the city is redefined: 'living in cities is an art, and we need the vocabulary of art, of style, to describe the peculiar relationship between man and material that exists in the continual creative play of urban living' (Raban 10). These are not simply social realist documents of immigration and prejudice. They are part of the process that would physically and culturally 'mould the fortunes of the city and its people well into the third millennium of its history' (J. White 131). Moreover, these experiences are London experiences, less reliant on the formulations of postcolonialism, or at the other extreme Enoch Powell, but of familiar narratives that have long contributed to the image and myth of the city.

6

London Revenant

The more uncanny a big city becomes, the more knowledge of human nature ...
it takes to operate in it.

Walter Benjamin, *Charles Baudelaire* (1973)

The history of the city has been of enduring interest to London writers since John Stow's sixteenth-century *Survey of London,* a 45-year project that consumed the time and effort of the writer to the point of abject penury. Stow's obsessiveness has a particular resonance within contemporary forays by novelists into the accreted past of London. While their writing has certainly proved more lucrative than Stow's experience – the writers to be considered in this chapter, Maureen Duffy, Peter Ackroyd, Iain Sinclair and Michael Moorcock, are successful novelists by any measure – it is significant that the form of London's history has been colonized, appropriated, popularized, if not fetishized by creative writers rather than by historians. That is not to say that there have not been several distinguished conventional histories of London in the post-war period, most recently Roy Porter's *London: A Social History* (1994) and Jerry White's *London in the Twentieth Century* (2001). Stow's work also initiated a long tradition of both popularist and more academic 'surveys' of London. Perhaps the best popular example in the post-war period intended for general readership was V. S. Pritchett's *London Perceived* (1962), with photographs by Evelyn Hofer. For more literary inflected surveys Ford Maddox Ford's 1905 *The Soul of London* has been influential and is something of a model – whether consciously acknowledged or otherwise – for Jonathan Raban's *Soft City* (1974).

More recently, versions of both the survey and the history have emerged, offering a dramatic reformulation of both forms. Iain Sinclair's *Lights Out for the Territory: 9 Excursions in the Secret History of London* (1997) and Peter Ackroyd's *London: The Biography* (2000) are, significantly, by writers better known for their fictional work. Unsurprisingly, therefore, both texts stray into realms recognized as the preserve of the creative writer rather than the historian and are indicative of the former's appropriation of the city's past. *Lights Out for the Territory* reformulates Pierre Nora's concept of place towards the urban: 'there are sites, *lieux de mémoire*, in which a residual sense of continuity remains' (Wolfreys 165). Such sites are highly personalized and subjective, but also draw upon recognizable literary and historical associations to create narrative structures that in turn form spatial syntaxes (de Certeau 115). Based on a metaphor of walking that is closely aligned with the practice of reading, Sinclair's text is recognizably of the 'survey' tradition, yet the shift towards the fictional and creative actively establishes a textual situation akin to Michel de Certeau's 'walking rhetorics':

> The long poem of walking manipulates spatial organizations, no matter how panoptic they may be: it is neither foreign to them (it can take place only within them) nor in conformity with them (it does not receive its identity from them). It creates shadows and ambiguities within them. It inserts its multitudinous references and citations into them (social models, cultural mores, personal factors). Within them it is itself the effect of successive encounters and occasions that constantly alter it and make it the other's blazon: in other words, it is like a peddler, carrying something surprising, transverse or attractive compared with the usual choice. These diverse aspects provide the basis of a rhetoric. They can even be said to define it. (de Certeau 101)

Yet in de Certeau's formulation the synchronic rather than diachronic is dominant – it is the present movement, the articulation of a rhetoric, that creates a poesis of walking in which the past becomes a 'reference' or 'citation' among a complex of social, personal and cultural factors. This suggests a further affinity to Sinclair's project. The textual itineraries of his 'excursions' punctuated by *lieux de mémoire* are static, synchronous nodes around which memory, history, social and cultural mores accrete. The 'excursion' a metaphor of movement has become the frame for the static site that accumulates knowledge and experience. Yet there is nothing in Sinclair's formulation equivalent to the dynamic of de Certeau's resistance via movement, even though Sinclair's writing is structured around a journey. The consequence of Sinclair's strategy is to reproduce a form of dominance of both history and space with the regularity of a textual map – the form of panoptic vision that de Certeau's practice of 'walking' would resist. As Paul Werth observes: 'Mental maps ... are built up not only from what we can perceive on any single occasion, but also on our memory of previous occasions, our knowledge of similar situations and inferences we can draw between all of these sources' (Werth 7). At the level of individual practice this aligns with de Certeau's liberationist conceptualization, but translated to the level of the textual Sinclair is dominating both space and place with his 'mental map' for others to trace. It is no longer memory, but discourse.

Peter Ackroyd also approaches London through metaphor. A 'biography' enacts a commonplace city image as an organic entity (Ford's 'soul' of London draws upon the same tradition). Indeed, Ackroyd's first chapter, 'The city as body', makes his intent clear, as does his suggestion that London is a labyrinth. These three images – 'biography', 'body' and 'labyrinth' – are a form of hyperbole; discursive strategies that attempt to limit and define. A 'biography' suggests a beginning and an end, while a body has discrete boundaries and also, as an organism, a definite beginning and end. A 'labyrinth', while perhaps endlessly perplexing, is still a structure with boundaries even if they are difficult to perceive from within. In contradiction, Ackroyd also claims that the city 'defies chronology' (Ackroyd 2001 2) so that despite this rhetorical containment, London escapes the one biological limit that determines the extent of all 'bodies' and 'life' histories. London is anthropomorphized into an entity which, bizarrely, hints at agency. Ackroyd goes so far as to hint at a Frankenstein's monster image for London, formed 'half of stone and half of flesh'. While this neatly encapsulates the nature of the city as a compound of inanimate structure and biological inhabitants, it also conjoins the living with the dead, inanimate matter with the bodies that swarm within. For a 'living body', the thematic taxonomy that follows is remarkably static. Chapter headings like 'The sea!', 'The stones', 'The crossroads' sit uneasily alongside the more conventional 'London's opera' and 'A London address', and the colloquial 'Silence is golden' and 'Raw lobsters and others'. And while there remains a chronology within his section and chapter headings, he is adamant that 'Contemporary theorists have suggested that linear time is itself a figment of the human imagination' (Ackroyd 2001 2). In narrative terms, his attempt to encapsulate an absent chronology is at odds with the linearity of story-time that lies behind any narrative, not to mention the actual chronology of the process of reading. In short, his text becomes an elaborate deceit to promote the conceit that London 'defies chronology'. If true, no narrative of the city would be possible.

The difficulty facing both Sinclair and Ackroyd is the essential problem of attempting to import aesthetic forms that privilege consciousness into a discourse, history, which proceeds on the assumption that the vagaries of consciousness can be minimized in a narrative of fact. As Hayden White argues:

> When we seek to make sense of such problematical topics as human nature, culture, society, and history, we never say precisely what we wish to say or mean precisely what we say. Our discourse always tends to slip away from our data towards the structures of consciousness with which we are trying to grasp them; or, what amounts to the same thing, the data always resist the coherency of the image which we are trying to fashion of them. (H. White 1).

In historical discourse, such slippage must be resisted and obscured, otherwise the conceit of objectivity is revealed to be tainted with subjectivity. In literary technique, a willingness to allow this slippage to occur between the structures of consciousness is the very aesthetic impetus that marks out the literary text. While both Sinclair and Ackroyd gesture towards such an aestheticization of historical discourse, their narratives never quite surrender to this impulse entirely. What results is the defamiliarization of London as narrative. In his essay 'Art as Technique', Victor Shklovsky argued that 'art exists that one may recover the sensation of life; it exists to make one feel things, to make the stone *stony*' (Rabkin 80). Literary representations of London's history therefore exist to create an impression, a representation, of the city as lived experience – not of course 'reality' itself. History attempts to reconstitute a record of life lived – not of course 'lived experience'. History relies on literary technique insofar as its narrative familiarizes and regulates the past. Literature relies on history insofar as narrative defamiliarizes and liberates the past, as Brian McHale observes: ' "A character cannot walk out of a fictional house and show up in a real café," writes Hrushovski. Of course not; but historical fiction often strives to give the illusion that the *opposite* can happen, that a historical figure can walk out of a real café and show up in a fictional house' (McHale 90).

But what of the city? The impetus behind both Sinclair's and Ackroyd's narratives is to make the commonplace unfamiliar. In an era where so much of the world is amorphous, mass produced, standardized and lacking in the sense of solidity and distinctiveness, reminding the reader of the uniqueness of place is a major task if the city is not merely to perform the function of background or incidental setting. How many post-war buildings have been constructed to last beyond a few decades? It is difficult to imagine a 1960s tower block still standing tall in London's skyline of 2060, or indeed the Millennium Dome, subject to a particularly sharp Sinclair diatribe in *Sorry Meniscus: Excursions to the Millennium Dome* (1999). Even the modern landmark building is largely assembled from glass and steel rather than brick and stone. Modern buildings have their obsolescence literally built into them; they are the ultimate prefabrications. This statement is not intended to promote nostalgia for a low-rise London of brick and stone in place of what is often a distinctive modern architecture (the idea that buildings might be renewed every few decades is in many ways an attractive one), but is indicative of a different kind of city conceptualization. As Stephen Barber suggests:

> The cities of Europe metamorphose rapidly. Each component is dispensable and may be restructured at will at any moment: the arrangement of the city is constantly cut, impacted, expanded. The flux between the city and its inhabitants is a site of ferocious visual tension,

with imaginaries generated that collapse and reformulate the perception of the city, its languages, its societies, its nationalities, its cultures.
(Barber 9)

Barber's 'ferocious visual tension' emerges between the visual permanence of the buildings of earlier – particularly Victorian – eras and
the visual disposability of the present. This is not to suggest that
Victorian or any other era's architecture actually embodies permanence, but rather the way in which modern building materials suggest
impermanence. This tension between the material artefacts of earlier
cities and the present is of course always present, and existed in the
Victorian and Georgian cities, and earlier. What has changed is the
way in which the contemporary moment only builds under the promise of erasure within a few decades. The status of the material vestiges of the past are reformulated and gain in mythic and aesthetic
significance within a perceptual uncanniness, as Vidler argues: 'the
"uncanny" is not a property of the space itself nor can it be provoked
by any particular spatial conformation; it is, in its aesthetic dimension
a representation of a mental state of projection that precisely elides
the boundaries of the real and the unreal in order to provoke a
disturbing ambiguity, a slippage between waking and dreaming'
(Vidler 11). It is no accident that Sinclair's and Ackroyd's engagement with the past in *Lights Out* and *The Biography* share a halluci-
nogenic tone.

When turning towards fiction, the polarities of the issue facing
Sinclair and Ackroyd in these essentially non-fictional texts are
reversed. The status of history in fiction demands different strategies.
The challenge of the contemporary city, however, remains constant.
This chapter examines three novels from the 1970s and 1980s,
beginning with Maureen Duffy's *Capital* (1975), Peter Ackroyd's
Hawksmoor (1985) and Michael Moorcock's *Mother London* (1988),
each of which tackles the eruptions of the city's past into a modern
fictional narrative. There are similarities in technique. All four novels
incorporate a split and fragmented narrative, but there is also distinct
development between them. It is no accident that the contemporary
moment for each text is either on the cusp of or soon after the
nation's turn to the right and what came to be known as Thatcherism.
In many respects, Margaret Thatcher's denial of contemporary
society, and desire to return to largely mythical Victorian certainties,
captures the urban sensibility that I have traced above. A disposable,
impermanent, consumerist urban present is no match for the imagined monolith of the past. Indeed, it would be Margaret Thatcher's
government that would undo the successor to the belated unity
granted the city in the form of the London County Council. The
demise of the Greater London Council (GLC) removed any unitary
authority for London as a whole, unique in Europe for a major city.

Yet not all the blame is a matter for Margaret Thatcher. The GLC was poorly conceived, the relationship between it and the London boroughs was a recipe for confusion and the left-leaning GLC leadership actively sought confrontation with a right-wing government, with little thought of the cost for London. This was a systemic failure of both the city's government and its status within the nation.

The contradictions of Thatcher's policies can be traced between this avowal of Victorian values 'intended to ... [evoke] a time when aggressive competition co-existed with tradition, family, religion, respectability and deference' (Sinfield 296), and fears that 'the free market has a tendency to subvert traditions having a turbulent effect upon culture and morality' (Graham and Clarke 86). The London that these texts incorporate is a city where urban identity is under threat. The response is an emphasis on the past. Indeed, in a period of regressive social and economic policies, all three novels are populated by economically marginal, disenfranchised Londoners who appear either centrally or on the fringes of the narrative. An underclass created by the inequalities of government policies, but an underclass onto which the burden of London, however disturbing, is thrust. The uncanny is not just a matter of city spaces, but also of people. Meepers, the co-protagonist of Duffy's *Capital*, is an obsessive London antiquarian who has been priced out of the district where he was born by gentrification. Now groundskeeper of the London square where he grew up, he lives covertly in his work shed in constant fear of eviction. The effect is estranging and marginalizing. Effectively homeless in his own home, it is upon him that the burden of London's past is loaded in the novel. The research question upon which his obsession rests is to seek nothing less than historical precedent to show that London and its culture will not collapse: 'If the city survived then I think it will again. It's threatened, you must see that ... We are out of love with it because we're out of love with ourselves. What might really destroy us is human self-disgust' (*Capital* 152). The two other narrative threads of the novel embody these two themes – love and historical continuity.

In the first, the co-protagonist of the narrative is an unnamed historian based at a fictional University of London college called Queen's (a fictionalized King's College, perhaps), who becomes increasingly involved with Meepers after he rejects an essay by him for his academic journal, *Studies in History*, as 'too early and conjectural' (*Capital* 116). In response, Meepers takes a job as a porter at the College and covertly joins a summer school being conducted by the historian. Meepers's act is a quiet challenge and it is clear that the historian has been rattled by his first encounter with him. When he begins to appear about college and then in his lecture, he grows more disturbed and reveals in a letter to his estranged partner in the United States: 'For a moment I really thought I'd gone mad or that I was mistaken and then he looked up and smiled at me. It was almost a relief' (*Capital* 31). His narrative begins as a series of letters to his partner in an attempt to fill the gap of her absence – such an epistolary narrative is rather apt, given his specialism in the eighteenth century. He is clearly out of love with himself as much as people are with the city, and this is the likely cause of their separation.

The third narrative thread is a series of short vignettes of past moments and lives throughout London's history. Beginning with the death of a Neanderthal mother and concluding with an experience from the Blitz, Meepers, the historian and others become part of the sequence by the conclusion of the novel. These interventions are not 'historical' in a formal sense, but 'fictional' and conjectural like Meepers's essay. Clearly, all three narrative threads are part of a larger investigation into the nature of London's past. Moreover, it is clear that formal history is not sufficient to do that past justice. The issue is dramatized in the novel when the historian is seeking a way to clarify his explanation of the South Sea Bubble and the National Debt, but is borne down with the enormity of what he is trying to explain – the 'enormous symbolic construct' finance (*Capital* 70). It is Meepers who manages to define the issue and a way through the historian's rhetorical aporia:

> Then the symbol was invented that could represent them all and be exchanged for any of them. Coin came to symbolize not only the things but their relationship to each other and then relationships between the people through whose hands it passed. Because it is a symbol not a reality money can be inflated or depressed not only by realities like famine or a rich harvest but by illusions, imagination, falls in confidence, alarms, jobbery. (*Capital* 70)

This passage draws attention to the multiple meanings of the novel's title; *the* capital is London, although capital is also money and financing – the roots of the city in commercial success is a factor within several of the micro-narratives of its past – but above all, cultural capital. Meepers has lost status and his home to the gentrification of his childhood neighbourhood, but retains a strong sense of cultural capital in his connection with the city. He represents an indigenous middle-class London identity – part of an 'organic' London community – that is being displaced by a socially mobile middle-class which is a post-war phenomenon identified as early as the 1950s in Gibbons's *A Pink Front Door*. Many of these incomers are scarcely Londoners in the 'traditional' sense and have little real investment in place. There is a tension in Gibbons's novel between James's nostalgia for an abstracted middle-class identity based on Victorian deference and Oxbridge (which he does not experience himself), and Daisy's attempt to reform or preserve a London community by propping up those who have come adrift in the city. In *The Lonely Londoners* it is the establishment of community that enables Tanty and Moses to become Londoners, even if that identity reflects an ongoing struggle. As a consequence of a failure of community, London begins to lose identity by becoming less distinctive. The contrast is replicated in the distinction between Meepers's and the Historian's disagreement over what represents valid historical discourse. Formal history is abstract and not embedded in local communities, and therefore does not value Meepers's conjectural feeling for London's past. Even though the historian comes from a working-class London background, he has risen in social and financial status by practising a culturally valued appropriation of the past within the academy, becoming detached from his own origins in the process.

In terms of relative wealth and cultural capital, the historian has risen while Meepers has declined. This has not been without cost for the historian: 'Any name is strong enough to break my bones since I no longer wear any stylistic shield to protect my damaged ego. How I long for some positive assertion of identity like a cloth cap and neckerchief, preferably red spotted' (*Capital* 45). Yet because of the modest origins of his forebears he is able to deflect responsibility for acts of oppression carried out by Britain in the past, such as empire and the slave trade. The contradiction, of course, is that by entering the academy he has inherited an intellectual tradition that is indelibly complicit with those acts. The displacement of this contradiction is expressed through his disconnection from London. By contrast to Meepers, he has lost his association with place, the neighbourhood where he grew up. It is only much later in the novel that he reconnects with the city in this fashion:

> ...on the way back with Meepers in the copcar, and maybe on the way over too but I didn't notice, we drove past where I was born and that I haven't seen for years. I don't even know if it's important. The city is a twenty-mile diameter cake. We live in a wedge of it, travel into the centre down our narrowing triangle, know the base of our portion, the bits to the right and left of us but no further as if it were indeed boxed, sliced into these segments by uncrossable chasms. Immediately opposite this wedge beyond the centre is the bit where I was born, where Meepers was fossicking about for his Roman remains. Yet it is further from me than Paris. And there we were driving through it.... I've never taken you there have I? I wonder why: I'm not ashamed of it, at least not consciously. But it had become irrelevant and perhaps that's wrong. I haven't been back since my father was killed. I went back for the funeral and didn't know what to do or say, not out of grief but because I'd lost the idiom ... (*Capital* 167–8)

The historian's image of London as a cake points to the lack of a unifying principle – community – that Meepers is seeking to recover. Even though he has culturally and physically traversed London to become an academic, this has meant cutting the ties to his past at each stage. In many respects, Albert in Johnson's *Albert Angelo* is a character at an earlier stage of this social process. For instance, his visits to his parents in Hammersmith – his original community – have become a duty and would probably not continue if he ever realized his dream to become an architect. Indeed, one could argue that his unwillingness to sever such ties is linked to his reluctance to actually take the final step and work at his designs. Even so, he has, like Duffy's historian, lost the idiom and finds it difficult to comprehend the working-class students of his final school.

History, as opposed to the past, is being likened to an 'enormous symbolic construct' that is in turn linked to class and power. The historian's model of London is a product of the city's historicization. By inserting himself into history, the historian unconsciously erases his past by accepting boundaries and restrictions that are not only psychological and cultural, but in effect become physical as the travel motif of his image suggests. This recalls de Certeau's distinction between form and use in the city: 'Use defines the social phenomenon through which a system of communication manifests itself in actual fact' (de Certeau 100). The historian has accepted the boundaries of his class and profession – the ideological form – and is, as a consequence, disassociated from the city as a whole. In a broader sense, this points to the formlessness of the city, which Meepers argues presages dissolution. His own practice by contrast, leans towards the archaeological rather than the historical. His desire to recover the physical artefacts of the past contrasts with the way formal history prefers to create narratives from eras that abound in textual evidence. Formal history is a discontinuous narrative; the gaps form when textual material is absent: 'It's the historical obscurity of that period in this country. Classical Rome and Greece fit in because they belong to recorded history even in decline. The Dark Ages are different, more like paleo and neo and so on. History isn't continuous' (*Capital* 116). But the accretion of the past *is* continuous and closely tied to the lived experience of the city. London may have a discontinuous historical record – particularly between records of the fall of the Roman Britain and the rise of the Anglo-Saxon city – but Meepers seeks proof that the city persisted. His strategy has some similarities to the utilization of the past in fiction rather than in formal history. As McHale argues:

> 'Classic' historical fiction from Scott through Barth tries to make this transgression as discreet, as nearly unnoticeable as possible, camouflaging the seam between historical reality and fiction ... by introducing pure fiction only in the 'dark areas' of the historical; by avoiding anachronisms; by matching the 'inner structure' of its fictional worlds to that of the real world. (McHale 90)

Meepers's unspecified conjectural history of the Dark Age city rejected by the historian serves the same purpose. By spanning the gap between recorded, textual history with a speculative narrative based on probabilities, he challenges disciplinary boundaries. The question, of course, is why the textual artefacts of the city's past should be more reliable?

Historical gaps are profoundly uncanny and so, by extension, are the aporias in the history of the city. In seeking to fill them, Meepers in fact conforms to the aims of the formal historian: 'Understanding is a process of rendering the unfamiliar, or the "uncanny" in Freud's sense of that term, familiar' (H. White 5). In the novel, this not only extends to London but also to some Londoners. The historian has forgotten or suppressed his past, and its rediscovery enables him to open up to feelings he has denied, in relation to both his father and his estranged partner. More cynically, one of his colleagues, Wandle, is busy writing 'an apologia for my generation' (*Capital* 46) to counter historical reappraisal that threatens his self-conceptualization. Both concern memory. The first is the recovery of self as feeling, the second a battle over self as discourse. But crucially they are also attempts to create or achieve understanding, to reconcile the 'uncanny' or unfamiliar in their respective pasts that have been made untenable by the revisions of the present. Once more, the comparison is between the conjectural and the discursive, but both are struggles over revision. The historian revises his feelings about his father and his modest childhood in a working-class neighbourhood; whereas Wandle wishes to revise negative contemporary accounts of movements he has aligned himself with in the past. Meepers's project in relation to London has the same impetus. As such, he too shares in the 'will to power' ethos of historical discourse. This can be mapped by the symbolic rise represented by his various 'squats' across London, which parodies his earlier decline in status. From the gardener's shed on the square where he grew up, he is forced to move to another caretaker's lodge in Hyde Park, a brief sojourn in the home of the historian back on the square, and next door to the one where he spent his childhood, and then a washroom on the 11th floor of an unoccupied office building. As his project nears completion, he achieves a residence with a panoptic view of central London. Yet rather than the sense of power initially felt by residents in Ballard's *High-Rise*, he feels their later self-diminishment:

> Aloft in his block index fingering the sky he still remained related to things he knew. He could look South as far as St Paul's riding floodlit into the night, serene as if incendiaries had never menaced it. But in this split level Ziggurat he felt himself dwarfed, overpowered, become less than a Lowry imp gangling matchstick limbs through a satanic factory townscape. (*Capital* 182)

This is an intriguing passage. Drawn 'to the things he knew', Meepers evokes one of the great iconic images of Second World War London, St Paul's eerily lit by the fires of surrounding bombed buildings but unscathed, while he 'felt himself dwarfed, overpowered'. Indeed, this iconic London vista is also compared to a 'satanic factory landscape'. It is London made unfamiliar, unhomely. Meepers is more than just cowed by the panorama of London, he is actively terrified. Yet a few paragraphs later he vehemently utters 'Let her live' (*Capital* 183).

The unease within this passage is of the present. Not only is Meepers seeking some assurance of continuity for the city, he wants to actively prognosticate that continuity. Through the historian he arranges to have programmed into a large computer at Queen's all the data that his investigation into the past have suggested to him as significant events indicative of the fate of the city. That he does not contemplate assembling such a narrative himself is suggestive. Unwilling to resort to the creative patchwork of narrative history, he chooses the systematic logic of a computer program. Yet the 'idea' of the machine introduces further complexities. On one level it enacts an image of similar provenance to Ackroyd's Frankenstein's monster image. Information assembled via the judgement of a man will be processed by the computer – the conjoining of the living with the inanimate. Rather than Ackroyd's image of London as 'half of stone and half of flesh', the city has become half imagination and half circuitry; *poiesis* and *tekhne.* Yet as the computer's programmer points out: 'There is a sense ... in which it can't tell us anything we don't already know – except that we don't know we know it' (*Capital* 85). As the historian interjects, 'that's metaphysics', but it is also a representation of the city. As Julian Wolfreys observes, 'London is unavailable to any generalisation' (Wolfreys 4), a conundrum which establishes a city that is intimately known, endlessly symbolized, but ungraspable. The signifier 'London' is unable to contain the content of the city, a 'proper name' around which forms the 'imaginary community' of the city. Likewise, a single governing body for London faces conflicting identitifications and conflicts over boundaries. Meepers's fear for the future of the city, and the historian's awareness of its fragmentation as a lived experience evokes the contemporary confusion over London's administration as a single entity, place and space:

> Maybe all this would not have mattered so badly had not the London Government Act shared so much power at local level between the boroughs and the GLC. Maybe, most of all, it would have mattered less had the times been more propitious. But the late 1960s and 1970s were years when there was fundamental disagreement over every element of change in London ... indeed, there was furious dispute ... Getting things done in such a tempestuous climate proved noisy, bloody and endlessly protracted. (J. White 389)

This returns the reader to the historical fragments that punctuate the contemporary narrative. What is their status? One possibility is that they are a selection from Meepers's material to be fed into the computer. They are certainly conjectural. The prehistoric examples begin with early human communities along the Thames valley, but then introduce elaborations of English myth: Arthur (Artor) and Merlin (Murddin), the former being transformed into the title of a tribal shaman (*Capital* 56–66); King Lud (Lludd) the mythical founder of London, who is conflated with King Lear and his daughters (*Capital* 72–4). With the initiation of the Roman period (*Capital* 81–3) the fantastic does not entirely disappear with the anthropomorphization of the thoughts of a plague-carrying flea (*Capital* 127–9), but there also emerges a ludic view of historical 'London' myths. Elizabeth I is characterized as King Elizabeth (*Capital* 158–60), and Dick Whittington is presented via a dramatic parody anticipating the future of his story as a perennial pantomime favourite (*Capital* 148–9). There are other clearly historical figures such Sir Thomas More in the tower (*Capital* 154–5). Later interjections increasingly focus on 'ordinary' Londoners in specific historical periods until the present day of the novel. All the interjections reveal the inner thoughts of the focalized characters within them, whether prehistoric, historic, or fantastic like the flea. The very conjecture rejected by formal history, but a recognizable strategy. The historical fantasies also create a particular rhythm. The novel is divided into five sections – 'The City of the Dead', 'New Troy', 'Respublica Londiniensis', 'Babylon' and 'Cockaigne' – all of which are of approximately equal length with the exception of the final section, which is half the length of the others. Proportionately, sections three and five ('Respublica Londiniensis' and 'Cockaigne') have the most historical interjections. Section three has eight interjections and section five has five (which, since it is half the length of the other sections, reflects a frequency equivalent to, if not slightly higher than, section three). Historically, section three takes us from the end of the eleventh century to the end of the sixteenth century, while the interjections in section five are all twentieth-century manifestations. All the other sections have three or four interjections and relate to varying lengths of chronological time.

There seems to be little connection between the historical span of the interjections and the frequency of their appearance in the narrative, although this is contrasted by the close correlation between the lengths of the sections with the exception of section five. On the one hand this careful division of the novel into sections represents a symmetrical pace; the duration and frequency of the interjections fluctuate, increasing considerably in sections three and five. There is a clear creative tension within the narrative between regularity and fluctuation that echoes the creative tension Meepers seeks between imagination and logic, by turning to the computer to both assess

London's past and prognosticate the future. Yet the increased frequency of section three also coincides with the formation of a closer connection between Meepers and the historian, when the latter rescues him from police arrest after one of his nightly archaeological expeditions. This closer relationship leads directly to the historian's proposal that Meepers's project should be submitted to the computer. Section five finds the characters awaiting the result of the computer analysis, which is never finally given – instead the narrative concludes with Meepers's death and the departure of the historian for the USA, to be reunited with his estranged partner.

Despite withholding the computer's output, the novel has provided the answer in advance. The prologue and epilogue reflect a future time when most of human civilization has abandoned the cities, presumably for some form of mass suburbanism in contrast to which the ruins of the cites are inexplicable and uncanny: 'Really weird. Kilometres of weeds and rusting iron between broken walls like a filmset' (*Capital* 221) – but London persists: 'Think of the organization needed to run a place like that, the energy and resources it would consume. I mean like not just fossil energy, human nervous energy, psychic energy' (*Capital* 221). As Burton Pike observes:

> Cities are a plural phenomenon: there are many of them, but though each has its individual history, they all seem to exemplify similar patterns. The most basic of these is the interpretation of past and present. On the one hand there is the visible city of streets and buildings, frozen forms of energy fixed at different times in the past and around which the busy kinetic energy of the present swirls. On the other hand there are the subconscious currents arising in the minds of the city's living inhabitants from this combination of past and present. (Pike 4)

Capital is an attempt to capture, or rather represent, these kinetic energies of the past and present in literary narrative, through a number of creative tensions. The most important of these is the encounter between the part mythic, part historical, and part conjectural conceptualization of London in Meepers's mind; the physical manifestation of the past codified by historical discourse; and the logical order of the technological mind, the computer. This is replicated through several levels of the novel – Meepers's partnership with the historian; the careful narrative pacing of the equal length of four out of the five sections, balanced against the variable frequency of the historical interjections which increase the pace in sections three and five; the tension between a past, validated by physical evidence and a historical discourse based on textual evidence; the familiarity of the city and its potential, at its experiential fault lines, to create moments of acute uncanniness. Yet is this novel an attempt to recreate London in narrative, or a narrative that actively creates London?

Writing on postmodern fiction, Brian McHale argues that such fiction 'revises the *content* of the historical record, reinterpreting the historical record, often demystifying or debunking the orthodox version of the past. Secondly, it revises, indeed transforms, the conventions and norms of historical fiction' (McHale 90). There is certainly something transformative about *Capital*. The conjectural fictionalization of London myth and history, the ideological and personal struggle over that transformation and the very structure of the novel, speak to this, but the object is not historical fiction as a genre, but London as a form of historical fiction enacted, manipulated, redefined in multifarious forms in the imaginations of its readers as 'spatial syntaxes'. The city has, of course, its physical artefacts and the material experience of everyday life, but as a concept it derives its existence from 'human nervous energy, psychic energy' (*Capital* 221) that cannot be reduced to the single formula Meepers desires. His final thoughts reflect on this impossibility: 'He couldn't keep track of it all. He had failed and they knew he had' (*Capital* 213). For Duffy, London is an open-ended process, a community, of which fragments can be traced or represented through metaphor and narrative form, but the city itself generates an energy that resists static definition.

The relationship between the material landmarks of London and the psychological manifestation of the city as past and present is very much the preoccupation of Peter Ackroyd's *Hawksmoor*. Here, too, there is careful narrative manipulation of the past as artefact and history as discourse. The novel offers two narratives. The first is the recreation of a first-person memoir by an early eighteenth-century architect. A survivor of both the Great Plague and the Fire of London who has risen to a responsible position in the Office of Works at Scotland Yard under the direction of Sir Christopher Wren, where he is commissioned to erect a series of new churches across central London and Westminster. The second is a contemporary narrative of a successful police detective investigating a string of serial murders at New Scotland Yard. The spatial continuity is a significant strategy in the novel, as is historical manipulation. The 1711 commission for the churches and the architect for those completed are a matter of historical record – Nicholas Hawksmoor – yet the character in the novel is named as Nicholas Dyer. The police detective of the contemporary narrative is, significantly, Nicholas Hawksmoor. This transposition is emphasized in the novel's title, which is not the fictionalized Hawksmoor–Dyer, but the real architect of the extant churches and the protagonist of the contemporary narrative. The fictional history of Nicholas Dyer bears no relation to what is known about the historical Hawksmoor beyond the church commission (little is in fact known about the private life and origins of Hawksmoor). The police detective of the contemporary narrative is more easily negotiable as fictional, despite the obvious historical association with his name.

The construction of the plot around definite, named, locales in London and focused on a series of landmark buildings requires that readers negotiate the relationship between the physical artefacts of the past and historical narrative. Or put more exactly in this context, the physical residue of the city's past in its buildings, and the narratives that create for those buildings a contemporary logic. Moreover, the novel is also explicitly intertextual, drawing attention to its origins in another text, Iain Sinclair's poem *Lud Heat*, in an acknowledgement on the final page of the novel:

> Any relation to real people, either living or dead, is entirely coincidental. I have employed many sources in the preparation of *Hawksmoor*, but this version of history is my own invention. I would like to express my obligation to Iain Sinclair's poem, *Lud Heat*, which first directed my attention to the stranger characteristics of the London churches. (*Hawksmoor* 218, unnumbered)

While appended to the final page of the novel, this acknowledgement is significant for a number of reasons. The first line – 'Any relation to real people, either living or dead, is entirely coincidental' – provokes a wry smile. In a narrative that deliberately contrasts a fictional narrative around both historical artefacts and figures, and then works to break down the usual barriers between historical and fictional narrative, this asserts the mischievous pattern of the whole. This is a real contrast to the serious tone of the 'historical' fictionalizations in *Capital*. Next, 'this version of history is my own invention' implies that history *is* invention woven around 'sources', presumably of a textual nature. This contrasts with the acknowledgement of another literary text from which the narrative, ironically, acquires its material grounding in the churches. Sinclair's *Lud Heat* provides the material referent which textual 'sources' do not, lending the literary 'source' material anchouring denied the historical 'record'.

This text is deliberately provocative. On the one hand, it is strongly mimetic. The eighteenth-century discourse of Dyer is convincing in the best traditions of the historical novel, while contemporary London and its various idioms is also 'believable'. And yet the representation of the churches within a contemporary landscape and as historical artefact challenges the very fundamentals of historical fiction, and indeed, history in literature. Lukács's formulation of history in literature indicates a more subtle possibility: 'What is being reflected in a correct work and failing to be reflected in an unmediated one is a whole objective *form* of reality, something which is far less immediate and tangible' (Forgacs 173). Indeed, as with *Capital*, it is the form and structure of the narrative that is the most striking initial feature of the novel; a facet of the text that is stressed within the two narratives. Dyer's narrative begins with a clear, spatial elaboration of the plot in the form of an instruction to his bumbling assistant:

'And so let us beginne; and, as the fabrick takes Shape in front of you, always keep the Structure intirely in Mind as you inscribe it. First, you must measure out or cast the Area in as exact a Manner as can be, and then you must draw the Plot and make the Scale' (*Hawksmoor* 5). While, Hawksmoor, the detective, an archetypal character in search of a plot, reflects: 'If I knew the end, I could begin, couldn't I? I can't have one without the other' (*Hawksmoor* 114), and a few pages later he describes the investigation as 'according to the book', only to admit 'perhaps there is no book in this case' (*Hawksmoor* 118). The architect and the detective – the former creating a plot physically inscribed in stone, and the latter searching for connections between events and places to unravel the narrative and reach the conclusion.

The relationship between the two narratives extends further than just the coincidence of place and the playful transposition of names. Dyer plots a series of murders around the construction of his churches in accordance with occult practices, and Hawksmoor unravels a corresponding series of murders about those same churches in the contemporary narrative. The narrative link is made clear early on in the novel. Hawksmoor the detective does not appear until chapter six, the two earlier contemporary chapters, two and four, relate the experiences of two victims, a young boy and a vagrant that mirror Dyer's murders. Both chapters introduce strong intimations of the supernatural, but not so far that the experiences could not be explained as uncanny since the 'victims' are hallucinating at the time of their death as a consequence of exhaustion, hunger and, in the case of the young boy, physical injury. When Hawksmoor enters the narrative, the parallel plots haunt each other as Dyer becomes increasingly paranoid as he feels hunted, and Hawksmoor becomes equally as paranoid, hunting a spectre that is always just beyond his grasp. Both, in the end, lose their position and the final chapter has them meeting in one of Dyer's/Hawksmoor's churches. Until this moment, the fantastic has been kept at bay and even at this moment they could both easily be interpreted as insane. While the two narratives are peppered with coincidences that seem to link them structurally, it is left up to the reader to choose a fantastic or uncanny explanation in his/her interpretation of the plot. Often, the hiatus is never quite so easy to resolve. The effect is sinister and disturbing, which returns us to Lukács and his observations about history and literary form. Are we to read this as a mediated '*form* of reality', in which case London is the object of scrutiny within the novel, which Ackroyd's acknowledgement suggests? If so, then what is being said about London?

The focus on physical locale generates a form of reification in which the balance of representation is shifted away from the relationship between the city's inhabitants towards the relationship between things. The major source of the disturbance this text creates is the way it prises the frozen forms of energy in the city – the streets and buildings – away from the kinetic energy of lived experience. In the process, all the human inhabitants of this London are marginal and borne down upon by the extreme uncanniness of the inanimate city, which becomes both monolithic and acutely disturbing, as Dyer concludes his instruction of his assistant: 'I have imparted to you the Principles of Terrour and Magnificence' (*Hawksmoor* 5). In a similar way, the dual narrative prises the contemporary away from the containment of the past, through the pacification of historical discourse. The past is a source of alienating disturbance, of domination, rather than reassurance and continuity. Indeed, the novel's final words are apocalyptic: 'And then in my dream I looked down at myself and saw in what rags I stood; and I am a child again, begging on the threshold of eternity' (*Hawksmoor* 217).

Yet the novel does not ignore the modern strategies of containment, if not hope, that we saw in Duffy's *Capital*, although with considerable ambivalence. Two scientific discourses are deployed against the past that set up points of comparison. They both replicate Meepers's hopes for the future – computer analysis and archaeology. In *Capital*, the material anchouring of the past through its physical artefacts was set in contrast to 'authorized' historical discourse based on the textual and archival record. In contrast to the reassuring domesticity of Meepers's Roman shard, the archaeological dig beside St Mary Woolnoth in *Hawksmoor* does not reveal any evidence of the phenomenal city, but rather compounded historical levels that have been dug through and back in time:

> 'What have you found here?'
> 'Oh, flint blocks, some bits of masonry. That's a foundation trench there, you see.' As she talked she was scraping the skin off the palm of her hand. 'But what have *you* found?'
> Hawksmoor chose to ignore the question. 'And how far down have you reached?' he asked her, peering into the dark pit at his feet.
> 'Well it's all very complicated, but at this point we've got down to the sixth century. It really is a treasure trove. As far as I'm concerned we could keep on digging for ever'. And as Hawksmoor looked down at what he thought was freshly opened earth, he saw his own image staring back up at him from the plastic sheeting. (*Hawksmoor* 161)

The manner in which Hawksmoor's question is thrown back at him – 'what have *you* found?' – forces a comparison between the respective activities of the archaeologist and the detective. Both are trying to discover what has happened in a defined location, in fact the same location – the church St Mary Woolnoth. Both seek to reconstruct the lives of the dead. Yet the implications for Hawksmoor's investigation are not good. For the archaeologist, the past does not have a definable beginning or an end: 'we could keep on digging for ever'. The point for the archaeologist is the record of and investigation into the residue of the past, not its containment into a narrative plot with beginning and an end – the dead and the trauma of death resolved and contained. That is the historian's and the detective's job. When Hawksmoor sees himself staring back at him from the past, the moment is disturbingly uncanny but also suggests continuity. It is *his* past as a Londoner of which the present succeeds. And yet, it is also the living as a revenant, the dead in the present, death in life. In much the same way as the physical monuments of the past persist in London, so people are being memorialized in this novel; the combination of past and present in the minds of the city's inhabitants represents a form of material trace, its *form* 'a social and historical reality with a dialectical shape' (Forgacs 172).

The opportunity held out by computer analysis replicates Meepers's hopes in *Capital* – to bring logic and accord to a mass of disparate information. Yet Hawksmoor the detective is singularly unimpressed by the mystique of technological resolution when his assistant, Walter – another doubled character, Dyer's assistant shares the same name – attempts to interest him in the police computer:

> 'But it's much more efficient, sir. Think of all the agony it saves us!' He now entered a different command, although his hands barely seemed to move across the keyboard. And yet despite his excitement it seemed to Walter that the computer itself only partly reflected the order and lucidity to which he aspired – that the composition of these little green digits, glowing slightly even in the morning light, barely hinted at the infinite calculability of the world outside. And how bright that world now seemed to him, as a face formed in an 'identikit' composition, flickering upon the screen with green shading in place of shadow so that it resembled a child's drawing. 'Ah,' Hawksmoor said, 'the green man did it.' (*Hawksmoor* 160)

The inside/outside opposition established by this passage has a thematic impact across the narrative. The world outside is of 'infinite calculability', whereas the world 'reflected' by the computer is one of 'order and lucidity', but there is little to link them. The illumination that excites Walter – 'how bright that world now seemed to him' – as the supposed face of the murderer is exposed, has no more status than a child's drawing. Ironically, it is with the death of children or adults with a child-like disposition that Dyer has sought to 'consecrate' the occult significance of his churches: 'and this Thought came to me ... need the Sacrifice be a Child, and not one who has become a Child?' (*Hawksmoor* 64). The implication for the computerized, partial representation of London is that it produces a child-like vision of the city which Dyer is attempting to sacrifice in recognition of the 'true' disorder. He seeks to expurgate a simply rendered, ordered and logical imaginary city to reveal the chaos below:

'But this Capital City of the World of Affliction is still the Capitol of Darknesses, or the Dungeon of Man's Desires' (*Hawksmoor* 47). A chaos only he can perceive, appreciate and ride. And yet, like Meepers, his attempt is a will-to-power desire. He compares his churches to the pyramids, monuments that attempt to exert human will after death: 'they seemed to the People to be reigning after their Death' (*Hawksmoor* 56).

In many senses, of course, the fabric of the city inherited from previous generations does just that. Buildings and street plans designed for one purpose can be adapted for new purposes, but the echo of the original design still casts a shadow over later use, moulding the experience of the material city for the inhabitant. This replicates materially Raymond Williams's insight that culture is formed from the residue of past practices intermingled with the emergent practices of the future. It is the task of history to reconcile this tension to form a coherent present. Dyer is attempting to control the future at the expense of the present, he is eventually ruined in the present but the novel suggests that he succeeds in his aim. Kevin Lynch observes that 'A landscape loaded with magical meanings may inhibit practical activities' (Lynch 138). Dyer's churches are invested with a hidden magical shape and influence their locales and the people who live and swirl around them. Hawksmoor, by contrast, the contemporary agent of order, is increasingly controlled by the past. He has failed to contain the contradictions of the present by sharing a simple optimism for the future that would occlude such contradiction. Dyer appropriates that future to the past by the perverse sacrifice of children; Hawksmoor can only tend towards the dead which draw him. This is, of course, an image of the city in crisis; a vision that this text shares with *Capital*, although it markedly increases the pessimistic vision of the earlier text – the city of this text has no future. London is overburdened by its past to the point that its history doubles back on itself, when Dyer and Hawksmoor impossibly meet at the novel's conclusion. This is a vision feared by Roy Porter in the opening chapter of his *London: A Social History* (1994): 'London seems to be becoming one of the historic towns of Europe: a museum piece – even a dinosaur – and in some ways an irrelevance' (Porter 471). In essence a culmination of the fear initiated by Duffy in 1975, intensified by Ackroyd in 1985 and reiterated by one of the city's most respected historians in 1994. London's present and future has become its past, and threatens to leave the city moribund.

Yet Porter also reveals the narrative weight felt by the contemporary historian in encapsulating a history such as his own: 'The temptation at the conclusion of a volume like this is to offer either a blueprint for metropolitan regeneration or a funeral oration' (Porter 471). The pressure is no less for writers of fiction. Yet when Ackroyd combines both fiction and history in his *Biography*, written on the cusp of a new century, he strikes a rather different note in relation to the city than he did in the 1980s:

> These relics of the past now exist as part of the present. It is in the nature of the city to encompass everything. So when it is asked how London can be a triumphant city when it has so many poor, and so many homeless, it can only be suggested that they, too, have always been a part of its history. Perhaps they are part of its triumph. If this is a hard saying, then it is only as hard as London itself. London goes beyond any boundary or convention. It contains every wish or word ever spoken, every action or gesture ever made, every harsh or noble statement ever made, every harsh or noble statement ever expressed. It is illimitable. It is Infinite London. (Ackroyd 2001 778–9)

Despite the obvious hyperbole of the passage, it is interesting to see Ackroyd reconstitute the city's disturbing 'relics' of the past, its poor and homeless, as part of a historical discourse that normalizes their fate in what is still a very wealthy metropolis. Despite challenging the boundary between fictional technique and historical discourse in the *Biography*, it is historical discourse that gains the upper hand by the end of the text, enabling a positive gesture to the future that resembles Walter Benjamin's assertion that 'our image of happiness is indissolubly bound up with the image of redemption' (Benjamin 2000 118). London is redeemed in Ackroyd's *The Biography* in a manner that is denied in both *Capital* and *Hawksmoor*, and indeed by Porter. Yet the period of relative composition is significant here. There is a certain millennialism in such messianicism. Ackroyd's conclusion to *The Biography* strikes an almost identical note to Ford Maddox Ford in *The Soul of London* in language that is even more strongly messianic: 'London with its vastness that will last their day, will grant the solace of unceasing mortals to be interested in' (Ford 112). Indeed, the final phrase of *The Biography* is taken directly from Ford's text – 'London is illimitable' (Ford 15). Ford almost bestows a benediction, but in common with Ackroyd's *The Biography* both texts are looking forward into a new century and form, an image of redemption for the city. By contrast, the images formed by *Capital*, *Hawksmoor* and Porter's *Social History* are apocalyptic – the city is on the brink of collapse and ruin. It is tempting to draw the historical comparison further. The co-texts to Ford's redemptive city narrative are novels like Gissing's *The Nether World* (1889), James's *Princess Casamassima* (1886) and Conrad's *The Secret Agent* (1907), in which the city also threatens to collapse or crush its inhabitants. H. G. Wells's *The War of the Worlds* (1898) and Richard Jefferies *After London* (1885) directly presage the city's annihilation. One might also point to a whole series of *fin de siècle* texts describing the terrible conditions of the working classes, such as Arthur Morrison's grim novels, or social documents like Jack London in *The People of the Abyss* (1903) (the modern equivalent of which – government and charity reports on poverty in London – Ackroyd glibly dismisses in the passage above).

A different challenge has been thrown down by Michael Moorcock's *Mother London*. Published in 1988, only three years after *Hawksmoor*, it too is concerned with the past, history and memory of London, but far more than either *Capital* or *Hawksmoor*, it is about the individual in London and collectively the people of London. In the earlier two novels the focus has been on London's fabric – its narratives, monuments, future and identity. While *Hawksmoor* embodies this more stridently than *Capital*, the fates of the historian and Meepers are part only of the continuing narratives of the city, as are the interjected historical narratives. In other words, only as fragments of the past are they significant to London. *Mother London* posits London as the creation of its people, not they of it. While the novel turns to another biological metaphor – London is the 'mother' giving birth and nurturing its people – this is different to conceiving of London as a body in which the people are reduced to involuntary functional processes. 'Mother' also evokes a nature symbolism absent from the two earlier novels by supplanting 'Earth' with 'London'. By contrast to the images of decay, death and destruction that underlie *Hawksmoor* and *Capital*, 'mother' London is a symbol of cyclical renewal, of decline and rebirth thereby promising the continuity that is the illusive object of the earlier two novels.

The structure of the novel reflects this differing emphasis. *Mother London* is certainly related to Duffy's and Ackroyd's novels, since the narrative manipulates textual and historical chronology by the use of several narratives associated with the three main protagonists: David Mummery, Mary Gasalee and Josef Kiss. Each chapter is focalized on one or other of these characters, while the novel is divided into six sections. The first and last are an introduction to and the final reflections of these three characters in the contemporary London of the novel. Chapters within each section are identified with a specific date, and succeeding chapters work forward or back from that date, creating a form of chronological oscillation between sections two to five. Section two begins with a chapter in 1957 and moves forward incrementally to a concluding chapter in 1985; section three begins in 1956 and moves backwards to 1940; section four begins in 1940 and moves forward to 1970; and finally section five begins in 1985 and moves back to 1959. Story chronology is therefore pointedly fractured and can be reassembled as follows: 1940, 1944, 1946, 1949, 1950, 1951, 1954, 1956, 1957, 1959, 1963, 1964, 1965, 1968, 1969, 1970, 1972, 1977, 1980, 1981, 1985. While the gap between these years ranges from one to four years, the novel presents quite a regular sample of life in London between 1940 and 1985. The former can be taken to be the chronological beginning of the story and the latter as the contemporary time period that frames the novel in sections one and six. Only three years are repeated: 1940, 1956 and 1985. The repetition of 1940 and 1985 are explained as the opening and closing years of the story, but why 1956?

Both chapters are focalized on Mary Gasalee, who has remained in a coma between the years 1940 and 1956. As a 16-year-old bride in 1940, her home is hit by a bomb during the Blitz. Mary manages to save her young baby but then slips into the coma, from which she does not recover until 1956. She awakes in Bethlehem psychiatric hospital where she is placed under observation. Both Josef Kiss and David Mummery are resident in the same institution and this is the first point in the story chronology that they are brought together and Mary initiates a sexual relationship with each man. Both episodes in 1956 relate to this encounter, despite being separated in different sections and by eight other chapters. As a consequence this episode is the fulcrum around which the narrative revolves. The significance of these three characters is that they share a supernatural ability to overhear the thoughts of other Londoners – the ability fades the further from London they travel – and this is the reason that Kiss and Mummery are under observation in a psychiatric hospital. Throughout the novel they are in and out of psychiatric care depending on the fluctuations of their condition. Once awakened, Gasalee shares the same experience. The ability they share directly recalls Lynda from Lessing's *The Four-Gated City*. She too has an ability to hear thoughts, which Martha the central character comes to share to a lesser degree. Lynda and others like her are able to hold together society after a catastrophic environmental disaster, but before this they are viewed as mentally unstable. In Lessing's novel this points towards a symbolism of community and city, and a similar organizing motif is to be found in *Mother London*.

In Moorcock's novel, however, the ability is more central to the psychological 'idea' of London. It is suggestive that all three texts discussed in this chapter resort to the fantastic to a greater or lesser degree in otherwise realist narratives. There is also a perceptible development in this fantastic turn between each novel. The conjectural historical interjections in *Capital* move some way in this direction since they are largely unverifiable, and the uncanny paralleling of the two narratives of *Hawksmoor* goes even further, to the point that the fantastic becomes overt by the conclusion of the narrative when the two protagonists impossibly appear to meet. In both these earlier novels, the fantastic element in the narrative remains a point of tension, to dramatize the issue of contemporary consciousness of the city and the interaction between the material artefacts of its past, myth and historical discourse. In *Mother London*, the fantastic is located centrally within the narrative and is significantly located around individual Londoners. It is no external organizing force or structure, but part of their characterization and thence woven into the fabric of the narrative.

The creation of 'imaginary communities' has been used by other authors often associated with magic realism like Salman Rushdie's *Midnight's Children* (1980) in which one hundred children born on the stroke of midnight on the day of India's independence are all endowed with supernatural abilities. Yet one child holds them together as a group thanks to the ability to overhear and transmit their thoughts. This resort to the fantastic is an elaborate symbolic framework to investigate national identity. In *Mother London* it is used to explore the city's identity – Josef Kiss, Mary Gasalee and David Mummery are the fictional means to hold together London's post-war experience. Unlike the resort to the inanimate found in *Capital* and *Hawksmoor* through computer analysis or archaeology, in *Mother London* the city is a state of mind. Moreover, the tie between the city-dweller and his/her environment is a matter of biological contingency:

> David Mummery's theory was that their mutual condition was a product of what he called urban evolution: as a Brazilian native of the rain forest was able to instinctively use all his senses to build up a complex picture of his particular world, so could a city dweller read his own relevant signs, just as unconsciously, to form an equally sophisticated picture. (*Mother* 30)

This would suggest that what appears in the text to be literally 'overhearing' the thoughts of others is the translation of 'relevant signs' into a form of characterization by Gasalee, Mummery and Kiss. The psychological distress which leads to their periodic institutionalization is a by-product of doing consciously what most city-dwellers do instinctively. Jonathan Raban argues that 'in a community of strangers, we need a quick, easy-to-use set of stereotypes, cartoon outlines, with which to classify the people we encounter' (Raban 29). Much the same could be said about the particular narrative structure of the novel. The complex fragmentation of chronological periods through the novel conforms to an overall pattern as discussed above, but also creates a local disorientation for the reader. As a consequence it is necessary to formulate contingent hypotheses about individual characters and update that view as more information becomes available in the dated chapters. There is not a single 'story' as such to be decoded from the plot, but a series of events from the fictional lives of these three characters. Rather than a chronological sequence that mimics our perception of time in the 'real' world, the narrative is also spatialized and builds a pattern that is, in turn, the summation of the city. The effect is distinctly defamiliarizing, as Eric Rabkin argues:

> In twentieth-century literature the structural device that seems most obtrusive is fragmentation. In considering works like Eliot's *The Waste Land*, critics have not only followed Frank's lead to see fragmentation as a spatializing (not spatial) technique but have also pointed out that

the fragmentation of twentieth-century literature is an analogue for the felt fragmentation of twentieth-century culture. And this is often true. The term 'fragmentation,' however ... may be seen as equivalent to the term 'attenuation' ... Attenuation, much more pointedly than fragmentation, indicates the effect of narrative technique in creating diachronically a synchronic suspension ... (Rabkin 95)

This would suggest that despite the novel's surface preoccupation with dates, the effect of its narrative structure is to create a synchronic, spatial, suspension of the city. The chronological fragmentation alone is not enough to create this effect, but the narrative is further organized around a myth – the myth of the Blitz: 'By means of certain myths which cannot easily be damaged or debased the majority of us survive. All old great cities possess their special myths. Amongst London's in recent years is the story of the Blitz, of our endurance' (*Mother* 5). The focal point for this myth in the novel is Josef Kiss, the sole character to contribute to relief operations during the war; David Mummery was too young and Mary Gasalee lapses into a coma after her home is bombed in a raid.

Indeed, Kiss is in many respects the physical embodiment of London. A minor theatrical talent, his preferred outlet was the variety act, which recalls Hamilton's Archie Prest in *The Slaves of Solitude*. Kiss's early success as a psychic, based on his ability to read or overhear the thoughts of other Londoners, was abandoned since it threatened his psychological balance. Finding post-war success through parts in television commercials, he manages to eke out a comfortable living assembling a series of small properties across London. His career has spanned many of the theatrical industries of the city from the variety stage, to rep, through minor film roles to creating characters for television advertising. His knowledge of London is extensive and intimate; sensitive to its changes and any evidence of decline. His day follows an itinerary that encompasses much of central London, as observed by David Mummery:

> Pubs were the nodes from which radiated Mr Kiss's lines of travel; lines so strictly maintained that after a while I could predict almost exactly where in certain circumstances he would be at any given time of day. I became his protégé. I would leave home early in the morning to seek him out. Even when I occasionally failed to find him I enjoyed exploring the city. I loved to see him in Holborn emerging from elaborate pub doorways, from nondescript Mayfair drinking-clubs, from mysterious Soho alleys. Once I witnessed his mountainous body running ponderously down leafy Haverstock Hill towards the tube station as he held his black felt hat, his stick and his gloves in his hand, his ulster flapping in the wind, all flamboyant, self-confident, knowing vulgarity. (*Mother* 337)

Kiss gives form to the city for Mummery as a 'spatial practice' that 'weaves places together' (de Certeau 97). The places woven by Kiss's itinerary are not the official London of monuments and great buildings, but the 'nondescript' city of pubs, drinking dens, or running for underground trains. It is the ordinary city, and like Kiss's appearance, those places and spaces could be characterized as 'flamboyant', 'self-confident' and certainly 'vulgar'. Mummery's daily search for Kiss becomes an exploration of the city both physically and in pursuit of its spirit.

Yet the essence of Kiss's character is practice. Despite his theatrical manner and appearance, the idea that London itself should become a theatrical parody of itself appals him: 'For almost his entire life London has been his living. Why shouldn't he benefit from the trend? Holborn Viaduct and Ludgate Hill, not to mention Blackfriars and Fleet Street, have until now largely escaped becoming mere themes but is there any point in further resistance? Mightn't it be better to join the final fantasy? It would amount to capitulation' (*Mother* 469). Yet Kiss himself embodies the risk of caricature, in the association of his person with London in the manner of a popularly packaged Dr Johnson, or any one of Dickens's rotund London philanthropists and saviours. There is an element of parody in the characterization of David Mummery and Mary Gasalee as well. Mummery is a London antiquarian and historian in the mould of Meepers, while Gasalee in her coma populates an imaginary London with actors and actresses from the popular cinema of her day. Through all three characters, London is a kind of stage on which Kiss struts directly, Mummery retrieves and re-enacts through his historical narratives, and Gasalee populates with film actresses. As a trio focused on Kiss, London is an enactment.

Indeed, the opening statement of the novel that the Blitz is London's most recent 'special myth' indicates a further conscious staging of the city in *Mother London*. It is not the city being performed, but a myth of its recent past and this has risks: 'It is certainly a distinguishing characteristic of mythical thinking, which, whatever else it may be, is always inclined to take signs and symbols for the things they represent, to take metaphors literally, and to let the fluid world indicated by the use of analogy and simile slip its grasp' (H. White 177). There is a strain in all three novels considered in this chapter to find a totalizing metaphor that will encompass the whole of London, while attempting to retain 'the fluid world indicated by the use of analogy and simile'. In this respect, one can understand the need in some texts to stress that London is 'illimitable', however contradictory this might be to metaphors that suggest systemic limitation, e.g. the city as organic body, that become suspiciously literal as a consequence of their iteration. The issue ultimately becomes a matter of the past and history.

In *Mother London*, the vision of the city offered is literally embodied in the three principal characters; that vision is thereby deliberately limited, subjective, and is a part of the narrative only in the form of characterization. London can only be read as a facet of simulated lived experience. This is a staged simulacrum of the city; an analogy, not a metaphor for London. The city of this text does not exist beyond the text and reference to the physical city and its past is contingent upon the localized vision of the characters who enunciate it. This contrasts with the representation of the past and the city's history in both *Capital* and *Hawksmoor*. Here the past is acutely disturbing as a presence beyond the text and not subject to the limitations of fiction and subjectivity. The city, in many respects, becomes a metaphysical concept that the narrative struggles to contain; an uncanny eruption into the fictive plane of the narrative. In both *Capital* and *Hawksmoor*, the past of the city is shaped into a struggle between apocryphal stories and established historical discourse that destabilizes the mimesis of the city otherwise promised by their narratives. As McHale observes:

> ...the effect is to juxtapose the officially-accepted version of what happened and the way things were, with another, often radically dissimilar version of the world. The tension between these two versions induces a form of ontological flicker between two worlds: one moment, the official version seems to be eclipsed by the apocryphal version; the next moment, it is the apocryphal version that seems mirage-like, the official version appearing solid, irrefutable. (McHale 90)

In never promising anything beyond the subjective and apocryphal – even references to the 'officially-accepted' history of London are incorporated within the localized reflections of individual characters – Moorcock suggests a city that is always personal and individual; an entity assembled from experience. The narrative enables the reader to resist the temptation to totalize London by enacting a narrative of the city as a process of lived experience. A conglomeration of spatial stories 'caught in the ambiguity of an actualisation, transformed into a term dependent upon many different conventions, situated as the act of a present (or of a time), and modified by the transformations caused by successive contexts' (de Certeau 117). This is history in process rather than discursive regulation. Above all, this is the city as imaginative home, a 'homely interior' rather than 'the fearful invasion of an alien presence' (Vidler 3).

7

Coda

The modern city is the locus classicus of impossible realities. Lives that have no business mingling with one another sit side by side upon the omnibus.
                                    Salman Rushdie, *The Satanic Verses* (1988)

No single thesis can encompass every facet of the representation of London in post-war fiction. Yet this has nothing to do with the idea that London is so large and polymorphous, illimitable and formless, that it resists representation and definition. There is a danger that overwhelmed by the richness of creative response to the city, discursive inquiry itself slips into defining metaphors for London. The city becomes both cause and symptom of the same discursive hesitation – equally image *and* thesis. There is a temptation too of reading London as a thing, an entity that somehow exists independently of the human lives that swarm and swirl within its borders. Julian Wolfreys argues that 'the being of a city is always a becoming, a process, a performative projection from within and overflowing the contours of any perceivable identity or particular identity' (Wolfreys 10). A process and performance, yes, but the detachment from 'perceivable' or 'particular' identity is to concede that London is an abstraction that is too easily cut asunder from lived experience. As Pierre Macherey argued in *A Theory of Literary Production* (1966), all texts are necessarily incomplete and contradictory, but it is not the case that representation and imagination are entirely divorced from the lived. This is a key factor when contemplating a social entity like a city. The physical form of a city does not precede the process and performance of its existence; it is an artificial environment that owes its very existence to an accretion of disparate human experience. With the passage of time and the physical evidence of residual and emerging cultural practices, this connection can be easily obscured and the city can appear to have a discursive 'life' of its own, but there is no city, no community, without individual identity. As a *production* of human interaction the city conveys 'creativity the abstract meaning of the spatial that is more than a descriptive act or a mimetic attempt to transcribe our lives' (Tew 2004 90). Anything that enters the text becomes something else but that 'something' has ontological status and as Lefebvre cautions: 'conspicuous by [their] absence from supposedly fundamental epistemological studies [are] not only the idea of "man" but also that of space' (Lefebvre 3). Narratives, images and histories of the city are the city in performance, in process; their circulation and adaptation form a complex ontology that it is false to discursively isolate from experience. The nature of that ontology is a process that reinscribes community(ies).

The overriding theme in all the novels examined in this study is community, as befits a vast conglomeration of human endeavour. Nostalgia for the war years often resolves upon the strong sense of community that brought classes together in universal resistance of the Blitz. Yet nostalgia is a collective fantasy of the succeeding era and signifies more about that time than the event from which it draws its inspiration. Post-war London in the literary imagination has represented nothing less than a crisis of community. This is a matter of people rather than place, as I. M. Young argues: 'Racism, ethnic chauvinism, and class devaluation ... grow partly from a desire for community, that is from the desire to understand others as they understand themselves and from the desire to be understood as I understand myself' (Young 311). As Meepers observes in Duffy's *Capital* 'we are out of love with [London] because we are out of love with ourselves' (152). In writing the city there is a creative tension between place and social space; to become alienated from one's own identity is to become estranged from the place that consciousness constructs around it. When the sense of community that defines the latter is in flux, the physical aspect of the city is increasingly dehumanized, inexplicable, unhomely. Insofar as the characters in the various novels analysed in this study find or reformulate a community in London the individual is enabled – the city is a liveable place. Insofar as they fail to do so, they leave or the city becomes a space of confused identifications or, at worst, terror. Quite often the city is a little bit of both, recalling Raymond Williams's formulation of residual and emergent cultural practices. Nobody ever entirely belongs to the city and the city never entirely belongs to any single group.

Of course Williams's argument was an observation about the social pattern of culture as a whole, but as civilization's greatest material artefact cities physically focus and concretely embody these cultural contradictions more strongly than other environments. As the French poet Henri-Martin Barzun noted in *Voix, rythemes et chants simultanés* (1913), city life provides 'proof of the existence of simultaneous realities' (Kern 72) and it is only in the realm of the aesthetic, specifically literature in this study, that 'simultaneous realities' can be brought together. The multifarious images, histories and narratives of the city, and their reformulation over time are a potent representation of the communities that are London even if not everyone becomes part of them. Their simultaneity is a distillation of the lived experience of the production and process of the city.

Bibliography

Note: Where a first edition is not used, the year of original publication is indicated in additional parentheses thus: [1996].

Ackroyd, Peter (1993) [1985], *Hawksmoor*, London: Penguin.
Ackroyd, Peter (2001) [2000], *London: The Biography*, London: Vintage.
Adebayo, Diran (2001) [1996], *Some Kind of Black*, London: Abacus.
Adorno, Theodore (1967), *Prisms*, trans. Samuel and Shierry Weber, London: Neville Spearman.
Adorno, Theodore and Max Horkheimer (1979) [1944], *Dialectic of Enlightenment*, London: Verso.
Ali, Monica (2004) [2003], *Brick Lane*, London: Black Swan.
Augé, Marc (1995) [1992], *Non-Places: Introduction to an Anthropology of Supermodernity*, trans. John Howe, London and New York: Verso.
Bachelard, Gaston (1994) [1964], *The Poetics of Space*, trans. Maria Jolas, Boston, MA: Beacon Press.
Ball, John Clement (2004), *Imagining London: Postcolonial Fiction and the Transnational Metropolis*, Toronto, Buffalo and London: University of Toronto Press.
Ballard, J. G. (1994) [1973], *Concrete Island*, London: Vintage.
Ballard, J. G. (2004) [1973], *Crash*, London: Vintage.
Ballard, J. G. (2000) [1975], *High-Rise*, London: Flamingo.
Barber, Stephen (1995), *Fragments of the European City*, London: Reaktion Books.
Barthes, Roland (1976), *Mythologies*, trans. Annette Lavers, St Albans: Paladin.
Benjamin, Walter (1997) [1972], *Charles Baudelaire*, London: Verso.
Benjamin, Walter (1999), *The Arcades Project*, trans. Howard Eiland and Kevin McLaughlin, Cambridge, MA and London: The Belknap Press or Harvard University Press.
Benjamin, Walter (2000), 'Theses on the philosophy of history', from Tamsin Spargo (ed.), *Reading the Past*, London: Palgrave, 118–26.
Bergonzi, Bernard (1993), *Wartime and Aftermath: English Literature and its Background 1939–1960*, Oxford and New York: Oxford University Press.

Bloom, Clive (2003), *Violent London: 2000 Years of Riots, Rebels and Revolts*, London: Sidgwick & Jackson.

Bloom, Harold (ed.) (1986), *Doris Lessing: Modern Critical Views*, New York: Chelsea House Publishers.

Bloom, Harold (ed.) (1987), *Elizabeth Bowen: Modern Critical Views*, New York: Chelsea House.

Bowen, Elizabeth (1998) [1948], *The Heat of the Day*, London: Vintage.

Bowen, Elizabeth (1999) [1980], *Collected Stories*, London: Vintage.

Bradbury, Malcolm (2001) [1993], *The Modern British Novel, 1878–2001*, London: Penguin.

Buchan, John (1999) [1913; 1915], *The Power House and The Thirty-Nine Steps*, London: B&W Publishing.

Burgess, Anthony (2000) [1962], *A Clockwork Orange*, London: Penguin.

Burke, Edmund (1953) [1756], *A Philosophical Enquiry into the Origin of Our Ideas of the Sublime and Beautiful*, London: Routledge & Kegan Paul.

Butler, Tim with Garry Robson (2003), *London Calling: The Middle Classes and the Re-making of Inner London*, Oxford and New York: Berg.

Calder, Angus (2003) [1991], *The Myth of the Blitz*, London: Pimlico.

Cassirer, Ernst (1996), *The Philosophy of Symbolic Forms. Volume 4: The Metaphysics of Symbolic Forms*, New Haven, CT and London: Yale University Press.

Churchill, Caryl (1989) [1979], *Cloud Nine*, London: Nick Hern Books.

Connor, Steven (1996), *The English Novel in History*, London and New York: Routledge.

Conrad, Joseph (1995) [1899], *Heart of Darkness*, London: Penguin.

Conrad, Joseph (2004) [1907], *The Secret Agent*, Oxford: Oxford University Press.

Couto, Maria (1990), *Graham Greene: On the Frontier, Politics and Religion in the Novels*, London: Macmillan.

de Certeau, Michel (1988) [1984], *The Practice of Everyday Life*, trans. Steven Rendall, Berkeley, CA: University of California Press.

Crisp, Quentin (1985) [1968], *The Naked Civil Servant*, London: Flamingo.

Deleuze, G. and F. Guattari (1988) [1987], *A Thousand Plateaus: Capitalism and Schizophrenia*, London: Athlone.

Delville, Michel (1998), *J. G. Ballard*, Plymouth: Northcote House in association with the British Council.

Drabble, Margaret (1968) [1965], *The Millstone*, London: Penguin.

Duffy, Maureen (1984) [1969], *Wounds*, London: Methuen.

Duffy, Maureen (2001) [1975], *Capital*, London: Harvill Panther.

Duffy, Maureen (1983), *Londoners*, London: Methuen.

Dunn, Nell (1966) [1963], *Up the Junction*, London: Pan.

Elden, Stuart (2001), *Mapping the Present: Heidegger, Foucault and the Project of a Spatial History*, London and New York: Continuum.

Eliot, T. S. (1936), *Collected Poems, 1909–1935*, New York: Harcourt Brace.

Emecheta, Buchi (1974), *Second-Class Citizen*, London: Allison & Busby.

Emecheta, Buchi (1979) [1972], *In the Ditch*, London: Allison & Busby.

Fabian of the Yard (1959) [1954], *London After Dark*, London: Panther Books.

Fanon, Frantz (1986) [1952], *Black Skin, White Masks*, London: Pluto Press.

Feldman, Gene and Max Gartenberg (eds) (1960), *Protest*, London: Panther Books.

Ford, Ford Madox (1995) [1905], *The Soul of London*, London: Everyman.

Forgacs, David (1991), 'Marxist Literary Theories', from Ann Jefferson and David Robey (eds), *Modern Literary Theory*, London: B. T. Batsford.

Frankl, Paul (2001) [1962], *Gothic Architecture*, New Haven, CT and London: Yale University Press.

Frosh, Stephen (1995), 'Time, space, and otherness', from Steve Pile and Nigel Thrift (eds), *Mapping the Subject: Geographies of Cultural Transformation*, London and New York: Routledge, 289–308.

Fuss, Diana (1989), *Essentially Speaking*, London and New York: Routledge.

Garland, Rodney (1995) [1953], *The Heart in Exile*, Brighton: Millivres Books.

Gibbons, Stella (1959), *A Pink Front Door*, London: Hodder and Stoughton.

Gilbert, Pamela K. (ed.) (2002), *Imagined Londons*, New York: State University of New York Press.

Giles, Judy and Tim Middleton (eds) (1995), *Writing Englishness, 1900–1950: An Introductory Sourcebook on National Identity*, London: Routledge.

Gissing, George (1999) [1889], *The Nether World*, Oxford: Oxford University Press.

Glendenning, Victoria (1977), *Elizabeth Bowen: Portrait of a Writer*, London: Weidenfeld and Nicholson.

Graham, David and Peter Clarke (eds) (1986), *The New Enlightenment*, London: Macmillan.

Greene, Graham (2001) [1943], *The Ministry of Fear*, London: Vintage.

Greene, Graham (2001) [1951], *The End of the Affair*, London: Vintage.

Haggard, Henry Rider (1998) [1886], *King Solomon's Mines*, Oxford and New York: Oxford University Press.

Hall, Stuart (1995), 'New cultures for old', from D. Massey and P. Jess (eds), *A Place in the World: Places, Culture and Globalisation*, Oxford: Oxford University Press.

Hamilton, Patrick (1990) [1941], *Hangover Square*, London: Penguin.

Hamilton, Patrick (1999) [1947], *The Slaves of Solitude*, London: Penguin.

Harrison, Paul (1983), *Inside the Inner City: Life Under the Cutting Edge*, London: Penguin.

Heidegger, Martin (1962), *Being and Time*, trans. Edward Robinson and John Macquarrie, Oxford: Blackwell.

Hoogland, Renee C. (1994), *Elizabeth Bowen: A Reputation in Writing*, New York and London: New York University Press.

hooks, bell (1991), *Yearnings: Race, Gender, and Cultural Politics*, London: Turnaround.

Hopkins, Harry (1964), *The New Look: A Social History of the Forties and Fifties*, London: Secker & Warberg.

Inwood, Christopher (2005), *City of Cities: The Birth of Modern London*, London: Macmillan.

James, Henry (1987) [1886], *Princess Casamassima*, London: Penguin.

Jameson, Frederick (1991), *Postmodernism, or the Cultural Logic of Late Capitalism*, London: Verso.

Jefferies, Richard (2005) [1885], *After London, or Wild England*, London: Echo Library.

Jefferson, Ann and David Robey (1991) [1982], *Modern Literary Theory*, London: B. T. Batsford.

Jenks, Chris (1995), 'Watching your step: The history and practice of the *Flâneur*', in Chris Jenks (ed.), *Visual Culture*, London and New York: Routledge.

Johnson, B. S. (2004) [1964], *Albert Angelo*, from *B. S. Johnson Omnibus*, London: Picador.

Karl, Frederick R. (1986), 'Doris Lessing in the sixties: The new anatomy of melancholy', from Harold Bloom (ed.), *Doris Lessing: Modern Critical Views*, New York: Chelsea House Publishers.

Keith, Michael and Steve Pile (eds) (1993), *Place and the Politics of Identity*, London and New York: Routledge.

Kenner, Hugh (1973), 'The urban apocalypse', from A. Walton Litz (ed.), *Eliot in his Time*, Princeton, NJ: Princeton University Press, 23–49.

Kern, Stephen (2003) [1983], *The Culture of Time and Space 1880–1918*, Cambridge, MA and London: Harvard University Press.

Kerr, Joe and Andrew Gibson (2003), *London from Punk to Blair*, London: Reaktion Books.

Kipling, Rudyard (1998) [1901], *Kim*, Oxford and New York: Oxford University Press.

Kirby, Kathleen M. (1996), *Indifferent Boundaries: Spatial Concepts of Human Subjectivity*, New York and London: The Guildford Press.

Lamming, George (1954), *The Emigrants*, London: Michael Joseph.

Le Corbusier (1970) [1923], *Towards a New Architecture*, London: Architectural Press.

Le Corbusier (1996) [1929], 'A contemporary city', from *The City Reader*, London and New York: Routledge, 317–24.

Lee, Hermione (1981), *Elizabeth Bowen: An Estimation*, London and Totowa, NJ: Vision and Barnes & Noble.

Lefebvre, Henri (1991) [1974], *The Production of Space*, trans. Donald Nicholson-Smith, Oxford and Cambridge, MA: Blackwell.

LeGates, Richard T. and Frederic Stout (eds) (2003) [1996], *The City Reader*, London and New York: Routledge.

Lessing, Doris (1978) [1969], *The Four-Gated City*, London: Panther.

Lessing, Doris (1992), *London Observed: Stories and Sketches*, London: HarperCollins.

Levy, Shawn (2002), *Ready, Steady, Go! Swinging London and the Invention of Cool*, London and New York: Fourth Estate.

Lewis, Wyndham (1951), *Rotting Hill*, London: Methuen.

Lodge, David (1993) [1960], *The Picturegoers*, London: Penguin.

London, Jack (2001) [1903], *The People of the Abyss*, London: Pluto Press.

Lukács, Georg (1978) [1970], *Writer and Critic*, trans. Arthur Hahn, London: The Merlin Press.

Lynch, Kevin (1979) [1960], *The Image of the City*, Cambridge, MA and London: The MIT Press.

Macherey, Pierre (1978) [1966], *A Theory of Literary Production*, London and New York: Routledge.

MacInnes, Colin (1985) [1957], *City of Spades*, Harmondsworth: Penguin.

MacInnes, Colin (2001) [1959], *Absolute Beginners*, London: Allison & Busby.

MacInnes, Colin (1961), *England, Half English*, London: MacGibbon & Kee.

Marx, Karl (1975) [1844], *Economic and Philosophic manuscripts of 1844*, from Karl Marx and Friedrich Engels, *Collected Works Vol.3, Marx and Engels, 1843–1844*, New York: International Publishers.

Massey, Doreen, John Allen and Steve Pile (eds) (1999), *City Worlds*, London and New York: Routledge.

McEwan, Neil (1988), *Graham Greene*, London: Macmillan.

McHale, Brian (1987), *Postmodernist Fiction*, London and New York: Routledge.

McLeod, John (2004), *Postcolonial London: Rewriting the Metropolis*, London and New York: Routledge.

Mo, Timothy (1999) [1982], *Sour Sweet*, London: Paddleless.

Moorcock, Michael (2002) [2001], *London Bone*, London: Scribner.

Moorcock, Michael (2000) [1988], *Mother London*, London: Scribner.

Morrison, Blake (2000), Introduction, in Anthony Burgess (2000) [1962], *A Clockwork Orange*, London: Penguin, vii–xiv.

Mudford, Peter (1996), *Graham Greene*, Plymouth: Northcote House.

Mumford, Lewis (2003) [1937], 'What is a city?', from Richard T. LeGates and Frederic Stout (eds) (2003) [1996], *The City Reader*, London and New York: Routledge.

Murdoch, Iris (1956), *Under the Net*, London: Chatto & Windus.

Naipaul, V. S. (1968) [1964], *An Area of Darkness*, Harmondsworth: Penguin.

Naipaul, V. S. (1967), *The Mimic Men*, London: Andre Deutsch.

Nalbantoğlu, G. B. and C. T. Wong (eds) (1997), *Postcolonial Space(s)*, New York: Princeton Architectural Press.

Nora, Pierre (1996), 'General Introduction: Between Memory and History', from *Realms of Memory: Rethinking the French Past*, under the direction of Pierre Nora, trans. Arthur Goldhammer, New York: Columbia University Press.

Nord, Deborah Epstein (1995), *Walking the Victorian Streets: Women, Representation, and the City*, Ithaca, NY and London: Cornell University Press.

Onega, Susana and John A. Stotesbury (eds) (2002), *London in Literature: Visionary Mappings of the Metropolis*, Heidelberg: Universitätsverlag C. Winter.

O'Prey, Paul (1988), *A Reader's Guide to Graham Greene*, London: Thames and Hudson.

Orwell, George (1983) [1949], *Nineteen Eighty-Four*, Harmondsworth: Penguin.

Patterson, Sheila (1965) [1963], *Dark Strangers*, Harmondsworth: Penguin.

Phillips, Lawrence (2002), 'Writing identity into space: Ethnography, autobiography, and space in Bronislaw Malinowski's *A Diary in the Strict Sense of the Term* and Claude Lévi-Strauss's *Tristes Tropiques*', from *Reconstruction*, 2.3 (Summer 2003).

Phillips, Lawrence (ed.) (2004), *The Swarming Streets: Twentieth-Century Literary Representations of London*, Amsterdam and New York: Editions Rodopi.

Pike, Burton (1981), *The Image of the City in Modern Literature*, Princeton, NJ: Princeton University Press.

Pile, Steve and Nigel Thrift (1995), *Mapping the Subject: Geographies of Cultural Transformation*, London and New York: Routledge.

Porter, Roy (2000) [1994], *London: A Social History*, London: Penguin.

Powell, Anthony (2002) [1964; 1966; 1968], *A Dance to the Music of Time: Autumn*, London: Arrow.

Pritchett, V. S. (1962), *London Perceived*, London: Chatto & Windus and William Heinmann.

Raban, Jonathan (1988) [1974], *Soft City*, London: Collins Harvill.

Rabkin, Eric S. (1981), 'Spatial form and plot', in Jeffrey R. Smitten and Ann Daghistany (eds) (1981), *Spatial Form in Narrative*, Ithaca, NY: Cornell University Press.

Read, Herbert (1941), *To Hell with Culture*, London: Kegan Paul, Trench, Trubner.

Reader, John (2004), *Cities*, London: William Heinemann.

Reid Banks, Lynne (2004) [1960], *The L-Shaped Room*, London: Vintage.

Rhys, Jean (2000) [1934], *Voyage in the Dark*, London: Penguin.

Richardson, Dorothy (1998), 'There's no place like home', from James Donald, Anne Friedberg and Laura Marcus (eds), *Close Up 1927–1933: Cinema and Modernism*, London: Cassey, 168–9.

Rushdie, Salman (1992), *Imaginary Homelands: Essays and Criticism, 1981 to 1991*, London: Penguin/Granta.

Rushdie, Salman (1995) [1980], *Midnight's Children*, London: Vintage.

Sandhu, Sukhdev (2004) [2003], *London Calling: How Black and Asian Writers Imagined a City*, London: Harper Perennial.

Schneer, Jonathan (2001), *London 1900: The Imperial Metropolis*, New Haven, CT and London: Yale University Press.

Selvon, Sam (1979) [1956], *The Lonely Londoners*, London: Longman.

Shklovsky, Victor (1965), 'Art as technique', from Lee T. Lemon and Marion J. Reis (eds), *Russian Formalist Criticism: Four Essays*, Lincoln, NE: University of Nebraska Press.

Silverman, Hugh J. (1994), *Textualities: Between Hermeneutics and Deconstruction*, New York and London: Routledge.

Simmel, Georg (1950) [1903], 'The metropolis and mental life', from *The Sociology of Georg Simmel*, trans. Kurt Wolff, New York: Free Press, 409–24.

Sinclair, Iain (2002) [1975], *Lud Heat and Suicide Bridge*, London: Granta.

Sinclair, Iain (1995) [1987], *White Chappell Scarlet Tracings*, London: Vintage.

Sinclair, Iain (1997), *Lights Out for the Territory: 9 Excursions in the Secret History of London*, London: Granta.

Sinclair, Iain (1999), *Sorry Meniscus: Excursions to the Millennium Dome*, London: Profile Books.

Sinclair, Iain (2002) [2001], *Landor's Tower*, London: Granta.

Sinfield, Alan (1997), *Literature, Politics and Culture in Postwar Britain*, London and Atlantic Highlands, NJ: The Athlone Press.

Sissons, Michael and Philip French (eds) (1963), *Age of Austerity*, London: Hodder & Stoughton.

Sizemore, Christine W. (1996), 'The London novels of Buchi Emecheta', from Marie Umeh (ed.), *Emerging Perspectives on Buchi Emecheta*, Trenton, NJ: Africa World Press, 366–85.

Smith, Zadie (2001) [2000], *White Teeth*, London: Penguin.

Smitten, Jeffrey R. and Ann Daghistany (eds) (1981), *Spatial Form in Narrative*, Ithaca, NY: Cornell University Press.

Soja, Edward (1989), *Postmodern Geographies*, London: Verso.

Spargo, Tamsin (ed.) (2000), *Reading the Past*, Basingstoke: Palgrave.

Stow, John (2005) [1598], *A Survey of London: Written in the Year 1598*, London: Sutton Publishing.

Steedman, Carolyn (1986), *Landscape for a Good Woman*, London: Virago.

Summerson, John (2003) [1945], *Georgian London*, New Haven, CT and London: Yale University Press.

Tew, Philip (2001), *B. S. Johnson: A Critical Reading*, Manchester and New York: Manchester University Press.

Tew, Philip (2004), *The Contemporary British Novel*, London and New York: Continuum.

Thrift, Nigel (1996), *Spatial Formations*, London: Sage.

Tinkler-Villani, Valeria (ed.) (2005), *Babylon or New Jerusalem: Perceptions of the City in Literature*, Amsterdam and New York: Editions Rodopi.

Umeh, Marie (ed.) (1996), *Emerging Perspectives on Buchi Emecheta*, Trenton, NJ: Africa World Press.

Vidler, Anthony (1992), *The Architectural Uncanny: Essays in the Modern Unhomely*, Cambridge, MA and London: The MIT Press.

Walkowitz, Judith R. (1992), *City of Dreadful Delight: Narratives of Sexual Danger in Late-Victorian London*, London: Virago.

Waller, Maureen (2004), *London 1945: Life in the Debris of War*, London: John Murray.

Weightman, Gavin and Steve Humphreys (1983), *The Making of Modern London, 1815–1914*, London: Sidgwick & Jackson.

Wells, H. G. (2005a) [1895], *The Time Machine*, London: Penguin.

Wells, H. G. (2005b) [1898], *The War of the Worlds*, London: Penguin.

Werth, Paul (1999), *Text Worlds: Representing Conceptual Space in Discourse*, Harlow: Pearson Educational.

Westwood, Sallie and John Williams (eds) (1997), *Imagining Cities: Scripts, Signs, Memory*, London: Routledge.

White, Hayden (1985) [1978], *The Tropics of Discourse: Essays in Cultural Criticism*, Baltimore, MD and London: The Johns Hopkins University Press.

White, Jerry (2002) [2001], *London in the Twentieth Century*, London: Penguin.

Wildeblood, Peter (1955), *Against the Law*, London: Weidenfeld and Nicolson.

Williams, Raymond (1977), *Marxism and Literature*, Oxford and New York: Oxford University Press.

Willis, F. Roy (1973), *Western Civilization and Urban Perspective: Volume II from the 17th Century to the Contemporary Age*, Lexington, MA: D. C. Heath.

Wolfreys, Julian (2004), *Writing London Volume 2: Materiality, Memory, Spectrality*, Basingstoke: Palgrave Macmillan.

Woodcock, George (1984), *Orwell's Message: 1984 and the Present*, Madeira Park (Canada): Harbour.

Woolf, Virginia (1998) [1929], *A Room of One's Own and Three Guineas*, Oxford: Oxford World's Classics.

Young, I. M. (1990), 'The idea of community and the politics of difference', from L. Nicholson (ed.), *Feminism/Postmodernism*, London: Routledge.

Zukin, S. (1992), 'Postmodern urban landscapes: Mapping culture and power', from S. Lash and J. Friedman (eds), *Modernity and Identity*, Oxford: Blackwell, 221–47.

Index

Achebe, Chinua 129
Ackroyd, Peter 6–7, 19, 38–9, 72, 96, 134, 135, 142
  Hawksmoor 9, 136, 145–50, 151, 152, 153, 157
  London: The Biography 13, 132, 136, 150–1
Adorno, Theodore 63, 76
Amis, Kingsley 'Socialism and the Intellectuals' 35
Arts Council 11

Bachelard, Gaston 5–6, 125
Bailey, David 59
Baldwin, James 129
Ball, John Clement 106, 107, 111
Ballard, J. G. 84
  High Rise 7, 35, 47, 48, 50–4, 83, 141
Banks, Lynne Reid *The L-Shaped Room* 8, 68–74, 79, 111, 114, 128
Barber, Stephen 50, 62, 123, 135–6
Barthes, Roland 41, 46–7
Barzun, Henri-Martin *Voix, rythemes et chants simultanés* 159
Baudelaire, Charles 117
BBC 113
Benjamin, Walter 6, 13, 65, 117, 118, 132, 151; see also *flâneur Charles Baudelaire* 132
Bennett, Arnold 91
Bergonzi, Bernard 12
Bhabha, Homi 13
Blitz 2, 7, 10, 12, 13, 15, 19, 21, 25, 26, 32, 80, 155, 156, 159
Bloom, Clive 94
Bloom, Harold 17
body, city as 3, 13, 20, 25–6, 134
Bowen, Elizabeth 7, 12, 13, 14, 36, 38
  The Heat of the Day 16–23, 24, 25, 26–7, 30, 31, 33, 60, 62, 120
British Union of Fascists 94
Bruno, Giuliana *Streetwalking on a Ruined Map* 56
Buchan, John *The Thirty-Nine Steps* 29
Bunyan, John *A Pilgrim's Progress* 73
Burke, Edmund 49

Burgess, Anthony *A Clockwork Orange* 7, 35, 47–50, 51, 54

Caine, Michael 59
Calder, Angus *The Myth of the Blitz* 11, 12, 13
Cassirer, Ernst 4
Chamberlain, Neville 15, 16
Churchill, Caryl *Cloud Nine* 119
Churchill, (Sir) W. S. 3, 13, 16, 34, 83
cinema 59, 61–5, 67, 74, 76, 79, 156
Civil Defence 18
Clarke, Peter *The New Enlightenment 137*
colonial; see empire
Commonwealth 106, 107, 108, 127
Conan Doyle, (Sir) Arthur 78
Connor, Steven 33, 34, 59
Conrad, Joseph *Heart of Darkness* 78, 107, 112, 121, 130
  The Secret Agent 151
Conservative Party 36
contact zone 8
Cooper, Susan 31
County Hall 36
Cubitt, Lewis 97

Dante (Durante degli Alighieri) 21, 101–2, 121
  The Divine Comedy 102
  Inferno 21, 101–2
Dave Clarke Five 59
Dean, James 64
De Certeau, Michel 13, 40–1, 44, 45–6, 58, 62, 90, 101, 116, 131, 133, 140, 155, 157
  practiced place 41
  spatial stories 4, 58
  spatial syntaxes 62, 145
  The Practice of Everyday Life 5
  'Walking in the City' 5
Deleuze, G. 77, 117
Delville, Michel 47
De Saussure, Ferdinand 45
Dickens, Charles 58, 78, 87, 156
Donovan, Terrance 59
Duffy, Maureen 9, 132
  Capital 8, 136, 137–45, 146, 148, 149, 150, 151, 152, 153, 154, 157, 159

172   *Index*

Dunkirk 20

Eliot, T. S. 94
    The Four Quartets 121
    The Waste Land 21, 26, 115, 154
Elizabeth I 143
Emecheta, Buchi *Second-Class Citizen* 8, 108,
    125–31
empire 36, 37, 57, 78, 106–7, 120, 121–2,
    128, 112, 123, 126, 139
Empire Windrush 107
Englishness 28, 83, 110

Fabian, Bob 114
Faith, Adam 59
Fanon, Frantz *Black Skin, White Masks* 117
fascism 15, 24, 27, 94, 110; see also Nazis
Faulkner, William 12
Feldman, Gene 35
Festival of Britain (1951) 36, 83
Fielding, Henry *Tom Jones* 60
film; see cinema
fin de siècle 151
Fire of London (1666) 145
First World War 1, 87, 89
flâneur 65, 117, 118, 123; see also Walter
    Benjamin
Ford, Ford Maddox *The Soul of London* 132,
    134, 151
Forgacs, David 146, 149
Forster, E. M. *Howards End* 90
Foucault, Michel 43, 57
    'repressive hypothesis' 57
Frankl, Paul *Gothic Architecture* 96
French, Philip 12, 31, 81
Freud, Sigmund 4, 48, 87, 141; see also
    uncanny *id* 48
Frosh, Stephen 69
Fuss, Diana 125

Garland, Rodney *The Heart in Exile* 8, 74–9,
    81, 83, 109, 113
gay London, 68, 70–1, 75–7, 79, 100, 109, 113–4
gentrification 80, 81, 83, 86
Gibbons, Stella *A Pink Front Door* 8, 83–91,
    98–9, 100, 102–3, 105, 138
Giles, Judy 30, 38
Gilroy, Beryl *Boy Sandwich* 106
Gissing, George 58, 78, 151
    The Nether World 151
Glendenning, Victoria 13, 23
gothic 17–18, 93
gothic architecture 95–6
Graham, David *The New Enlightenment* 137
Great Plague (1665) 145
Greater London Council (GLC) 136–7, 142
Green, Henry 12
Greene, Graham 12, 41
    'At Home' 32
    The End of the Affair, 24, 30–4, 61
    The Ministry of Fear 14, 15, 24, 27, 78

Guattari, F. 77, 117

Hamilton, Patrick 7, 12, 15
    Hangover Square 14, 16, 24
    The Slaves of Solitude 24, 25, 26–30, 34, 60,
        110, 113, 119, 154
Hall, Stuart 123
Harrison, Paul 50
Hastings, Macdonald 11
Hawksmoor, Nicholas 145
Heidegger, Martin 4, 104
    Being and Time (Sein und Zeit) 4
    'Letter on Humanism' 104
Hemmingway, Ernest 12
Hitler, Adolf 15, 16, 27, 89
Hofer, Evelyn 132
homosexual; see gay London
Hoogland, Renee 14, 23
hooks, bell 71, 81, 83, 100, 104
Horizon 12
Horkheimer, Max 63
Howard, Anthony 14
Hughes, David 81
Humphreys, Steve 2

imperial; see empire
Inwood, Christopher 2

James, Henry *Princess Casamassima 151*
Jameson, Frederick 81, 83
Jefferies, Richard *After London* 151
Jefferson, Ann 41
Johnson, B. S. *Albert Angelo* 8, 83, 91–100,
    103, 105, 140
Johnson, (Dr) Samuel 156
Joyce, James 101

Kafka, Franz 101
Karl, Frederick R. 101
Keith, Michael 71, 103, 111
Kenner, Hugh 121
Kern, Stephen 159
Kipling, Rudyard *Kim* 78
Kinks 59
Kurieshi, Hanif 106

Labour Party 35, 36, 81, 83, 89
labyrinth, city as 19, 23, 134
Lancaster, Burt 74
Le Corbusier 53
Lee, Hermione 16–17
Lefebvre, Henri 5, 47, 53, 92, 99, 101, 159
Lehman, John 11
Lehmann, Rosamund 12
Lessing, Doris *Children of Violence* 100
    The Four-Gated City 8, 83, 100–5, 153
Levy, Shawn 56, 57, 59
Lewis, Wyndham 55, 57
    Rotting Hill, 35–7, 63
lieux de mémoire 133; see also Pierre Nora

Lodge, David *The Picturegoers* 8, 59–68, 71, 74, 75, 79, 85, 114, 118
London County Council (LCC) 136
London, Jack *The People of the Abyss* 151
'London Particular' 72
Lukács, Georg 146, 147
Lynch, Kevin 1, 5, 23, 108, 150
   The Image of the City 1

McHale, Brian 135, 140–1, 144–5, 157
McLeod, John 107
Macherey, Pierre *A Theory of Literary Production* 158
MacInnes, Colin 57, 59, 111
   City of Spades 8, 108–14, 118, 119, 122, 123, 124, 129
Mackinder, Halford 25–6
Madison, Guy 74
Marlowe, Christopher 97
Marx, Karl, 6, 129
   Economic and Philosophical Notebooks 6
Merleau-Ponty, Maurice 90
Metropolitan Police District 1
Meyhew, Henry 78
Middleton, Tim 30, 38
Ministry of Information 18, 38, 44
miscegenation 118
Mitchum, Robert 65
misogyny 66, 75, 100, 118–19
modernism 7, 91
Monet, Claude 72
monster, city as 3, 27–8
Moorcock, Michael 132, 157
   Mother London 9, 136, 152–6
More, (Sir) Thomas 143
Morrison, Arthur 78
Morrison, Blake 47
Mosely, (Sir) Oswald 94
Mudford, Peter 31
Mumford, Lewis 95
music hall 29, 110
myth 4, 7, 46–7, 107–8, 131

Naipaul, V. S. *An Area of Darkness* 107
   The Mimic Men 8, 108, 119–24
Nalbantoglu G. B. 106
National Debt 138
Nazis 36, 56; see also fascism
Nora, Pierre 133; see also *lieux de mémoire*
nostalgia 86–8, 130, 135, 138, 159
Nwapa, Flora 129

O'Prey, Paul 25, 32
Orwell, George *Nineteen Eighty-Four* 7, 35, 37–47, 48, 50, 51, 54, 111

Palladian architecture 84, 93, 95–6, 101
Panter-Downes, Mollie 11
Patterson, Sheila *Dark Strangers* 109
permissive society 8, 56
picaresque 114, 131

Pike, Burton 19, 22, 38–9, 52, 72, 99, 107–8, 115, 144
Pile, Steve 54, 71, 103, 111, 117, 119
Poe, Edgar Allen *The Fall of the House of Usher* 87
Porter, Roy *London: A Social History* 132, 150, 151
postcolonial 108, 131
postcolonial London 2, 106
Pound, Ezra 94
Powell, Enoch 131
Pretty Things (The) 59
Pritchett, V. S. *London Perceived* 132
prostitution 40–1, 71–3, 101
Proust, Marcel 101

Raban, Jonathan 9, 21, 47, 58, 71, 86, 96, 100, 131, 132, 154
Rabkin, Eric S. 42, 135, 154–5
Read, Herbert *The Hell With Culture* 89
Reader, John 34
Rhys, Jean *Voyage in the Dark* 68
Richardson, Dorothy 61, 63–4
Rider Haggard, (Sir) Henry *King Solomon's Mines* 78
rock 'n' roll 66, 75
Rolling Stones 59
Rushdie, Salman 123
   Midnight's Children 154
   The Satanic Verses 158

Sandhu, Sukhdev 107, 115
Schneer, Jonathan 106–7
Scott, Gilbert 97
Selvon, Samuel 121
   The Lonely Londoners 8, 108, 115–19, 120, 122, 123, 126, 130, 131, 138–9
Senate House (University of London) 38, 44
Shapiro, Helen 59
Shaw, Sandie 59
Shklovsky, Victor 135
Simmel, Georg 11, 12, 57
Sinclair, Iain 96, 134, 146
   Lights Out for the Territory: 9 Excursions in the Secret History of London 132–3, 136
   Lud Heat 146
   Sorry Meniscus: Excursions to the Millennium Dome 135
Sinfield, Alan 46, 66, 89, 107, 109, 113, 128, 137
Sissons, Michael 12, 35, 81
Sizemore, Christine 130
Small Faces 59
Smith, Zadie 106
Soja, Edward 100
South Bank 36, 80
South Sea Bubble 138
Special Relationship 56
spiv 14, 37, 81
Stamp, Terence 59
Steedman, Carolyn 59

Stow, John *Survey of London* 132
suburban 2, 15, 18, 25, 26–7, 29–31, 58,
    60, 62, 64, 67, 70, 75, 85, 120–1,
    123
Suez 57
suffragettes 89
Summerson, John *Georgian London* 80, 81
swinging London 8, 56, 57, 105

Teddy Boys 65–6, 67, 76, 79, 81
Tew, Philip 81, 91–2, 98, 158–9
Thatcher, Margaret 83, 136–7
Thompson, James *City of Dreadful Night* 80
Thrift, Nigel 54, 110, 117, 119
Tory, see Conservative party
Twiggy 59

Uncanny 4, 9, 17, 19, 86, 90, 103, 136, 141,
    144, 147; see also Freud
University Settlement 78
USA 14, 36, 56, 144
USSR 14

Victorian London 1, 3, 31–2, 44, 77–8, 95,
    136
Vidler, Anthony 6, 86, 87–8, 90, 136, 157
violence 10, 16, 17, 18, 19, 21, 49–50,
    54, 61, 65–6, 90, 94, 97, 109, 111–2

Waller, Maureen 10, 11
Waugh, Evelyn 12
Weightman, Gavin 2
Wells, H. G. 4, 151
    The War of the Worlds 151
Werth, Paul 47, 99, 133
Westwood, Sallie 12–13
White, Hayden 6, 134, 141, 156
White, Jerry 2, 10, 31, 35, 41, 54–5, 57, 58,
    59–60, 67, 81, 93, 105, 107, 110, 131,
    132
Whittington, Dick 143
Who (The) 59
Wildeblood, Peter 77
Williams, John 12–13
Williams, Raymond 150, 159
Wolfreys, Julian 13, 133, 142, 158
Wong, C. T. 106
Woodcock, George 37
Woolf, Virginia 57, 91
    A Room of One's Own 104
    'Kew Gardens' 58
    Mrs Dalloway 57, 89
Wren, (Sir) Christopher 145

Young, I. M. 159

Zukin, S. 74

Lightning Source UK Ltd.
Milton Keynes UK

173595UK00001B/112/P